The McGraw-Hill
Small Business
Tax Advisor

Other Books by Cliff Roberson

THE MCGRAW-HILL PERSONAL TAX ADVISOR, 2ND EDITON
THE BUSINESS PERSON'S LEGAL ADVISOR, 2ND EDITION

AVOIDING PROBATE: TAMPER-PROOF ESTATE PLANNING
FIGHT THE IRS AND WIN: A SELF-DEFENSE GUIDE FOR TAXPAYERS

The McGraw-Hill Small Business Tax Advisor

Understanding the Tax Law

Cliff Roberson, LLM, Ph.D.
University of Houston-Victoria

Second Edition

McGraw-Hill, Inc.

New York   St. Louis   San Francisco   Auckland   Bogotá
Caracas   Lisbon   London   Madrid   Mexico   Milan
Montreal   New Delhi   Paris   San Juan   São Paulo
Singapore   Sydney   Tokyo   Toronto

Library of Congress Cataloging-in-Publication Data

Roberson, Cliff
    The McGraw-Hill small business tax advisor : understanding the tax law /
Cliff Roberson. — 2nd ed.
        p.   cm.
    Rev. ed. of: The small business tax advisor. 1st ed. c1987.
    Includes index.
    ISBN 0-07-053111-0   — ISBN 0-07-053110-2 (pbk.)
    1. Small business—Taxation—Law and legislation—United States. 2. Tax
planning—United States. I. Roberson, Cliff, Small business tax advisor. II. Title.
    KF6491.R63 1992
    343.7306′8—dc20   91-24902
    [347.30368]   CIP

Contents

Preface

*An old saying has it that the art of taxation
consists in so plucking the goose as to get
the most feathers with the least hissing.*
        From the court opinion: USLIFE
        v. Harbison, 784 F.2d 1238

The Revenue Reconciliation Act of 1990 resulted in the largest tax increase in U.S. history. Over the next five years, this act will increase the total amount of taxes that taxpayers pay by approximately 5 billion dollars.

The purpose of this book is to provide small business owners and managers with a general introduction to income taxation of businesses and corporations. There have been eight major changes since 1975 to the tax code. The Tax Reform Act was the most extensive change to occur in the past 30 years. The book provides current and accurate tax guidance to small business persons regarding tax-saving strategies. One of its strong points is the numerous tax-saving pointers that are scattered throughout the book.

What is presently known as the Federal Tax Law consists of more than 3500 pages of complicated tax statutes and an additional 6000 pages of tax regulations designed to explain the statutes. In researching the provisions of the new laws, two things are apparent. First, the recent changes do not simplify the tax law as they were designed to do. Second, the more the law changes, the more it remains the same.

Regarding the statement that the recent tax legislation does not simplify tax preparation, the truth of this statement is apparent to any one who attempts to read the recent changes to the tax code. As in all other tax statutes, the new legislation was written by lawyers and accountants for lawyers, and accountants. It is not designed for the average person to read and understand. The recent changes to the tax law have been nicknamed the "full employment for attorneys and accountants acts."

Many tax experts contend that the complexity in our income tax law is due to three factors:

1. The inherent complexity of our diverse economy

2. The use of the income tax system to promote social interests, resulting in special favors and concessions to varied taxpayer groups

3. The "dynamic complexity" condition caused by new regulations adopted to close loopholes in the tax code, thus forcing taxpayers to rearrange their affairs to find new tax advantages which in turn results in more regulations; causing a never-ending process

The distinctions between various forms of business organizations are very important for federal income tax purposes, because certain organizations such as sole proprietorships and partnerships are not considered as taxable entities, and income or loss is passed through to the individual owners. Corporations are either S corporations or C corporations. An S corporation is one subject to certain limitations which qualify it to be treated as a partnership for income tax purposes. A C corporation is defined as any corporation not qualifying as an S corporation. Since a C corporation is considered as a separate taxable entity, it is required to file and pay income taxes.

Cliff Roberson

The McGraw-Hill
Small Business
Tax Advisor

1
New Income Tax Rules for Businesses

Introduction

This chapter contains a brief summary of the principal changes in income tax rules and regulations involving corporations and businesses set forth in the Tax Reform Act of 1986 and amended in the 1990 Tax Act. A detailed discussion of the effects of each change is included in subsequent chapters. The general theme of the Tax Reform Act is that it favors savings and penalizes borrowing.

In 1986, Congress enacted the most comprehensive tax reform act in history. We were led to believe that this was *the* great tax reform act. Each year since then, however, Congress has continued to tinker with the tax law. Although there is no constitutional mandate for Congress to change the tax law each year, they continue to do so.

Summary of Recent Tax Changes

The 1990 and 1986 acts make it difficult for small business owners and managers to save taxes by the use of traditional tax shelters. Taxpayers should redirect their tax-saving efforts in new directions (see Chapter 2). A summary of the major tax changes follows.

- There are now three official tax brackets; 15, 28, and 31 percent. (For a detailed discussion, see the section on tax brackets later in this chapter.)

- The surtax for the 15 percent bracket and personal exemptions has been eliminated.

- The maximum tax bracket for net capital gains is 28 percent. Net capital gains is the excess of net long-term capital gains for the year over the net short-term capital loss for the year.

- Personal exemptions are phased out for married taxpayers filing jointly with adjusted gross incomes (AGIs) of $150,000 or more; singles with AGIs of $100,000 or more; and heads of households with AGIs of $125,000 or more. Persons with high AGIs also lose part of their itemized deductions.

- The estate tax freeze created by the 1986 Tax Reform Act was repealed retroactively and replaced with a new set of rules designed to require the payment of gift taxes when a freeze is implemented.

- Small businesses can receive a tax break for complying with the Americans with Disabilities Act of 1990.

- A 10 percent luxury tax was imposed on expensive automobiles ($30,000 and up), aircraft ($250,000 and up), boats ($100,000 and up), and jewelry and furs costing over $10,000.

- Any cellular telephone or similar telecommunications equipment placed in service in 1990 or later will be considered as listed property for depreciation purposes. If listed property is not used more than 50 percent for qualified business use during any tax year, it must be depreciated using the modified accelerated cost recovery system (MACRS) method of the life of the property (see Chapter 7).

- Generally, the cost of cosmetic surgery is no longer deductible as a medical expense. This change, alone, is expected to raise approximately $269 million over the next 5 years.

- The alternative minimum tax rate has been changed from 21 to 24 percent.

- The temporary federal unemployment surtax was extended through 1995.

- The Medicare portion of the social security tax now applies to the first $125,000 of wages. This is up from $51,300.

- The 25 percent health insurance deduction for self-employed and certain S corporation shareholders was extended through 1991. S corporations are defined in Chapter 3.

- The value of child care provided under any federal or state program is not an employment-related expense for purpose of the dependent care tax credit.

- Large corporate tax underpayment now incurs higher interest charges.

- The IRS was given additional authority to issue regulations that expand the definition of cash for purposes of business cash reporting requirements.

- Taxpayers must now provide social security numbers for claimed dependents over 1 year old.

- The period for the IRS to begin collection proceedings and to refile tax liens has been increased from 6 to 10 years.

- Tax refunds may now be used by the government to offset any overpayment of social security benefits.

- Tax return booklets published by the IRS must include graphs of federal income and outlays.

- Medical care reimbursements under self-insured medical reimbursement plans are no longer subject to wage withholding.

- The alternative minimum tax exemption amount for children under 14 who are subject to the "kiddie tax" has been increased under certain circumstances.

- The present tax code provides for "indexing" to adjust for inflation. The indexing applies to tax rate brackets, standard deductions, and personal exemptions. The adjustments will be rounded down to the next lowest multiple of $50. The calendar year 1990 is now used as the base year for determining inflation adjustments.

- The unauthorized disclosure of tax returns and return information by persons who provide services to the IRS are now subject to the same penalties as are unauthorized disclosures by IRS employees.

- Form 1040A has been expanded to include IRA payments, pensions and annuities, taxable social security benefits, and credit for the elderly and disabled.

- There have been changes in various penalties related to accuracy, such as the penalties for negligence and substantial understatement of income tax. In addition, the penalties for failure to file or failure to supply the required social security numbers when fraud is involved have been increased.

- Taxes have been raised by the amount indicated on the following items: $0.05 per gallon of gasoline, $0.16 per fifth of 80-proof liquor,

$0.16 per six-pack of beer, $0.04 per pack of cigarettes, and $0.18 per bottle of table wine.

Items Left Unchanged

Despite the numerous changes, some income, expense, and deduction items were left unchanged. They include the following:

- Contributions and benefits to a qualified group legal services plan established by an employer for prepaid services for employees were extended.
- Child support payments made to the custodial parent are not taxable income.
- Gifts, bequests, devises, and inheritances are not subject to income taxes, but any income from them remain subject to income taxes.
- Certain amounts received for personal injuries or sickness, including payments under workers' compensation and employer-provided accident or health insurance plans, are not taxable income.
- Certain employee achievement awards recognizing safety or length of service are not taxable income.
- Car pool reimbursements to automobile owners by fellow employees are not taxable income as long as the taxpayer does not make a profit on the car pool.
- Life insurance proceeds paid on the death of the insured are not taxable income.
- Meals and lodging provided for the convenience of the employer and provided on the business premises are not taxable income.
- Certain scholarships for tuition, books, and course-related fees are excluded from taxable income.
- The once-in-a-lifetime election by homeowners 55 years or older to exclude gain from the sale or exchange of their principal residence, up to $125,000 (or $62,500 for married filing separately) was retained by the recent legislation.

Important Reminders

Earned Income Credit.   You, as an employer, must notify employees who worked for you and from whom you did not withhold income tax about the earned income credit.

Form W-4. You should make new Forms W-4 available to your employees and encourage them to check their income tax withholding for each tax year. Those employees who owed a large amount of tax or received a large refund for last tax year may need to file a new Form W-4.

Children Employed by Parents. Wages you pay to your children age 18 and older for services in your trade or business are subject to social security taxes.

Employees' Tips. All tips reported by an employee are subject to the employer portion of the social security tax. Thus, you must pay the employer social security tax on the total amount of tips and wages up to the social security maximum.

Information Returns (Form 1099 Series). If you make total payments of $600 or more during the year to another person, other than an employee or a corporation, in the course of your business, you must file information returns to report these payments for the year.

Tax Brackets and the Marginal Tax Rate

Probably the area of the greatest confusion since the 1986 Tax Reform Act and carried forth in the 1990 Tax Act is that of tax rates and brackets. It is important that taxpayers understand their marginal tax rates. A *marginal tax rate* is that rate that applies at the margin to your top dollar income. For example, if your highest tax rate is 31 percent, then for each additional dollar of taxable income that you make, 31 cents goes for federal income taxes. If you are at the 15 percent bracket, then only 15 cents of each additional dollar goes to federal income taxes. Under our graduated tax system, as your income rises, not only do your taxes rise, but the percentage of that income that is paid as taxes also rises.

From 1986 to 1990, we had two official tax rates, 15 and 28 percent. But because of the "bubbles" created by a phaseout of certain deductions, a portion of high income was taxed at 33 percent. Now, there are three official tax rates—15, 28, and 31 percent. However, because of the phaseout of certain deductions, the 1990 act also created bubbles that are even more complicated than those of the original act. For example, there is a 31.93 percent bubble if an adjusted gross income before exemptions and itemized deductions is over $100,000. You lose $30 worth of deductions for every $1000 that is over the threshold; i.e., the IRS gets to tax $1030 rather than $1000, which has the effect of raising the tax rate to 31.93 percent. In addition, there are bubbles at 32.46, 39.2,

42, and 47.96 percent. Since most of these do not apply to the majority of taxpayers, they will not be discussed further in this book.

Prior to the 1986 Tax Reform Act, long-term capital gains were taxed at approximately 50 percent of other income. The 1986 act eliminated the long- term capital gains favorite tax treatment. Starting in 1990, capital gains once again receive a favorable tax treatment. Presently there is a maximum tax rate of 28 percent on net capital gains. *Net capital gains* is defined as the excess of net long-term capital gain for the year over the net short-term capital loss for the year.

The maximum 28 percent may be somewhat deceiving since it may push your total gross income into an area where you fit into one of the tax bubbles and, therefore, pay an additional rate. For example, a capital gains could push your total adjusted income up to a point where you would be required to pay taxes on social security benefits or lose part of your itemized deductions.

The *marginal tax rate* applies to each additional dollar of income of a taxpayer. Economists contend that it is important because it affects a taxpayer's motivation to earn more money. For example, a taxpayer in the 15 percent bracket keeps 85 percent of income after federal taxes compared to a taxpayer in the 31 percent bracket who keeps only 69 percent after federal taxes. At one point, shortly after the Second World War, the marginal tax rate was 90 percent. This meant that a taxpayer would keep 10 cents on each additional dollar that he or she made. The knowledge of your marginal tax rate is important in order to rearrange your financial affairs to legally pay the minimum tax. For example, a taxpayer in some situations with an adjusted gross income of $110,000 may be allowed to deduct up to $20,000 for loss on a rental income. If, however, the taxpayers' income is increased by $1000, the deduction on rental income would be reduced by $500, which means that the landlord would lose $500 of the rental loss deduction.

Personal Exemptions

Prior to 1990, the deductions for personal exemptions were phased out for taxpayers having taxable incomes above several specified levels. For example, such deductions were phased out for taxpayers filing joint returns whose adjusted gross income exceeded $162,770; the phaseout was accomplished by increasing the tax rate for such taxpayers by 5 percent of their taxable gain within certain ranges. The 1990 Tax Act, however, repealed the 5 percent rate adjustment, and, in lieu of the adjustment, provided for the phaseout of deductions of personal exemptions for taxpayers whose gross income exceeded threshold amounts. The phaseout percentage is 2 percent for each $2500 by which the adjusted gross income exceeds the threshold amount for such taxpayer. For married individuals filing separately, the applicable percentage is 2 percent for each $1250 in which the AGI exceeds the threshold amount. Note that the percentage cannot exceed 100. For 1991, the threshold amounts for phaseout of personal exemptions are $150,000 for joint returns or returns of surviving spouses, $125,000 for returns of heads of households, and $100,000 for returns of single taxpayers.

The tax code now provides that the threshold amount, beginning in 1992, will be automatically adjusted for inflation, and, accordingly, the AGI threshold amounts are increased by the percentage, if any, in which the consumer price index (CPI) exceeds the CPI for base year 1990. In effect, this means the inflation adjustment, or the popularly called indexing, will be based on the new base year of 1990 rather than an earlier year.

Filing Status

Your filing status is determined by your circumstances on the last day of the year. The requirements for head of household or for a couple filing a joint return were not changed. If you are a U.S. citizen, your filing requirements depend on your filing status, your gross income, and your age. Gross income includes all income you received in the form of money, goods, property, and services that are not exempt from tax. If your gross income is less than the threshold amount, you must file if you owe other taxes such as self-employment taxes, social security taxes on tips received, alternative minimum tax, or tax on an IRA.

Alternative Minimum Tax

The present tax code has modified the alternative minimum tax for noncorporate taxpayers. The alternative minimum tax (AMT) rate has been increased from 21 to 24 percent. The AMT is computed by applying the AMT rate to a tax base, and if the resulting amount is more than what the taxpayer would be required under normal tax rules, then the taxpayer must use, in most cases, the alternative minimum tax. It is interesting to note that, presently, for purposes of determining whether or not a taxpayer is required to file under the alternative minimum tax rules, capital gains are not treated as tax preferences. In addition, a charitable contribution of capital gains property that created a deduction for regular tax purposes equal to the market value of the contribution may be affected by the AMT (except for the tax year 1991). Accordingly, any taxpayer who is considering making a donation of appreciated tangible personal property as discussed in Chapter 6 should determine the maximum tax benefits of the proposed gift.

To prevent profitable corporations from avoiding significant tax liability, an alternative minimum tax for corporations was included in the code.

Investment Tax Credit

There is an interesting history regarding the investment tax credit. It seems that every major tax reform act has either increased or eliminated the investment tax credit. Most tax experts predict that it will be reenacted within the next few years. Despite pressure to restore investment credits, Congress failed in 1990 to reenact the tax credit. In 1986, to offset the repealed investment tax credit, the prior accelerated cost recovery system (ACRS) for depreciation expenses was changed to provide generous depreciation allowances for business property other than real estate. For real estate, however, the depreciation allowances were severely limited.

Deductions

Our present tax code retains most of the popular itemized deductions for home mortgage interest, state and local income taxes, state and local real and personal property taxes, charitable contributions, medical expenses, and casualty losses. Medical expense deductions, however, now have a higher floor.

Benefits no longer are available to individual taxpayers include interest deductions on consumer items, income averaging, second wage-earner deduction, many of the miscellaneous deductions previously available on Schedule A, and the capital gains exclusion.

Instead of additional standard deductions for elderly and blind taxpayers, additional $800 deductions will be allowed for each individual who is age 65 or over. There is an additional deduction of $650 for blindness ($800 if 65 or over).

Certain categories of itemized deductions have traditionally been subject to specific percentage limitations. For example, otherwise allowable medical expenses can be deducted only to the extent they now exceed 7.5 percent of the adjusted gross income, and miscellaneous item deductions are deductible only to the extent that in the aggregate they exceed 2 percent of the AGI. Presently allowable itemized deductions are reduced by the lesser of 3 percent of the AGI over a threshold amount (presently $100,000) or 80 percent of the amount of the itemized deductions otherwise allowable for the year. This 3 percent reduction for high-income taxpayers is often referred to as the Pease plan, since it was originally proposed by Representative Don Pease. It serves to reduce itemized deductions—i.e., contribution taxes, mortgage interest, etc.—for high-income taxpayers, but it cannot eliminate more than 80 percent of the itemized deductions. This 3 percent reduction in total itemized deductions under the Pease plan has the effect of increasing the marginal tax rate of an affected 31 percent tax bracket by 0.93 percent for high-income taxpayers.

The marriage penalty has been increased. The so-called marriage penalty is where a two-income, married couple with relatively equal incomes pays more taxes than two unmarried individuals with the same combined income as the married couple. Because recent legislation reduces otherwise allowable itemized deductions for taxpayers with AGIs over $100,000, the marriage penalty has increased for many taxpayers.

Prior to 1990, the deductions for medical expenses included the cost of cosmetic surgery, i.e., face lifts, hair removal through electrolysis, and other medical procedures designed to improve a taxpayer's personal appearance. For most purposes, the IRS did not distinguish between procedures which were medically necessary and those which were purely cosmetic. Beginning in 1991, the amount paid for cosmetic surgery or similar procedures cannot be taken as a medical deduction unless the surgery or procedure was considered necessary to ameliorate a deformity existing from or directly related to a congenital abnormality or to a personal injury resulting from an accident or trauma or a disfiguring disease. Apparently, Congress felt that expenses for purely cosmetic procedures should not be deductible in computing taxable income. Cosmetic surgery is considered any procedure that is directed toward improving a person's appearance, and that does not meaningfully promote the proper function of the body or prevent illness or disease. Cosmetic surgery is deductible if it is necessary to correct a deformity as noted above.

Since cosmetic surgery is generally not deductible, then any part of premiums paid for insurance coverage for nondeductible cosmetic surgery would also be nondeductible as a medical expense.

Employee Benefits

For tax purposes, as an employer you must treat as wages any amounts you pay your employees as reimbursement of their employee business expenses if these amounts are paid or are treated as paid under a nonaccountable plan. This means that you must report the amounts as wages on your employees' W-2 forms. You must withhold and pay employment taxes on these amounts.

Excess Pension Funds Excise Tax

Prior to the 1990 Tax Act, there was a 15 percent excise tax imposed on pension fund amounts that were transferred to the plan sponsor (normally the employer) after the plan had terminated and its obligations were satisfied. Now there is a two-tier excise tax rate. The rates are now 20 and 50 percent. The tax rate is 50 percent of the amounts transferred, except under the following conditions, where the rate is 20 percent: the plan sponsor is in Chapter 7 bankruptcy or similar proceedings; the sponsor provides for "pro rata benefit increases" under the terminating plan; or a "qualified replacement plan" is established or maintained.

Employee Education Benefits Exclusion

Prior to the 1990 act, an employee was not taxed on the value of educational benefits (up to $5250 per year) received from an employer's qualified educational assistance program. Now the exclusion also applies for graduate study of the kind normally taken by an individual pursuing a program leading to law, business, medical, or other advanced professional degree. The $5250 exclusion for non-job-related educational assistance is scheduled to end after tax year 1991.

Group Legal Services Plans

The 1990 Tax Act extends the exclusions from taxable income for employer-paid contributions to qualified group legal services plans through tax year 1991. The tax-exempt status was scheduled to expire for tax years beginning after September 30, 1990. The new legislation also extends the tax-exempt status of organizations that provide exclusive legal services as part of a qualified group legal services plan.

Tax Credits

Disabled Access Credit

Starting in tax year 1991, eligible small businesses may elect to apply a credit against income tax of up to 50 percent of the amount of disabled access expenditures for the year that are over $250 and not more than $10,250. Congress established the credit to assist those small businesses that, under the Americans with Disabilities Act of 1990, were faced with the obligation to make structural changes to facilities to accommodate the disabled and handicapped. To be eligible, a small business must have a gross income of not less than $1,000,000 for the tax year before that in which the credit is elected and must employ no more than 30 full-time employees. Apparently, a business in its first tax year would qualify for the "disabled access credit" because for the prior year it would not have gross receipts exceeding $1,000,000 or 30 full-time employees.

Eligible disabled access expenditures are amounts paid or incurred by an eligible small business to enable the business to comply with the disability act. They include amounts paid to remove architectural, communication, physical, or transportation barriers that prevent a business from being accessible or usable by individuals with disabilities. They also include amounts paid to provide qualified interpreters or other effective methods of making material available to people with hearing impairments and/or visual impairments. Only those amounts that are considered reasonable by the IRS are deductible. Expenditures which are not required in order to comply with the disabilities act are not eligible for the credit. For the purposes of this deduction, the term *disability* is as defined in the Americans with Disability Act of 1990.

For partnerships and S corporations, the maximum of $10,250 for the disability credit applies to the partnership as a whole, not to each individual partner or corporation S stockholder. For example, if a partnership had three partners and the partnership otherwise qualified, the partnership is entitled to an access expenditure credit of $10,250. A partner with 50 percent interest would be entitled to a credit based on 50 percent of $10,250.

Prior to 1990, taxpayers were given the option of expensing (deducting out of current income) up to $35,000 for certain expenses paid or incurred to make facilities more accessible to handicapped and elderly individuals. The 1990 act reduced the amount to $15,000. Accordingly, any authorized expenditures above $15,000 must now be capitalized rather than expensed as current income.

Targeted Jobs Credit

Employers who employ disadvantaged individuals who are certified as members of one of the "targeted" groups may claim a tax credit of 40 percent of the first-year wages not to exceed $6000 of wages per eligible employees ($3000 for qualified summer youth employees). This credit was scheduled to expire on September 30, 1990, but was extended by the 1990 Tax Act to employees hired before November 5, 1990. Congress has modified this date with almost every new tax act. Accordingly, there is a good possibility that it will be extended.

Research Tax Credit

Like the targeted jobs tax credit, the tax credit for qualified research expenses has been extended by recent legislation. It is now extended through 1991 and may be further extended. Under this program, employers may qualify for a 20 percent research expense credit for qualified incremental research expenses paid or incurred during the year, and expenses paid during the calendar year to universities for qualified research.

Earned Income Credit

The 1990 legislation modified the earned income tax credit. Presently, certain low-income persons are allowed a refundable tax credit equal to a percentage of their income. The tax credit is the amount equal to the sum of the "basic earned income credit" and the new health insurance credit. The 1990 act also changed the phaseout percentage of the tax credit for earned income in excess of a threshold amount. Now the phaseout percentage depends on the number of qualified children that may be claimed. The new law also increased the credit percentage and adjusted it for family size. The maximum earned income credit allowable was 14 percent of $6810, or $953. The projected amount for tax year 1991 is $2009. *Note:* The exact amount depends on the adjustment for indexing.

The health insurance credit is determined in the same basic manner as the basic earned income credit except that the credit percentage is 6 percent and the phaseout percentage is 4.285 percent. The health insurance credit cannot exceed the actual amount paid for insurance coverage. In addition, amounts reimbursed by state or federal governments may not be used in determining the credit.

Low-Income Housing Credit

The low-income housing credit is a business tax credit for persons owning residential rental property that qualifies as low-income housing. A higher tax credit is now allowed for new housing that is not financed

with tax-exempt bonds. The 1990 legislation increased the credit allocation limit amount. The legislation also permits certain individual taxpayers to elect to presently claim credits that would otherwise be
allowed in future years.

Penalties

The following penalties for late tax deposits and late information returns are based on the length of time a deposit or information return is
late. The penalty for furnishing statements to payees, however, is not
time-related.

Late Tax Deposits

The penalty for a late tax deposit is:

- 2 percent for the first 5 days late
- 5 percent for the sixth through the fifteenth day late
- 10 percent for more than 15 days late
- 15 percent if the deposit is not made within 10 days

after the IRS issues the first notice demanding payment

Late Information Returns

The penalty for filing a late information return applies if you do not file
by the due date, if you do not include all required information, or if you
report incorrect information. The penalty is:

- $15 for each return filed within 30 days after the due date, up to a
  maximum of $75,000
- $30 for each return filed after the 30-day period but by August 1, up to
  a maximum of $150,000
- $50 for each return filed after August 1, or never filed, up to a maxi-
  mum of $250,000

Small businesses pay the same penalty for a return, but the maxi-
mums are lowered to $25,000, $50,000, and $100,000. A small business
is one with average annual gross receipts of $5 million or less for the last

3 years ending before the calendar year the return is due, or since the business began, if shorter.

Late Payee Statements

A $50 penalty applies for each statement you do not furnish a payee by the required date up to a maximum of $100,000. The penalty also applies if you do not include all required information, or if you report incorrect information.

Miscellaneous Rulings

Change of Address

If you change your mailing address, you should use Form 8822, "Change of Address," to notify the IRS of your new address. Be sure to include your suite, room, or other unit number. If you are changing both your home and business addresses, you must complete two separate forms. However, individuals who are also household employers and file Form 942 can use one form. Send the form to the Internal Revenue Service Center from your old address.

New $100,000 Deposit Rule

Undeposited social security and withheld income taxes that reach $100,000 or more in any eighth-monthly deposit period must be deposited on the next banking day. However, you are still required to make deposits within 3 banking days when undeposited taxes reach at least $3000 at the end of an eighth-monthly deposit period.

Estimated Tax Payments for S Corporations

An S corporation must make quarterly estimated tax payments if its expected liability is $500 or more for the tax on net recognized built-in gain, or excess net passive income, and on any increase in tax for which the S corporation is liable because of the recapture of investment credits. (See Chapter 5 for a more detailed discussion of S corporations.)

Impact of Tax Changes on Individual Businesses

As with any change in economic systems or tax reforms, there are winners and losers. Accordingly, some businesses are winners with the recent tax changes and others are losers. In general, the winners are labor-intensive businesses, software companies, retailers, stock brokerages, and other service-sector companies. The losers are capital-intensive companies, banks, utilities, real estate companies, oil companies, small businesses, and some manufacturers. Companies that depended on tax breaks such as the investment credit and other deductions are losers since their lost deductions will not be offset by the lower tax rates.

Banking Institutions

Banks were hurt under the tax reform in several areas. Listed below are some of the most prominent areas:

Elimination of the Deduction for Carrying Costs for Municipal Bonds and Other Municipal Obligations.   About one-third of all municipal bonds are held by banks. Prior to the tax change, banks could deduct 80 per-

---

Businesses Considered as Winners

  Electronics

  Publishing

  Retail companies

  Consumer products companies

  High-tech companies

Businesses considered as losers

  Real estate

  Banks

  Property and casualty insurance companies

  Utilities

  Steel industry

cent of the interest they pay on money borrowed to buy the munici-pal bonds. Interest expenses on loans for investment capital for mu-nicipal bonds are limited under the new law. This will increase the cost of the bonds, and thus the banks will need a higher return than previously needed to make the same profit.

Limitations of Foreign Tax Credits.   The new limitations on foreign tax credits reduce the feasibility of foreign loans. Prior to the tax change, banks pooled all taxes paid to foreign governments and used these payments to offset taxes on their U.S. tax returns. This change will reduce the long-term benefits of foreign loans, and it puts U.S. banks at a disadvantage in competition with international banks from other countries.

Loss of the Deductions for Bad Debt Reserves.   This change alone could cost banks as much as $4 billion in higher taxes over the next 4 years. Now banks with over $500 million in assets may write off bad debts only when the individual loans are declared as worthless. Some tax experts contend that this change will also encourage banks to fore-close sooner on problem loans, since they can not take a deduction for a bad loan until the debt is written off the bank's books. Small banks with less than $500 million in assets may still use the reserve method of accounting for bad debts.

Leasing Changes, Including Elimination of the Investment Tax Credit.   Banks are involved in a large percentage of equipment leasing in the United States. Loss of the investment credit of 10 percent make leases less at-tractive to the banks.

Property-Casualty Insurance Companies

As noted above, insurance companies are also losers under the tax re-form act. Life insurance companies are less affected by the change than property-casualty companies. The major changes affecting these com-panies are twofold: Insurers are required to include premiums in their taxable income sooner than in the past, and they are required to wait longer before deducting some claims expenses.

Deferral of expenses and early reporting of income causes the com-panies to lose the use of these funds earlier. This treatment of capital eliminates tax breaks that casualty insurance companies have enjoyed since 1921. Life insurance companies lose some of their special tax breaks, but these may be offset by the lower tax rates.

Heavy Industry

Heavy industry was a definite loser under the tax reform act mainly because of the loss of the investment tax credit and the modification of the depreciation schedules. An additional tax benefit loss is the requirement for modification of accounting procedures for installment sales. See Chapter 8 regarding the accounting procedures for installment sales.

Retailers

One of the biggest winners in the recent tax reform are retailers. There are some disadvantages caused by loss of the investment credit and new rules dealing with credit. Overall, the favorable tax rates are very helpful for retailers who do not use the investment credit to the same extent that other types of business use it.

In addition, it is anticipated that the change in tax rates should produce more discretionary income for consumers and thus spur spending. Since most retailers have a rapid turnover of inventory, the change in accounting rules regarding inventory is not expected to have much impact on retailers.

Broadcasting Companies

Like retailers, broadcasting companies should fare well under the act. CBS Inc. reported that, in 1985, their tax rate was 43 percent. Thus, with the maximum rate of 34 percent, they should experience a significant reduction in income taxes. Capital Cities/ABC Inc. reported a similar situation.

Publishing Companies

Loss of investment credit should not adversely affect publishing companies since the industrywide investment tax credits in 1985 amounted to only about 5 percent. The drop in tax rates and a possible increase in consumer advertising should help this industry.

Small Businesses

Small businesses will probably suffer more from the increased accounting requirements than any other aspect of the new law. The accounting procedures are much tougher and more complicated than under the prior law. Some small businesses will benefit from the reduced tax rates on the first $50,000 of their income (at 15 percent).

A summary of the impact on small businesses is as follows (note that the first five items are adverse effects and the last two are beneficial):

1. Elimination of investment tax credit

2. Less generous depreciation allowances

3. Elimination of tax benefits of leasing property

4. Requirement that certain inventory costs be deducted only when inventory is sold

5. Required changes in pension plans regarding vesting and nondiscrimination rules

6. Simplified LIFO (last in–first out) inventory accounting

7. Lower tax rates

High-Tech Companies

The repeal of the investment tax credit and changes in capital gains should be offset by the lower tax rates. In addition, the reduction in development cost writeoffs from 25 to 20 percent should also be offset by the lower tax rates.

2
Reducing
Tax Liability

To reduce your tax liability, there are four possible approaches that an individual taxpayer may take. They are:

- Taking steps to reduce your gross income. This may be accomplished by converting ordinary gross income into other forms of income that receive tax preference or by delaying recognition of such income. While this approach is not as significant as in prior years because of the recent tax changes, there are still steps that a taxpayer may take to reduce gross income.
- Using full advantage of special tax credits and deductions allowed to lower final tax liability.
- Rearranging activities so that personal deductions are allowable as business deductions.
- Shifting income to other persons to ensure maximum use of the lowest tax rate bracket. This approach was also limited by the recent tax changes; however, there are still situations where income shifting will reduce the overall tax liability of the taxpayer.

While the recent tax changes generally have reduced the tax advantages that can be gained by using the above approaches, there are still significant tax benefits available to the tax-wise individual. In this chapter, possible tax saving strategies and suggestions are examined. The advisability and availability of each depend on your particular situation.

Judge Learned Hand once stated in a U.S. Supreme Court opinion, "There is nothing sinister in arranging one's affairs so as to keep taxes as low as possible." The judge was indicating that while it is a crime to evade the payment of taxes legally due, there is no duty to pay taxes that are not due. Accordingly, it is not wrong to rearrange your affairs in order to reduce your tax liability.

Reducing Adjusted Gross Income

There are many ways of reducing your adjusted gross income for tax purposes. The sections below list some of those ways.

Personal Income

- Make gifts of income-producing property to family members under 14 years of age and other gifts to minors (there are certain restrictions on this).
- Save losing lottery or other betting tickets to offset any winnings.
- Defer income on the sale of property by delaying the closing date of the sale or delaying the settlement of a pending dispute over an item of income.
- Welfare assistance payments, such as aid to the blind, are not taxable income in most cases.
- Generally, life insurance proceeds are not included in the taxpayer's gross income.

Business Income

- Net operating losses for a business may be carried back 3 years or forward for 15 years to offset income. If you feel that your income will be higher in the future, then carry it forward. If, however, you do not anticipate higher income in the future, it may be to your advantage to carry it back to offset income from 1 or more of the 3 previous years.
- Corporations whose stock is owned by five or fewer persons should check their estimated income to make sure that their corporation is not classed as a personal holding company. The personal holding company classification can result if 60 percent or more of adjusted gross income is personal holding company income. If your company is in danger of this, it may be advisable to take steps to shift income to a different tax year.

- Since a partner's share of a partnership loss is deductible only to the extent of the partner's basis in the partnership, it may be advisable for the partner to increase his or her capital contribution during the tax year that the loss will occur.

- The entire profit from the sale of a business or other item is ordinarily taxable in the year of the sale. Using an installment method, however, may defer a portion of the gain to later tax years.

- If you have depreciation deductions that are eligible for expensing, consider which ones require you to pay less taxes in the long run.

- If you are self-employed and need to defer income, consider delaying billing your customers until the year's end.

- If you receive year-end bonuses and/or commissions, request to defer some of them into the next year.

- If you have an office in your home, take depreciation on that part of the home that is used as an office. Office furniture, business machines, and the like can also be depreciated.

- An employee's personal use of a company car must be valued and reported as part of gross income. There are three acceptable methods that can be used in valuating the benefit. If you fall into this category, be careful and use the method that produces the smallest addition to gross income.

Investment Income

- Postpone or defer income and interest to a later tax year. This may be accomplished, for example, by investing in deferred interest bonds. In some cases, deferring earned interest from November or December to January will postpone income taxes on the interest for a year.

- Consider investing in real estate investment trusts (REITs) that plan for growth and/or income rather than tax savings.

- If you can make deductible IRA (individual retirement account), Keogh, or other pension contributions, make them early in the year so that they will earn more tax-free interest.

- In buying preferred stock, consider whether it pays dividends in January or December.

- Consider using savings bonds purchased after December 31, 1989, to pay for college or other educational costs. In many cases, the interest earned on savings bonds purchased after 1989 is tax-free when used for educational purposes.

- Cash method taxpayers may use bank certificates with maturities of 1 year or less to defer interest if the certificate provides that the interest won't be paid or made available before maturity without penalty.

- Unearned income of children under 14 is generally taxed at their parents' top tax rate. Avoid this by giving the children Series EE savings bonds and not electing to have the interest recognized as it accrues.

- If you sell stocks or securities and rebuy within 30 days, it may be considered as a "wash" sale. To recognize loss on the earlier stocks or securities, wait at least 31 days before buying the same stocks or securities.

- No gain is recognized on the exchange of property held for productive use in a trade or business or for investment if such property is exchanged for "like" property. Consider exchanging rather than selling your property.

Maximizing Deductions

Deciding whether or not to itemize deductions is an important consideration for every taxpayer. If your itemized deductions are only slightly above those for the standard deduction, before deciding to itemize consider the impact of state taxes. In many states, if you itemize on the federal return, you are required to itemize on the state return. If you fall short by a small amount each year by itemizing rather than using the standard deduction, consider shifting your deductions to another tax year. It may work out that you can itemize every other year. This would be accomplished by either paying possible deductions prior to December 31 or delaying as many as possible until after January 1.

Maximize deductions by using the strategies listed.

- Rather than use consumer loans to buy consumer products, use home mortgage loans for which the interest expense may be deductible.

- Keep accurate records for use of an automobile in business, travel to a second job, etc.

- A casualty loss isn't sustained and therefore not deductible to the extent that the taxpayer has a claim for reimbursement of the loss and there is a reasonable expectation of recovery. Accordingly, a taxpayer who suffers a casualty loss in one tax year should consider whether it would be better to speed up the settlement process or postpone it to the next tax year.

- Under certain circumstances recreational vehicles and boats may qualify as second homes. In this case, the mortgage interest expense may be fully deductible.

- Charitable contributions are deductible in the year that they are mailed, even if received by the charity the next year.
- Contributions to charity made by charge card are deductible in the year charged even if the charge is not paid until the next year.
- Taxes are deductible in the year that they are paid, regardless of the year they relate to.
- To obtain a higher deduction for state and local taxes, consider paying January's installment before December 31.
- Donate appreciated securities to charity and receive a deduction for the full market value of the securities.

Medical Expenses

- Medical expenses may be deducted only in the year in which they are paid; therefore, consider bunching them into one tax year if possible.
- Childbirth classes may be deductible to the extent that they prepare the mother for an active role in the process of childbirth.
- Fees paid to attend stop-smoking and weight-loss programs may be deductible if they are necessary to alleviate a specific ailment.
- Home alterations for medical reasons may be deductible as medical expenses.
- Costs of medical treatments for drug and alcohol abuse are generally deductible.
- If you furnish more than half the support of your parents, you may deduct the medical expenses paid for the parents, subject to the 7.5 percent floor. *Note:* This deduction would be available even if you cannot claim the parents as dependents because of the gross income test.
- Travel expenses for trips that are primarily for and essential to medical care may be deductible medical expenses

Travel and Business Expenses

- If a trip is primarily for business, the cost of traveling there and returning is generally tax-free even if you spend a few days at the location for recreation.
- The expenses of your spouse traveling with you on your business trips are normally not deductible unless your wife's presence serves bona fide business purposes. Accordingly, if your spouse is expected

to socialize extensively with customers, his or her expenses may be deductible.

- If during your business travel, your spouse's travel is not deductible and you stay at a hotel where single rooms cost $100 and doubles cost $130, you may deduct $100 of the $130 as a business expense. In this situation, always request that your receipt also indicate the cost of a single room.

- Fees paid to a country club or other association may be deductible as long as the club is used for business purposes more than 50 percent of the time.

- Expenses for job searches are deductible as long as they relate to your present line of work. Such expenses include résumé preparation costs, mailing costs, travel costs, etc.

Maximizing Exemptions

To maximize exemptions, take advantage of every avenue available. If possible, keep your taxable income below the point at which exemptions are lost because of the phaseout rules.

Partial blindness can qualify a taxpayer for the blindness exemption. An individual is blind if his or her central visual acuity does not exceed 20/200 in the better eye with corrective lenses or the field of vision is not more than 20 degrees.

Claiming Dependents

If there is a question as to whether you are providing more than 50 percent support to an eligible dependent, increase your contribution in December to ensure that you can take advantage of this deduction. For example, if your son who attends school makes $7000 a year and of this amount spends about $4000 on his support and you send him $300 a month or $3600 a year, it may be to your benefit to send him an extra payment of $225 for December and have him bank $225 of his money that he was going to use for support. In this case, you would provide $3825 for support and he would provide $3775; i.e., you could claim him as a dependent.

When a person approaches age 65 and his or her income is primarily from nontaxable sources, it may be a good strategy to allow one of his or her children or a close relative to claim him or her as a dependent.

Filing Status

A taxpayer who is a U.S. citizen or resident and is married to a nonresident alien normally may not file a joint return. The taxpayer, if he or she maintains a household, may be eligible for head-of-household filing status.

A taxpayer who is separated from his or her spouse and has been separated for the last 6 months of the tax year may qualify to file as a single taxpayer or head of household rather than as married filing separately.

Tax Reduction Changes

Make estimated tax payments on time and in sufficient amounts to avoid any tax penalties, which are stiffer under the Tax Reform Act. Determine as soon as possible whether you are liable to be hit by the alternative minimum tax (AMT). If so, devise a strategy to avoid or minimize it.

As a result of the Tax Reform Act, the large drop in tax rates have made tax- free municipal bonds a less attractive investment. At a 28 percent tax rate, it takes a 5.84 percent tax-free yield to equal 8 percent. Prior to the Tax Reform Act, with a 50 percent tax rate a 4 percent tax-free yield was equal to the 8 percent. Now, however, it appears that tax-exempt bonds may once again be a good investment. For example, some bonds pay high yields of 7 percent, which can be the equivalent of as much as 12 percent for many investors in states with high state tax rates. Accordingly, take a second look at the tax-free bonds in your portfolio.

If you realize that you have missed a deduction, exemption, etc., after you have filed your taxes, file an amended return. One of the most overlooked tax credits is the child-care credit. If you pay for child or other dependent care, take advantage of this credit.

High-income taxpayers who intend to make maximum use of 401(k) plans may not be eligible to contribute the stated maximum. Penalties can result for overcontributing to a 401(k) plan. Watch this carefully if you are a high-income taxpayer. Also, while you cannot borrow from your IRA without paying a penalty if you are under age 59½, by rolling over the IRA once a year you can use the proceeds as a personal loan for 59 days.

3
Corporations

There are certain key concepts involving the income taxation of corporations. Every corporation, unless it is specifically exempt or has dissolved, must file a tax return even if it had no taxable income for the year and regardless of the amount of its gross income for the taxable year. A corporation with no assets is not required to file a return after it stops doing business and dissolves.

Certain small corporations may elect to be treated as S corporations and thus taxed as partnerships; all other corporations are considered C corporations. The income tax form for C corporations is Form 1120. Form 1120S is used by S corporations. Every corporation, including S corporations, must have an employee identification number (EIN).

A corporation files its returns with the Internal Revenue Service center serving the area where the principal office of the corporation is located. A corporation's tax return is due on or before the fifteenth day of the third month following the close of the corporate tax year or, in the case of corporations using the calendar year, March 15 of the next year. A corporation may receive an automatic 6-month extension for filing a return by submitting an application for an extension on Form 7004. There is a substantial penalty for failure to either file on time or pay tax due on time. The penalty may be excused by the IRS if the corporation can establish that the failure to file or pay tax on time was due to a reasonable cause.

Corporations are allowed a deduction for a percentage of certain dividends received during the taxable year. Normally, the basis of stock held by a corporation is reduced by the untaxed portion of extraordinary dividends paid. The top corporate tax rate is 34 percent.

The Corporate Entity

Because corporations are not consumers, many economists contend that they should not be taxed as separate tax entities, but treated like partnerships where the profits are passed through the partnership and thus taxed to the owners. This, however, appears to be politically unacceptable. The average person fails to realize that most corporations are not large companies but small businesses.

Corporate income taxes have steadily declined as a share of federal revenues, from approximately 24 percent in 1960 to only about 6 percent in 1984 (the last year for which complete statistics are available). The Tax Reform Act was designed to increase the corporate share of income taxes and reduce the percentage paid by individual taxpayers.

In this chapter, C corporations and associations that are considered by the Internal Revenue Code as separate tax entities are discussed. S corporations, also known as Subchapter S corporations, are discussed in Chapter 5.

The earnings of a corporation are subject to three types of taxes: a corporate income tax, an accumulated earnings tax, and a personal holding tax. The income tax has been imposed on corporations since the first Income Tax Act of 1913. The accumulated earnings tax has been imposed on corporations since 1921. The personal holding company tax was first imposed on corporations in 1934.

While the legal meaning of a corporation or what constitutes a corporation is well defined in American law, it has a special and somewhat different meaning under the Internal Revenue Code. The code defines a corporation to include associations, joint stock companies, trusts, insurance companies, and certain partnerships that actually operate as associations or corporations, i.e., are considered as separate tax entities. This definition of corporation has been contained in the Internal Revenue codes since 1917.

In determining whether or not a corporation exists for income tax purposes, federal law takes precedence over state law. The federal law, therefore, will determine whether or not an entity should be taxed as a corporation. For example, the failure of a corporation to pay its franchise tax does not affect its status as a taxable entity under federal law unless its charter is revoked by the state.

The doctrine of "corporate entity" provides in general that, for purposes of income tax recognition, a corporation is a separate and distinct entity from the stockholders who own the corporation stock. The fact that the corporation as an entity may be completely dominated and controlled by one stockholder will not of itself mean that it is not a separate and distinct entity.

In one tax case the U.S. Supreme Court stated that, as a general rule, the court is not justified in disregarding the fact that a corporation is a separate entity simply because the taxpayer was dealing with the corporation in which he alone owned controlling interest. Accordingly, the court determined that there was no reason for disregarding the fact that taxpayer and corporation were separate tax entities.

In *Commissioners v. Southern Bell and Telegraph Company,* the Court of Appeals for the Sixth Circuit stated that a corporation is not a fiction but a creature of the law; and its ownership is a "nonconductor" that makes it impossible to attribute an interest in its property to its members.

In addition, the court concluded that the corporate entity is unaffected by changes in stock, ownership, name, business site, or type of business. Thus, a change of stock ownership does not result in a new corporation for tax purposes, nor does a change in name, business site, or type of business.

There are cases, however, where the general rule that the corporation stockholders are separate and distinct tax entities from the corporation has been disregarded. In those cases, the courts have looked beyond the corporate entity to the stockholders as the real parties in interest.

In one case, the Supreme Court disregarded the separate corporate entity when the court determined that the corporation was a mere agent for the stockholders, and that the corporation and the stockholders' businesses were so intermingled as to constitute a single business enterprise for practical purposes.

In another case, the Supreme Court disregarded the corporate entity for a holding company that held all the stock of a number of subsidiaries except for the necessary qualifying shares and all the companies were related to a single enterprise of buying, transporting, refining, and selling oil. When the subsidiaries became unable to pay their debts and the holding company took over their accumulated earnings and surplus, it was held that the parent company's taking over the assets of the subsidiaries was a mere bookkeeping transaction and thus not a dividend to the parent corporation. Therefore, the parent company was liable for the debts of the subsidiaries.

The Supreme Court has stated that the IRS can disregard the corporate tax entity when it is used solely for tax fraud or tax avoidance. In cases of fraud, tax avoidance, or other lack of bona fide transactions, and in cases in which the corporation has no real business purpose, the courts may disregard the corporate entity and look through the form to the substance of the organization and thus to the taxpayers.

If, however, the corporation is conducting its own business, the courts have shown a greater reluctance to disregard the corporate entity status even though the corporation may have been formed for the purposes of gaining an advantage under the law of the state of incorporation or to avoid or comply with the demands of creditors or to serve the stockholders' personal convenience. The key factor in such cases is whether or not the corporation is actually conducting its own business.

The use of a corporate form of business to reduce taxes is not considered tax avoidance. In fact, one of the first considerations that most businesses take into account is tax status and the relative advantage of using one procedure versus a different procedure. Therefore, the form of business that the taxpayer chooses is not necessarily illegal merely because it results in a tax savings for the taxpayer. In another Supreme Court case, the court said a taxpayer is not to be penalized for electing a legal or legitimate procedure that carries the least tax liability, i.e., a corporation in this case.

In an earlier Supreme Court case, the Court disregarded the corporate entity where it was used as a mere conduit for purposes of reporting gain on a transaction from an installment sale. Even so, the courts have held that the presence of a tax avoidance motive is of itself not sufficient to disregard the corporate entity as long as there were legitimate business purposes for using a corporate form of organization. The court in that case recognized the general rule that taxpayers might avail themselves of ever proper means of reducing tax liability.

As noted, in trying to determine whether to recognize a corporation as a separate entity, the IRS considers whether or not the corporation has a real business purpose. Whether the corporation should be disregarded as a valid entity depends, therefore, on all the surrounding facts and circumstances of the particular case in question. Although escaping business taxes is not considered legitimate corporate business, the disregard of the corporate entity by the IRS is the exception and not the rule.

Income of Corporations

The income of a corporation is computed similarly to that of an individual taxpayer. The Internal Revenue Code states that gross income includes "all income from whatever source derived including but not limited to" fifteen specific items, among which are compensation for services, fees, commissions, income derived from businesses, gains from dealing in property, rents, royalties, dividends, income from discharge of indebtedness, etc. It is noted that these items would also be income to an individual taxpayer.

The gross income of a corporation does not include any contributions to its capital. Contributions to capital normally arise in three situations: (1) contributions by stockholders at the time of incorporation; (2) contributions by stockholders subsequent to incorporation; and (3) contributions made by nonstockholders at any time. In each case, such contributions are not included in the corporation's gross income.

Sometimes it is difficult to determine whether the amounts given to a corporation are contributions to capital or payment for goods or services. If the funds are for the payment of goods or services, then they must be considered income.

The key factor, according to one court, is the motive or purpose and intent in making the contribution. If the motive for payment is an enhancement of a shareholder's proprietary interest, the payment is then considered a capital contribution. If, however, the primary motive is payment for goods or services rendered by the corporation or corporate personnel, then the contribution should be considered income to the corporation.

Assessments paid by stockholders—in one case, tenants of an apartment building—to help retire the bonds of the corporation were considered capital contributions and not payments of rent. In another case, a court held that a parent's corporation cancellation of indebtedness of its wholly owned subsidiary immediately before the merger of that subsidiary into another wholly owned subsidiary of the corporation was contribution to the capital of the debtor subsidiary.

Special Classes of Corporations

The Internal Revenue Code treats certain classes of corporations differently from ordinary corporations. In Chapter 5, the S corporation is discussed. All other corporations are considered C corporations, with the exception of insurance companies. The code makes special provisions for the taxation of life insurance companies, mutual insurance companies, and companies other than fire, marine, or flood insurance companies issuing perpetual policies.

Types of corporations receiving special treatment under the code are domestic corporations deriving a large part of their income from U.S. possessions, foreign corporations (i.e., corporations not engaged in trade or business in the United States), and bank and trust companies.

The code defines *bank* to mean a bank or trust company incorporated in doing business under the laws of the United States, the District of Columbia, or any state of which a substantial part of the business consists of receiving deposits, making loans, and exercising fiduciary powers similar to those permitted by national banks under the authority of the Comptroller of Currency.

One principle contained in the Internal Revenue Code is that some trusts are treated as separate entities and are thus taxable as such. One such unincorporated association is known as a "Massachusetts Trust." This business organization has a highly complex organizational structure and many of the same attributes as a regular corporation. Such organizations have existed in Massachusetts for more than 100 years, and thus have acquired their nickname.

An *association* under the code is defined as an organization created by agreement, declaration of trust, statute, or otherwise for the transaction of designated affairs or the attainment of some object. As with a corporation, the association continues even though the members or owners may change.

In determining whether or not an organization is a separate tax entity, the code and IRS regulations provide, in part, that a trust will be taxable as a trust and not as an association when the purpose of the organization is to vest in the trustees the responsibility for the property for beneficiaries who cannot share in the discharge of such responsibility. That is, a trust is created to protect or conserve property for beneficiaries, whereas any organization created by a beneficiary to carry on a profitmaking business would normally be classified as an association and, therefore, would be taxable as such.

One Fifth Court of Appeals case stated the criteria to determine whether or not an association is taxable as a corporation are as follows:

1. Ownership of property as an entity
2. Centralized management
3. Property status unaffected by death of beneficial owners
4. Easy transferability of beneficial interest
5. Ability to include large number of participants
6. Limitations of personal liability of the beneficial owners

It would appear, according to court cases, that at least three of the six elements must be present in order to classify the association as an entity and thus for it to be taxable as a separate entity, i.e., corporation.

The Internal Revenue Service stated in one of their regulations that the major characteristics of a separate tax entity are as follows:

1. Associates
2. An objective to carry on business and divide the gains therefrom
3. Continuity of life
4. Centralization of management
5. Liability for debts limited to the association's property
6. Free transferability of interest

The IRS, in their regulations, seem to imply that the absence of one of the above six items would not of itself prevent the association from being considered a separate tax entity. The test set forth by the IRS is that an organization will be treated as a taxable entity (association) if it more nearly resembles a corporation than a partnership.

Green Mail Payments

Prior to the Tax Reform Act, many corporate taxpayers were taking the position that the expenditures incurred to repurchase stock from stockholders to prevent a hostile takeover of the corporation by such shareholders (so-called green mail payments) were deductible business expenses. Green mail gains are subject to a 50 percent excise tax.

Green mail is presently defined as any consideration transferred by a corporation or a person acting in concert with a corporation to acquire, directly or indirectly, the stock from a shareholder under the following circumstances:

1. The shareholder from whom the corporation acquired the stock held the stock less than 2 years before agreeing to transfer it.
2. The acquisition was under an offer not made to all shareholders.
3. During the 2-year period ending with the date of the corporation's acquisition, a takeover was threatened.

To clarify that green mail payments were not deductible business expenses, the Tax Reform Act denies a deduction for any amounts paid or incurred by a corporation in connection with the redemption of its stock. This provision, however, is not limited to hostile takeover situations but applies to any corporate stock redemption. The theory is that the purchase of stock, including the repurchase by an issuing corporation of its own stock, should generally be treated as a capital transaction that does not give rise to a current deduction.

The change in the law was also made to help offset a case where the court found that as a result of extraordinary circumstances the amount paid by a corporation to repurchase its stock may be deductible in a year of the repurchase. In that case, *Five Star Manufacturing Company v. Commissioners* (355 F. 2d 724: 5th Circuit, 1966), the court relied on the fact that liquidation of the corporation was imminent, and, in the absence of repurchase, that no value would have been realized by the shareholders on such liquidation. The court, therefore, upheld the tax deduction of payment. Later cases, however, have limited the holding in the Five Star Case to its peculiar facts or have questioned its validity. The general rule is that a current business deduction may not be taken for stock exemption payments.

The Supreme Court has held that the requirement that stock redemption payments be capitalized extends not only to the amount representing consideration for stock itself but also to expenses such as legal, brokerage, or accounting fees incident to the acquisition. This limitation includes amounts paid to repurchase the stock, premiums paid for the stock, and legal, accounting, brokerage, transfer agent, appraisal, and similar fees incurred in the connection with the repurchase. Also included are any other expenditures necessary to or incident to repurchase where the representing costs incurred by the purchasing corporation or by the selling shareholders are thus paid or reimbursed by the purchasing corporation.

The provision is also intended to apply to any amounts paid by corporations to a selling shareholder pursuant to an agreement entered into as part of or in connection with the repurchase of stock whereunder the seller agrees not to purchase, finance a purchase, acquire stock, or in any way be a party or agent to the acquisition of stock of the corporation for a specified or indefinite period of time. This latter agreement is called a "standstill" agreement.

The limitation, however, does not apply to any interest that is deductible. Also, it does not apply to amounts constituting dividends related to payments for the purposes of the accumulated earnings, personal holding company, and foreign personal holding company taxes or for the purposes of the regular income tax in the case of regulated investment companies and real estate investment trusts. Such amounts, thus, will continue to qualify as a dividends-paid deduction to the same extent as under previous law.

The limitation also does not apply to otherwise deductible expenses incurred by a regulated investment company that is an open-ended mutual fund in connection with redemption of its stock upon demand of a shareholder. For example, costs incurred by a company in processing applications for redemption and issuing checks in payment for redeemed shares would be deductible to the same extent that they are under previous law.

Personal Holding Company

As noted earlier, there is a special tax or an additional tax designated as a personal holding company tax on corporations that fall within the classification of a personal holding company. Personal holding companies have been used as a "corporate pocketbook" to shelter a high-income taxpayer's passive investment income from stocks, bonds, etc. The classification can also apply to situations where a company receives payments for the personal services performed by one of its stockholders. For example, a baseball player who requires that the baseball club pay his salary to a company and not to him would be subject to the personal holding company rules.

The code defines *personal holding company* as a corporation in which at least 60 percent of gross income during the taxable year is personal holding company income, and 50 percent or more of the value of outstanding stock is owned directly or indirectly by not more than five individuals. Certain personal holding companies may elect to be treated as regulated investment companies and thus be taxed at the highest corporate rate on their undistributed income.

Personal holding company income includes dividends, interest, royalties (other than mineral, oil, or gas royalties, or copyright royalties), annuities, and gains from the sale or exchange of stock, securities, or futures transactions in commodities.

Also included under personal holding company income is income from estates and trusts, and amounts received under personal service contracts. In certain situations, payment for use of corporate property by a shareholder is also included as personal holding company income, as are rents, including interest constituting rent. The code excludes certain types of corporations meeting the above tests from the definition of personal holding company. These are exempt corporations, banks, domestic loan and building and loan associations, life insurance companies, security companies, foreign personal holding companies, and lending and finance companies of which 60 percent of ordinary gross income is derived directly from the active and regular conduct of a lending business and not more than 20 percent of ordinary gross income is personal holding company income.

Income that is subject to a personal holding company tax is defined by the code as undistributed personal holding company income. In computing the undistributed personal holding company income subject to the tax, dividends paid are reduced from that amount, as are certain allowable deductions.

Dividends paid after the close of the tax year and on or before the fifteenth day of the third month following the close of the tax year are considered as having been paid in the last day of the tax year. The purpose of this is to give personal holding companies additional time after the close of the year to determine more accurately the personal holding income, and thereby to enable them to pay additional dividends in order to escape the payment of the personal holding tax.

Also excluded are consent dividends. A consent dividend is a statutory fiction, which means that no dividends have been paid by the corporation but the stockholders consent to include in their returns their respective shares of the dividends, and treat those shares as though the dividends were paid by the corporation. This in effect constitutes a contribution to the capital of the corporation, allowing the shareholders to claim the deductible since otherwise taxable income is being given to the corporation.

Real Estate Investment Trust

A *real estate investment trust* (REIT) is an entity that receives most of its income from passive real estate–related investments and that receives conduit treatment for income that is distributed to the shareholders. To qualify as a REIT, an entity must be, for its entire tax year, a corporation or an unincorporated trust or association that would be taxable as a domestic corporation but for the REIT provisions. It must also meet the following requirements:

- It must be managed by one or more trustees.
- The beneficial ownership of its members must be evidenced by transferable shares or certificates of beneficial interest.
- The beneficial ownership must be held by 100 or more persons.
- At no time can 50 percent of the outstanding stock be owned by five or fewer persons.

In addition to the above requirements, there is a threefold gross income test, as follows:

1. At least 75 percent of entities' income, excluding gross income from prohibited transactions, must be income from rents or from real

property, interest on obligations procured from mortgages on real property or interest on real property gained from the sale or disposition of real property or distributions from another REIT, gain from the disposition of interest in an REIT, and income or gain derived from property that qualifies as foreclosure property.

2. At least 95 percent of its income must be derived from the avenues listed in item (1), plus any dividends, interest, or gain from the sale or disposition of any stock or securities.

3. Less than 30 percent of its income can be derived from securities or stock held less than 1 year, property disposed of in a prohibited transaction, and real property held less than 4 years (except for involuntary conversions).

REITs are required to distribute 95 percent of income, other than capital gains, within 12 months of the end of the tax year.

A REIT's sale of property that it holds primarily for sale to its customers in the ordinary course of its trade or business is considered a *prohibited transaction*. Prohibited transactions of a REIT are defined to include the fact that the number of sales of property that a REIT may make within what the law calls a "safe harbor" is increased to 7. In addition, the expenditures that a REIT may make within 4 years of sale is 30 percent of the net selling price of the property. The Tax Reform Act of 1986 also provided an alternative safe harbor whereby the REIT may make any number of sales during the tax year provided that the gross income from such sales does not exceed 15 percent of the REIT's taxable income. In addition, for penalty purposes the Tax Reform Act provided that in computing the amount of net income derived from prohibited transactions, losses from prohibited transactions may not be taken into account. For example, if a REIT has a net gain of $100 from a prohibited transaction, a net loss from a prohibited transaction of $50, a net rental income of $200, and no other income or deductions, the REIT would be subject to a tax on the gain from its prohibited transaction in the amount of $100 since the loss cannot be counted. Thus net income would be $300.

Real Estate Mortgage Investment Conduits and Taxable Mortgage Pools

Real estate mortgage investment conduits (REMICs) are multiclass vehicles for investing in real estate mortgages. They are not considered taxable entities, and their taxable income must be reported by the persons holding interests in them. A REMIC is subject to tax on income from foreclosure property and may be subject to a 100 percent tax on prohibited transactions.

A REMIC is any entity that has made an election to be treated as a REMIC, is composed of regular interests or residual interests, and has only one class of residual interests. In addition, substantially all assets must consist of qualified mortgages.

A taxable mortgage pool (TMP) is, however, treated as a corporation and is thus taxable as a corporation. A TMP is any entity other than a REMIC whose assets consist primarily of debt obligations and more than 50 percent of the debt obligations consist of real estate mortgages or interest in real estate.

4
Partnerships

The partnership is one of the most common forms of doing business. Special rules apply to partnership income, deductions, and transactions. In some cases, partnerships are treated as only a collection of individuals, and in other cases as entities in their own right. In this chapter the income tax treatment of partnerships and partnership interests will be discussed. For income tax purposes, a *partnership* is the relationship between two or more persons who join together to carry on a trade or business, with each person contributing money, property, labor, or skills and each expecting to share in the profits or losses of the business. No formal agreement is necessary to constitute a partnership.

An agreement between two corporations to manufacture equipment and divide the profits and a syndicate which bought and developed acreage and distributed subdivided lots to its members each of whom later sold the lots have been held to be partnerships for federal income tax purposes.

However, a shell partnership with no present intention to conduct an enterprise for a business purpose, a boxer and the fight promoter who didn't participate in management of the fight, and a feedlot operator who participated with a cattle owner in 10 percent of net profits on the sale of cattle have been held not to be partnerships.

If taxpayers file partnership returns, the IRS has the option of accepting or denying the designation. Generally, taxpayers will not be allowed to retroactively disclaim the existence of a partnership for tax purposes. In addition, a partner who files a tax return indicating that he or she is not a partner is generally barred from later claiming that he or she was a partner for the tax year in question. Since each tax year is considered separately, however, the partner barred from claiming he or she is a partner for the year in question may claim partnership status for a different tax year.

A partner may split his or her share of the partnership gains and losses with a nonmember of the partnership. In this case, a "sub-partnership" may be created.

Spousal Partnerships

Spouses who are in a family business may elect to file only a joint income tax return or they may treat the business as a partnership and file accordingly. If they elect to use the partnership concept, then the parties must file an information return for the partnership. The advantages of filing as a partnership is that it may increase the number of social security credits that each party may claim.

Family businesses are frequently operated as partnerships. It may be possible to gain tax savings where the partners are parents and children or brothers and sisters. If there are going to be substantial losses, family partnerships are usually not recommended. In cases of loss, the IRS requires the partners to allocate the losses for tax purposes in the same ratio as profits. Accordingly, losses allocated to low-income members of the family may not fully utilize the tax benefits associated with carrying losses back or forward.

Partnership as Tax Entity

A partnership is not considered a tax entity for purposes of income tax. However, any partnership is required to file an informational income tax return. Each partner is required to take into account separately in their individual tax return for that year the distributive share of the partnership whether or not any income, profits, etc., were distributed.

Treatment of any income or distributive share of a partner shall be determined as if such income or share were realized directly from the source from which it was realized by the partnership or incurred in the same manner as incurred by the partnership. Thus, the tax burden of the partnership passes through to each partner in the percentage that the partner shares in the gains or losses of the partnership.

In a community property state where husband and wife are both domiciled within the state and only one spouse is a member of the partnership, if separate returns are filed by husband and wife, any part of the distributive share of the partnership is required to be equally reported by husband and wife. In a non-community property state, the distributive share would go to the partner spouse who has the interest in the partnership.

Determination of the partner's interest in a partnership is required to ascertain that portion of the partner's tax liability and is normally required to be made only at the end of the partnership's tax year. In certain cases, the adjusted basis of a partner's interest in a partnership may be determined by reference to the partner's share of the adjusted basis of the partnership's property that would be distributable to the parties upon termination of the partnership. Thus, for example, if a partner owned 50 percent interest in the property of the partnership and shares 50 percent of the proceeds of the partnership, then that partner would normally be liable to claim on the income tax return 50 percent of the gross income of the partnership.

As noted earlier, the general rule is that each partner is required to report on his or her individual tax return that portion of the partnership profit that is attributable to that partner whether or not a distribution has been made.

Tax Year

In computing a partner's taxable income for the tax year, the partner is required to include his or her distributive share of the partnership items for any partnership year ending within or with the tax year. The tax year of a partnership is determined as if the partnership were a taxpayer. A newly formed partnership may adopt a tax year that is the same as the tax year of all of its principal partners, or the same as the tax year to which its principal partners are changing without seeking prior approval of the IRS. In addition, a partnership may adopt a calendar year without securing prior approval. For the adoption or change in a tax year, the partnership must first obtain permission from the IRS, except as noted above. In addition, an existing partnership may not change its tax year without approval from the IRS unless all principal partners are using the same tax year to which the partnership is changing or unless all principal partners concurrently change to the new tax year. Note, in this regard, that a partner cannot normally change his or her tax year without securing approval from the IRS. For purposes of this regulation, a *principal partner* is defined as a partner who owns an interest of 5 percent or more in the partnership's profits or capital of the partnership.

In order to request a change in tax year, an application must be forwarded to the Commissioner of Internal Revenue, Washington, D.C. 20224. It must be filed on IRS Form 1128.

In the case of a newly formed partnership where prior approval of the IRS is required for the adoption of the tax year, the form shall be filed with the Commissioner of the IRS on or before the last day of the month following the close of the tax year to be adopted.

When prior approval is required, the partnership or business must establish to the satisfaction of the commissioner that there is a legitimate, bona fide business purpose for the modified tax year. When a partner retires or otherwise disposes of his or her entire interest in the partnership, the partnership tax year shall close with respect to that partner; in addition, that partner is required to claim on his or her individual income tax return the profit or loss of the partnership as of the day that the entire interest was disposed of in the partnership. For example, if a partner disposes of her interest on June 1, at which time the partnership shows a profit of $6000 for that year, the partner would be required to show on her individual income tax return that portion of the $6000 that represents her interest in the partnership. This would be required even though the partnership may lose money in the second half of the tax year and thus end the year with a loss.

When a partner dies, however, the partnership tax year shall not close with respect to that partner until the end of the partnership tax year. Therefore, the deceased partner's distributive share for tax purposes would be determined on the basis of the entire tax year of the partnership.

The final return of a deceased partner shall include only his or her share of the partnership's taxable income for any partnership tax year or year ending with the last tax year for the partnership. The distributive share of any partnership's taxable income ending after the decedent's last tax year is included in his or her estate or successor in interest. Thus, if the deceased taxpayer was on a fiscal year, i.e., July 1 to June 30, and the partnership of which he was a member was on a calendar year and the taxpayer died in May, then the close of the last tax year for which he or she was a partner would be June 30. Therefore, the only partnership distributive income would be what was included at the close of the partnership year prior to death of the partner, i.e., December 31 of the prior year; and the distributive income from the partnership that was computed at the end of the partnership year would then be considered gross income to the estate of the deceased taxpayer.

If a partner sells, exchanges, or reduces his or her interest in a partnership, the partnership's tax year will continue to its normal end. In this case, the partner's distributive share shall be determined by taking into account his or her varying interest in the partnership during the partnership's tax year. If a taxpayer makes a gift of a partnership's interest, then that gift, even though it may completely dispose of the taxpayer's interest in the partnership, does not close out the tax year until the end of the normal partnership year. The taxpayer would be required to include on his or her individual income tax return that portion of the partnership income attributable to him or her for that portion of the year prior to the date of the gift. That portion attributable to that share after the date of the gift would be taxable to the donee of the gift, i.e., the person who received the gift.

In the case of transactions between partners, the partner who engages in the transaction in other than in a capacity as partner shall be treated for allocatable income determinations as if he or she were not a partner to the partnership. However, sales or exchange of property with respect to controlled partnership losses would normally be denied.

Termination of Partnerships

A partnership shall terminate when operations of the partnership are discontinued and no further business continues to be carried on by any of the partners in the name of the partnership. In addition, a partnership shall be considered to have terminated when 50 percent or more of the total interest in the partnership capital and profits is sold or exchanged within a period of 12 consecutive months. The 50 percent or more interest means at least 50 percent interest ownership of the partnership's capital and at least 50 percent interest in partnership profits. For tax purposes, a partnership does not terminate upon the death of a partner if the remaining partners continue to operate the partnership business.

If two or more partnerships merge and consolidate into one partnership, then the new partnership shall be considered as a continuation of the prior partnership that had the greatest assets, providing the stockholders of that partnership own at least 50 percent of the stock and obtain at least 50 percent of the derivative share of the income. If partnerships do not meet that test when they are merged with other partnerships, then they shall be considered as terminated on the date of the merger.

If a partnership divides into two or more partnerships, then those partnerships which acquire less than a 50 percent interest in the capital and profits of the prior partnership shall be considered as terminated. If one of the partnerships acquires 50 percent or more of the capital and profits of the prior partnership, then that partnership shall be considered a continuation of the earlier partnership before the split. The resulting continuing partnership is required to file a return for the tax year of the partnership that has been divided. The return is required to indicate that the partnership is a continuation of a divided partnership and must set forth separately the distributive shares of the partners for periods prior to and after the date of the division.

Organizational Expenses

Organizational expenses of a partnership may be treated as deferred expenses, or the partnership may amortize the organizational expenses over a period of not less than 60 months on a straight-line basis. The period must begin with the month that the partnership commences business. A partnership on a cash basis of accounting, however, cannot make any allowances with respect to any expenses not yet paid.

If the partnership is terminated prior to a complete writing off of the organizational expenses, then the partnership in its last tax year must deduct the unamortized amount of the organizational expense in that final tax year. No deductions are allowed for capitalized syndication expenses. In other words, an expense for syndication rather than an organizational expense must be capitalized and cannot be amortized.

Organizational expenses are defined by Section 709(B2) of the Internal Revenue Code as expenses that are necessary to the creation of the partnership; are chargeable to the capital account; and are of a character which, if expended incident to the creation of a partnership having an ascertainable life would, except for Section 709(A), be amortized over such life.

In order to qualify as an organizational expense, the expenditure must meet each of the three criteria. In addition, the expense must be incurred during the period beginning at a point which is a reasonable time before the partnership begins and ends with the date prescribed by law for filing of a partnership return for the tax year that the partnership begins business. The item must also be of a nature normally expected to benefit the partnership throughout the entire life of the partnership, such as legal fees for services incident to organization of the partnership, negotiation and preparation of the partnership agreement, and accounting services in preparation of the partnership's filing fees. Expenses that are not considered organizational expenses within the meaning of Section 709 include the following:

1. Expenses connected with acquiring assets for the partnership or transferring assets to the partnership.

2. Expenses involved with the admission or removal of partners other than when the partnership is first organized.

3. Expenses associated with a contract relating to the operation of the partnership trade or business.

4. Syndication expenses (brokerage fees, registration fees, legal fees to the underwriter or placement agency, etc.). As noted earlier, syndication expenses must be capitalized.

For purposes of determining organizational expenses, the date that a partnership begins business is normally when it starts business operations. The mere signing of a partnership agreement is not of itself sufficient to create the partnership. The acquisition of operating assets necessary to carry on the partnership business has or will in certain cases constitute for beginning of business for the partnership.

Partnership Property

If partnership property is contributed to the partnership by a partner, its basis is the adjusted basis of such property to the contributing partner at the time the asset is transferred to the partnership. Thus, the property has the same basis in the hands of the partnership as it had in the hands of the contributing partner. The holding period of such property by a partnership may in most cases include the period for which it was held by the partner.

The basis of a partner's interest is the amount of money contributed plus the adjusted basis of any property contributed by the partner. The adjusted basis of the property is determined on the day of acquisition by the partnership.

Distributions

The general rule regarding distributions is that when money is distributed by a partnership to a partner no gain is recognized to the partner except to the extent that the distribution exceeds the adjusted basis of the partner's interest in the partnership immediately before the distribution. The advances or drawings of money or property by a partner is considered as current distributions made on the last day of the partnership's tax year with respect to such partner.

Losses are normally recognized only when the entire partnership interest is liquidated. Moreover, money distributed to the partner that is not partnership income or gain may be considered in most cases a return of capital and, therefore, is not included in the partner's individual tax return for that tax year unless it exceeds the taxpayer's adjusted basis. It does, however, reduce the partner's basis in the partnership.

If property in lieu of money is distributed to a partner, then that property is either a return of capital or a distributive share of partnership gain, and it is valued at its fair market value on the date of distribution.

Partnership Profits

Unless otherwise agreed to, the general rule is that the parties share in the profits and losses in the partnership in the same ratio as their investments. However, parties may agree otherwise. A partnership determines its income in much the same way that individual taxpayers determine income.

Profits and any other income are not taxed to the partnership but pass to the taxpayers as taxable income. Even though the profits pass to the taxpayers, in most cases elections or choices regarding the profits of the partnership are made by the partnership and not the individual taxpayers. A few choices are made by the individuals.

Areas in which decisions are usually made by the partnership include the method of partnership accounting (cash or accrual); the method of computing depreciation, amortization, and depletion of partnership property; and nonrecognition of gain on exchanges of partnership property.

Areas in which decisions are made by individual partners when individual tax returns are filed include the treatment of foreign and U.S. possessions taxes, certain mining and exploration expenditures, investment interest limitations, and income from the discharge of an indebtedness.

Master Limited Partnerships

Publicly traded partnerships such as master limited partnerships (MLPs) are generally treated by the IRS as corporations, or their income will be treated as portfolio income. An MLP is one method that may be used to offset the restriction on "passive" losses and loss of certain tax benefits by real estate investors. Unlike traditional partnerships, MLPs are publicly traded. Therefore, holders of MLP interests can sell their interests almost at will. As with other partnerships, tax deductions are passed through the partnerships to the individuals.

In recent years, MLPs have been used in the petroleum industry. There are two basic types of MLPs, the "rollup" or the "rolldown" (the rolldown is also called the "dropdown").

A rollup MLP is one that is formed from two or more separate entities (usually limited partnerships). The separate entities are "rolled up" into one MLP.

The rolldown type is usually formed by a large company (sponsor) that may be a potential takeover target. The assets of the company are spun off into an MLP which remains under control of the sponsor. Interests that are not retained or acquired by the sponsor are sold to the public, which brings additional assets into the MLP. An alternative to selling the interests is distributing the partnership interests through a partial or complete dissolution of the sponsor.

The MLP is taxed as a partnership because it violates at least two of the six corporate characteristics required to prevent being taxed as an association, i.e., corporation. The six characteristics that the IRS uses to determine corporate status are:

1. Associates or shareholders
2. An objective to carry on business and divide the gains therefrom
3. Continuity of life
4. Centralization of management
5. Liability for debts limited to the association's property
6. Free transferability of interest

In most cases, when the MLPs are formed, neither the partners nor the partnerships are required to recognize gain or loss on the transfer of property necessary to form the MLP. The partners assume a substituted basis for their partnership units. The popularity of the MLP is the fact that partners can sell their shares like stock in a corporation; yet they retain most of the advantages of a partnership form of business organization.

Some tax experts state that, with the increasing popularity of MLPs, a substantial question exists as to whether the IRS will attempt to treat MLPs as tax entities, which could mean fewer tax benefits for individual interest holders. In 1984, the IRS proposed that if an MLP had more than 35 partners it would be considered as a separate tax entity, i.e., corporation. However, this proposal was never adopted as a regulation.

5

S Corporations

An eligible domestic corporation may avoid the double taxation by electing to be treated as an S corporation under the rules of Subchapter S of the Internal Revenue Code. The income of an S corporation is attributed to the shareholders, similar to a partnership.

Recent tax changes involving S corporations include the requirement that an S corporation pay estimated tax payments if its expected liability is $500 or more for the tax on net recognized built-in gain, excess net passive income, and any increase in tax for which the S corporation is liable from the recapture of investment credits. Also, if you are more than a 2 percent owner in an S corporation, you may be treated as self-employed for the purpose of contributing to a health insurance plan for yourself, your spouse, and your dependents. If eligible, you may deduct up to 25 percent of the amount paid on your behalf during the tax year for this health insurance. (This deduction has been extended at least through the tax years beginning before January 1, 1992.)

With regard to tax status of corporations, there are two general types of corporations, C and S. The C corporation, a regular corporation, is considered a separate tax entity and thus is required to file and pay income tax. (See the discussion of regular corporations and associations in Chapter 3.) The second type of corporation is the S corporation.

The S corporation has been more commonly referred to as a partnership type corporation. It first came into being in 1958. Except for the lack of a requirement to pay a corporate income tax and the ability to pass through income or loss to the shareholders (like a partnership), a Subchapter S corporation enjoys all the benefits of a standard corporation. For an S corporation taxable income is computed in substantially the same manner that partnership income is computed.

S corporations were originally called Subchapter S corporations.

Subchapter S refers to Subchapter S of Chapter 1, Subtitle A, of the Internal Revenue Code of 1954, as amended. Subchapter S is entitled "The Election of Certain Small Business Corporations as to Tax Status." Basically, the law was designed to permit small, closely held corporations to be treated more like partnerships for income tax purposes. This provision was first enacted in 1958, substantially modified in 1982, and further modified by the Tax Reform Act of 1986.

As noted above, the concept of an S (or Subchapter S) corporation is to permit small corporations to be treated like partnerships. This is accomplished by exempting the S corporation from income tax and allowing the passing of income and losses to the shareholders as if they were partners in a partnership. In this chapter, the basic principles involving S corporations and their tax treatment will be discussed. This is a highly complex area, and, therefore, only the major principles are addressed.

Pursuant to the Subchapter S Revision Act of 1982, corporations that were qualified for the designation under Subchapter S are officially designated as S corporations, and corporations that do not have the S corporate status (other corporations) are designated by the act as C corporations because they are subject to the rules set forth in Subchapter C of the Internal Revenue Code. While the terms *Subchapter S* and *S corporation* are used interchangeably, technically all such corporations should be listed as S corporations.

Advantages of S Corporation Status

The primary advantage of an S corporation is that it is not considered a separate tax entity; instead its income and losses are computed in much the same way that partnership income and losses are computed. Basically, the profits and losses are passed through the corporation to the stockholders. Normally, an S corporation is not subject to an accumulated earnings tax, a personal holding company tax, or a minimum tax because of preference items and adjustments. Preference items include accelerated depreciation, intangible drilling costs, bad debt deductions, and so forth.

Another advantage of an S corporation is that stockholders enjoy the nontax advantages of operating in a corporate form—freedom of owners from personal liability for business debts, free transferability of stock, and the continuity of business upon a change of business owners. In addition, the S corporation avoids the double tax on corporation earnings.

Since a corporation may lose money during its first few years of operation, electing S corporation status will allow those losses to pass through to the shareholders, whereas a C corporation would not be able to take advantage of those losses until the corporation started earning profits. While the same advantages are available to a business operating as a sole proprietorship or a partnership, the advantage that the S corporation has over the proprietorship and the partnership is the limited personal liability.

While capital losses of a C corporation can be carried back for only 3 years and the corporation must have a profit before the losses can be utilized as tax advantages, an S corporation, by passing its losses through to its shareholders, can use those losses to offset income (subject to certain restrictions) of the shareholders.

Many people in the past have used the S corporation as a method of splitting family income to channel some of the profits of the business to other members of the household. There is a question as to the practical effects of the Tax Reform Act on this income-splitting use of the S corporation. It appears, however, that if the child is in fact a bona fide shareholder in the S corporation, then that child would not be subject to the parental income restrictions established by the Tax Reform Act.

Another advantage of an S corporation is that if it does not have earnings and profits accumulated from its previous existence, if any, as a C corporation, it can have unlimited amounts of passive income. If it has earnings and profits carried forward from prior existence as a C corporation, then as long as the passive income does not exceed 25 percent of the gross receipts for 3 consecutive years, it would not be subject to the personal holding company tax and the problems associated with paying a personal holding company tax.

While the taxable income of an S corporation is generally computed in the same manner as the taxable income of an individual, there are several important exceptions to this general rule:

- Items of income have to be separately stated if their separate treatment could affect the taxpayer's tax liability.
- Certain personal deductions and exemptions may not be taken by an S corporation.
- There are limits on loss deductions for losses incurred in transactions with related persons.
- Fringe benefits for shareholders owning 2 percent or less of the corporation may not be deductible.

Disadvantages of S Corporation Status

There are certain situations where an election to be treated as an S corporation would not be advisable for the shareholders. Those include situations where the shareholders have excessive income, since the income of the S corporation would pass through the corporation to the shareholders and, therefore, would raise their taxable income even if not distributed.

Corporations that earn substantial profits that normally would be reinvested in the corporation would be unable to take advantage of the S status in that the earnings would be taxable to the shareholders in the year earned.

Since S corporations have a rule limiting deductions for certain expenses to gross income, the use of an S corporation for "hobby" enterprises is not advisable. C corporation status may be more appropriate since the hobby-loss rule does not automatically apply to C corporations. *Note:* With regard to "hobby" enterprises, an S corporation must be formed for profit.

Another problem that may exist is that many states do not recognize S corporations as partnerships for their own state income tax determinations. Therefore, an S corporation may be required to pay state income taxes, and then in those states that base individual income tax on the federal tax, the taxpayer would be required to pay twice.

Liquidations of S Corporations

The sale of stock and the acquisition of stock in an S corporation is handled in much the same way as for a C corporation, with the major exception that, as noted earlier, certain shareholders may affect the eligibility of a corporation to be treated as an S corporation.

The sale of the business is very similar to the sale of a regular corporation. The sale of assets, holdings, etc., of the S corporation is treated as are the sale of assets of a C corporation, and reorganizations are similarly treated.

S Corporation Designations

For a corporation to be eligible for treatment as an S corporation, it must meet all the requirements set forth below:

1. It must be a domestic corporation.

2. It must not be an ineligible corporation.

3. It must have no more than a specified number of shareholders.

4. It must have only individuals, estates, or certain trusts as shareholders.

5. It must have no nonresident alien shareholders.

6. It must have only one class of stock.

S Election

If a corporation meets the six requirements, the corporation may elect to be treated as an S corporation. The election must be made within the prescribed time and must be consented to by all the shareholders.

Domestic Corporations

As noted, an S corporation must be a domestic corporation. The Internal Revenue Code designates that a domestic corporation is one which is created or organized in the United States under state or federal law. For an election to be valid, the corporation must on the date of the election have acquired a legal existence. For example, in one tax court case, there was a question as to whether or not a corporation had been formed pursuant to the laws of the state of Texas. The Texas courts determined that the effective date of the corporation formation was not until May 1, 1972. The election by the corporation to be treated as an S corporation was made prior to that date. On that basis, the tax court concluded that the election was invalid on two grounds: first, that an election was made prior to the legal existence of the corporation; second, no evidence was submitted that all the stockholders had consented to the election.

While an S corporation is taxed similarly to a partnership, it is not a partnership, and there are some subtle distinctions between an S corporation and a partnership.

The S corporation election is available only when the corporation is operated for profit or with the intention of making a profit. The S status is not available to a corporation maintained as a hobby or for personal gratification of shareholders.

Ineligible Corporations

The ineligible corporations as defined by Section 1361(B)(2) of the Subchapter S Revision Act of 1982 are corporations that fall in the following categories:

1. A member of an affiliated group as defined under Section 1504 (see below)

2. A financial institution to which Section 585 or 593 applies (both sections provide for special bad debt deductions)

3. An insurance company subject to tax under Subchapter L (a special rule exists for casualty insurance companies)

4. A corporation to which an election under Section 936 applies (Puerto Rico or U.S. possession tax credits)

5. A DISC (domestic international sales corporation) or former DISC

A member of an affiliated group noted in category 1 is defined as two or more corporations connected to a stock ownership with a single common parent corporation. Thus, there will also be one parent and one or more subsidiaries. To be considered a parent, the parent must own directly at least 80 percent of the voting and nonvoting stock of at least one of the subsidiaries. Accordingly, the only time the affiliated group prohibition applies is when the corporation directly owns 80 percent or more of another corporation's stock. If an S corporation acquires a greater than 80 percent interest in another corporation, then that acquisition would disqualify the S corporation and terminates its S corporation status. A corporation which is otherwise qualified to be treated as an S corporation but not qualified because of the fact that it owns 80 percent or greater interest in another corporation may divest itself of that percentage of ownership of stock in the other corporation to reduce it to less than 80 percent. Once the percentage is reduced below 80 percent, then the corporation is no longer barred from becoming an S corporation because of the affiliated group prohibition.

Another exception to the affiliated group limitation against S status is where a parent S corporation owns 80 percent or more stock in a subsidiary which has not begun business and has no gross income. If the subsidiary engages in active business operations during the tax year, this automatically disqualifies the parent corporation from being treated as an S corporation.

Life insurance and casualty insurance companies are ineligible for S status if they are covered by Subchapter L. A casualty insurance company may qualify, however, as an exception to this rule if it meets any one of the three following requirements:

1. It was a Subchapter S casualty insurance company on or before July 12, 1982.

2. The corporation was formed prior to April 1982 and had made an election prior to that date to be treated as a Subchapter S corporation.

3. The corporation was approved for membership on an established insurance exchange pursuant to a written agreement entered into before December 31, 1982.

Any casualty insurance company claiming S status by meeting one of the above requirements is also required to have made a Subchapter S election in its first tax year beginning after 1984.

Number of Shareholders

An S corporation may have no more than 35 shareholders. A husband and wife who own stock in an S corporation are treated as one shareholder for purposes of the shareholder number limitation regardless of the form of ownership, i.e., separate, joint, or both. This joint treatment continues upon the death of either or both so long as the stock continues to be held by the surviving spouse or one of the spouse's estates. For stock being held by nominee, agent, or guardian, the individual for whom such stock is being held is considered the shareholder and not the nominee, agent, or guardian. Thus, the 35-shareholder restriction cannot be evaded by the appointment of one agent to hold stock for more than one shareholder.

Types of Shareholders

As noted, the only shareholders an S corporation may have are individuals, estates, and certain types of trusts. In addition, a shareholder must not be a nonresident alien, nor may a foreign trust be a shareholder. Accordingly, partnerships and other corporations cannot be shareholders in an S corporation.

As noted, qualified shareholders include certain trusts. The first Subchapter S legislation prohibited any trust from being a shareholder in an S corporation. This was modified in 1982.

The Subchapter S Revision Act of 1982 broadened the concept and allowed the following types of trusts to be shareholders in an S corporation:

1. A grantor trust (a trust which is wholly owned by the grantor, providing the grantor is a U.S. citizen and for purposes of the S corporation is treated as a shareholder of the S stock)

2. A trust of which someone other than the grantor is a substantial owner (under this type of trust, someone other than the grantor has the power to vest the trust raise or trust income)

3. A testamentary trust or trust receiving Subchapter S stock pursuant to probation of a will (in this case, the trust may continue to hold the S stock for a period of 60 days beginning from the date that the stock is transferred to it)

4. A qualified Subchapter S trust

Class of Stock

As noted, an S corporation must have only one class of stock. In determining whether or not a corporation has one or more classes of stock, only outstanding stock is considered. Accordingly, a corporation which may issue or has authority to issue both common or preferred stock that has not issued one of the two (e.g., preferred stock) may still qualify as an S corporation. If, however, it issues the preferred stock, then since it would have issued two types of stock, it would be disqualified.

The one-class-of-stock limitation has been held to mean that each share of stock must be identical to every other share of stock with regard to income and distributions of the corporation.

The IRS recently ruled that a stock purchase agreement which restricted the transfer of only one of four shareholders' stocks did not create a second class of stock. In that case, the one shareholder was restricted from transferring his stock unless he obtained consent of the other three shareholders, and if such consent could not be obtained, he could sell his stock only to the corporation or to other shareholders at book value. In addition, the purchase agreement for the stock gave the corporation or a majority of other shareholders the right to purchase his stock in the event of his termination of employment, disability, or death. It was contended that, since the stock held by one of four stockholders was restricted under the above-stated terms, it was a different class from the other stock, which could be freely transferred or sold and over which the company had no right of redemption. The IRS, however, held that there was only one class, and concluded that the one-class-of-stock rule should be interpreted to mean that each share of stock must be identical to every other share of stock with respect to the profits and assets of the corporation.

Based on this decision and the 1982 revision to the S corporation statutes, voting rights can now be concentrated among active shareholders, while stock without voting rights can be given to inactive shareholders (such as children) as long as each share of stock is identical to any other share of stock with respect to profits and assets of the corporation.

Estimated Taxes

In a recent IRS ruling, the pass-through ability of an S corporation was discussed in a case involving the requirement to pay quarterly estimated taxes. The IRS stated that closely held S concerns don't pay corporate taxes and that they pass profit or loss through to owners for tax purposes. The shareholders, therefore, are required to pay quarterly estimated taxes on S corporation income attributed to them.

In a separate ruling the IRS considered the question of how to compute the quarterly payments. In that case, the question revolved around whether the shareholders could use seasonal losses to trim quarterly estimated tax payments. The S corporation expected a loss for the first half of the year but an overall profit for the entire year. The IRS held that a year-to-date method may be used to compute quarterly payments. Therefore, if in the tax year to date (as of the end of the quarter) the S corporation had not made any profit, then no quarterly estimated tax payment was due. In addition, the taxpayer could use the attributed share of the loss to date to offset earnings from other sources in computing the quarterly payments.

Election Requirements

As noted, one of the requirements for an S corporation is to make a timely election for S corporation treatment. The election is made by using standard IRS Form 2553, which must be signed by a corporate officer who is authorized to sign the corporation's tax returns.

A corporation, otherwise eligible, may make an election at any time to be considered an S corporation for the following tax year. For the election to be effective in the year that it is made, however, the election must be made on or before the fifteenth day of the third month of the tax year, the corporation must have been eligible to make the election for the entire year, and each stockholder in the corporation during the portion of the year prior to the election must consent even if that person is no longer a stockholder on the date the election is made.

The IRS has continually taken the position that for the election to be valid for the entire tax year, not only must it be made within the first 2½ months of the tax year, it also must be filed prior to the end of the tax year.

If a corporation makes an election within the first 2½ months but is otherwise not qualified during that tax year, the corporation may under certain circumstances be treated as having made the election for the next tax year if the restrictions barring S corporation status are removed prior to the beginning of the next tax year. However, the corporation *must* be a legal entity at the time the election is made.

A newly formed corporation, in order to be considered an S corporation from its start, must make its election no later than the fifteenth day of the third month of its first tax year, and it must also file such election prior to the end of that first tax year. In one case, a corporation began its tax year on December 14, 1983. The corporation received permission for its first tax year to be from December 14 to December 31, 1983. The corporation filed its election and consent on January 6, 1984. Even though the election was filed within 2½ months of the start of the tax year, the IRS concluded that it was not filed within the first tax year and thus the corporation did not make a proper election to be treated as an S corporation, and the tax court so agreed.

A corporation's first tax year begins when one of the following three situations or events occurs:

1. The corporation has shareholders.

2. The corporation acquires assets.

3. The corporation begins doing business.

Filing Requirement

As stated, to qualify under Subchapter S, the corporation must file with the IRS. The courts and the IRS have strictly enforced the filing deadlines for corporation S elections. Filing consists of placing the form in the mail properly addressed and with sufficient postage.

For example, in one case (*J. Simons*, 208 F. Supp. 744), the deadline for filing a Subchapter S election was December 1. Had the election been postmarked on that date, the filing would have been considered timely even though it would not have reached the district director's office until after December 2. On December 2, the document was personally delivered to the district director's office. The court held that the filing was not timely and, therefore, the corporation did not qualify for Subchapter S treatment even though the regularly mailed election would not have been received until after December 2.

In one Sixth Circuit Court of Appeals case, the court held that an election was not filed properly because at the time it was filed, the corporation had not yet acquired legal existence.

In another court case, the taxpayer was allowed to prove by secondary evidence that a timely election had been filed even though the IRS contended that it had not received such election. It would appear in this case that the taxpayer could have avoided the court litigation had the election been sent by certified or registered mail.

In a recent case, the tax court found that a valid Subchapter S election was timely filed even though the IRS had no record of ever having received Form 2553. In this case, the taxpayer produced evidence from himself, his mother, and his accountant to prove that the election form had been prepared, signed, and mailed. According to the court, the evidence indicated a presumption of delivery which the IRS was not able to counter.

If the final date for filing a form is a Saturday, Sunday, or a day that is a legal holiday in the District of Columbia, the filing is considered timely if made on the next succeeding business day. Therefore, if the final day for filing is a Saturday, an election filed the next Monday would be considered timely filed.

Termination of Status

Corporation S status automatically terminates when a disqualifying act occurs or the corporation is no longer qualified to be treated as an S corporation. The disqualification is automatic. However, a provision that allows for an S corporation not to lose its S status exists in the case of inadvertent termination. In such cases, an S corporation may retain its status under the following conditions:

1. The IRS or the tax court determines that the termination was inadvertent.
2. Within a reasonable period after discovering the disqualifying item steps are taken to requalify the corporation.
3. Both the shareholders and corporation involved agree to make adjustments required by the IRS.

Once a corporation's Subchapter S status has been either terminated or revoked, generally the corporation must wait 5 tax years before it or a successor corporation may elect S corporation status again. For purposes of this limitation, a successor corporation is one in which 50 percent of the stock is owned directly or indirectly by the same shareholders who own 50 percent or more of the stock of the former S corporation, and the new corporation has acquired a substantial portion of the assets of the former corporation.

The IRS is permitted to consent to a reelection prior to the end of the 5-year waiting period under the following circumstances: if there is more than a 50 percent change in ownership in the corporation; if the event causing the termination was not reasonably within the control of the corporation or shareholders with a substantial interest in the corporation; or if the determination was not planned or participated in by substantial shareholders.

Consent of Shareholders

All shareholders must consent to the election. Consent is normally made on IRS Form 2553. However, individual shareholders may consent on a separate statement attached to Form 2553 providing the separate statement includes the name, address, taxpayer identification number, the shareholders in the corporation, the percentage or number of shares owned by the stockholder, and the date on which the stock was acquired.

Once a stockholder has consented, the consent is binding and may not be withdrawn after a valid election is made by the corporation. There are provisions for the IRS to grant extension of time for filing consents.

The general rule is that each person who is a stockholder at the time the election is made by the corporation must file a consent. As noted earlier, if the election is to be retroactive to the first of the tax year, all persons who have owned stock in the company during that period of time for which it is retroactive must file a consent even if they do not own property at this time. If stock is owned as community property by a husband and wife, both must consent. In the case of a minor, consent must be by the minor's legal guardian. In one case where a stockholder held the stock in his name but in trust for his brother, both were required to consent.

A new stockholder does not have the power to revoke a valid S election unless the new stockholder owns more than 50 percent interest in the voting stock. Accordingly, on change of stockholders, the S corporation status continues until it is either terminated by a disqualifying act or voluntarily revoked by the corporation. Persons who become stockholders after a valid election are not required to consent to the election.

Tax Year

Every S corporation electing the Subchapter S status after October 1982 is required to have as its tax year a "permitted" year. A permitted year is defined as a calendar year ending on December 31 or any other tax year with prior IRS approval. For the IRS to approve a year other than a calendar year, the corporation must show a good business purpose.

The Tax Reform Act requires that S corporations conform more closely to the tax years of their owners. This change is directed at professionals who structure their practice as S corporations. Prior to the tax reform, these persons could postpone taxes on a portion of their income by putting the business on a different tax year from the calendar year they used for their personal taxes. If an S corporation's tax year ends after the personal tax year, then any profits from the corporation are not required to be reported as income until the year in which it is paid, i.e., the next personal tax year. Congressional tax writers estimated that requiring an earlier reporting of income would raise approximately $1.7 billion in the next 5 years. There is in the act a provision, which many accounting firms may request, that permits the IRS to approve a different tax year. As one accountant stated, most of an accounting firm's work is in the first quarter of the calendar year. Therefore, it is more natural for them to use a fiscal year (July to June) for tax purposes. Undoubtedly, the IRS will be called on to decide this issue.

Terminations

As noted, once a corporation qualifies as an S corporation, that status is retained until a terminating event occurs or the election is revoked by the corporation with consent of the majority of the stockholders.

Since a termination or revocation is no longer automatically retroactive to the beginning of a tax year, in many cases, a corporation that has its Subchapter S status either terminated or revoked during the tax year may have to file two tax returns for that year, one for that portion of the year in which it was entitled to S corporation treatment and another for the balance of the year when it is considered a C corporation.

Termination of Subchapter S status occurs when any of the necessary designations is violated, specifically if:

1. The number of shareholders exceeds 35.

2. The corporation acquires 80 percent or more of the voting stock of another corporation.

3. The corporation issues a second class of stock.

4. A corporation, partnership, or ineligible trust becomes a stockholder.

5. A nonresident alien becomes a stockholder.

6. The corporation ceases to be a domestic corporation.

Passive Investment Income

In addition, a corporation's Subchapter S status may be revoked because the corporation has excessive passive investment income. The revocation would occur only if in 3 consecutive years as an S corporation, it had earnings and profits that were accumulated at the time the corporation was not eligible for S status and before it had made a valid election to be treated as an S corporation; and for each of these 3 consecutive years, the corporation had a passive investment income of 25 percent or greater of its gross receipts. When the above passive investment income limitation is exceeded, then the corporation's Subchapter S status is terminated at the end of the third consecutive year. This restriction does not apply to an S corporation that has no accumulated earnings and profits from a prior C (regular) corporate status. Thus, if the S corporation never had any other status, it is not subject to a limitation on passive investment income.

Passive investment income includes gross receipts from royalties, dividends, interests, rents, annuities, sale and exchange of stock, and securities. Rental income is not considered passive investment income if the corporation rendered significant services as part of the rent compensation.

Filing Requirement

A corporation is required to file a notice of disqualifying event with the district director of the IRS. The notice must include the name, address, and tax identification number of the corporation, the cause of the termination, the date of the occurrence, and the facts surrounding the event which led to the termination.

Revocation

An S corporation may voluntarily give up its S status if the majority of stockholders on the day in which the revocation is made consent to the revocation. If the revocation is made on or before the fifteenth day of the third month of the tax year, then the revocation is effective as of the first day of the tax year. If the revocation is made after that date, then it becomes effective the following year unless the corporation chooses otherwise. The corporation can specify the date on which the revocation will take effect, either the date it was filed or some subsequent date rather than the first day of the tax year.

If the corporation selects a revocation date during its tax year, then the corporation will be considered to have had two short years and must file two tax returns, one covering each period.

IRS regulations require a written revocation. The statement revoking the Subchapter S election must be signed by a corporate officer authorized to sign tax returns and must contain a statement that the corporation is revoking its Subchapter S election, indication of the number of shares of stock issued and outstanding at the time the revocation is made, and indication of the date on which the revocation is to be effective.

Distributions to Shareholders

Distributions to shareholders, i.e., profits, losses, etc., pass through to shareholders whether or not the items are actually distributed to the shareholders.

S Corporation as Tax Entity

The tax courts in several cases have ignored the existence of an S corporation where there was no valid reason for its existence. In the *Sue B. Packard* case, decided in September 1985, a partnership had purchased cattle feed from an S corporation on an installment sale setup. The corporation was then liquidated and the assets were assumed by the partnership less than 2 months after corporation was created. The court ignored the sale to the corporation and treated the partnership as if it had been the one that entered into the S corporation's transactions.

In a Seventh Circuit Court case, the taxpayer was unable to shift income to his children, who were in a lower tax bracket, by use of an S corporation. A district court had determined that where there was no material change in circumstances from earlier years, the transfer of S corporation stock lacked sufficient economic reality to permit the income to be taxed to the children.

The IRS may, pursuant to Section 482 of the code, reallocate income and expenses among related entities. This, accordingly, has been used by the IRS to reallocate income among shareholders and members of shareholders' families in S corporations. The general rule in transfer of S corporation stock to related family members is that the transfers must have sufficient economic reality to permit the income of the Subchapter S corporation to be taxed to the transferee rather than the transferor of the stock. In one case, the Seventh Circuit Court of Appeals stated that four questions should be used to determine whether a transfer of stock has economic reality:

1. Are the transferees within the family able to effectively exercise ownership rights over their shares?
2. Did the transferor continue to exercise complete dominion and control over the transferred stock?
3. Did the transferor continue to enjoy the economic benefits of ownership after the conveyance of stock?
4. Did the transferor deal at arm's length with the corporation?

In another case involving the same question, a Wisconsin district court stated that there was no sufficient economic reality to permit the income to be transferred to the children because the major shareholders (the fathers) borrowed large, unsecured interest-free loans from the corporation; the nominal shareholders (the children) received minimal cash distributions approximately equal to their tax liability for the S corporation income; and the fathers retained control of the corporation as officers, directors, and employees.

On the basis of these rulings, for a transfer of stock to children in an S corporation to be legal, it must be more than a nominal transfer.

6
Business Property

In starting a new business or continuing an existing one, property is a necessary investment. The recovery or repayment of the investment is a complicated tax issue. In this chapter, the tax treatment of business property will be discussed. The most common type of business property is business assets. Business assets are property that is used in the trade or business for the production of income and that has a useful life in excess of 1 year. Most business assets are recovered by depreciation, which is discussed in depth in Chapter 7.

Capital Expenditures

Capital expenditures must be distinguished from the other costs of doing business since, in most cases, capital expenditures may not be deducted simply as normal expenditures. There are three kinds of capital expenditures; (1) startup expenditures, (2) business assets, and (3) improvements to existing business assets. Each of these will be discussed in turn.

Startup Expenditures

Startup expenses are those expenses you incur before beginning business operations. They include cost of advertising, travel, connecting utilities, rent deposits, and employee wages prior to the start of operations. Such expenses are considered operating expenses if incurred after business operations have commenced. In many cases, these expenses must be capitalized, i.e., added to the basis of the business.

Business Assets

As noted, business assets are the property used in the business that has a useful life in excess of 1 year. They include land, buildings, office machines such as computers and typewriters, furniture, books, patents, and franchise rights. The cost of most tangible business assets that have a predictable useful life may be recovered by use of depreciation (see Chapter 7).

Improvements to Assets

The costs of making improvements to a business asset are also classed as capital expenditures if the improvements add to the value of the asset, appreciably lengthen the useful life of the asset, or adapt it to a different use. The cost of the improvement is added to the basis of the property in most cases. Improvement costs are normally recovered through annual depreciation deductions. Examples of improvements include a new roof, a new engine, new plumbing, etc.

Repairs, unlike improvements, can be deducted only in the year incurred and are not added to the adjusted basis of the property. Examples of repairs include routine maintenance, tuneups for automobiles, minor adjustments to machine parts, and so forth.

Adjusted Basis

The basis of business property is used to ascertain the amount and type of investment in an asset. The purchase price of the asset is its original basis. The cost of any improvements or modifications to the asset is added to the original basis, and the value of any tax deductions or value received from disposition of any part of the asset are subtracted from its basis. The total after any additions and deductions from the cost make up the asset's adjusted basis.

Normally, improvements or additions increase the adjusted basis of an asset, whereas casualty losses and depreciation deductions decrease the basis.

Recovery

Normally, the taxpayer cannot deduct the cost of capital expenditures. The costs are usually "recovered" by deducting a percentage of the costs each year through depreciation, depletion, or amortization. Most tangible business asset costs are recovered by use of depreciation deductions. Since depreciation is such an important aspect of business assets, it is discussed in detail in Chapter 7.

Amortization is used to recover only certain types of capital expenditures, such as startup costs and organizational costs (see the discussion below on amortization). Depletion is used to recover the cost of an economic interest in timber, minerals, and other natural resources.

First-Year Expensing

A taxpayer can choose to deduct a limited amount of certain capital expenditures in the tax year in which they are incurred. The maximum limit is $10,000 a year. The deduction is limited to property that is purchased for use in a taxpayer's trade or business. Property held merely for the production of income does not qualify for this treatment. Recovery property is depreciable new or used property. Neither a depreciation deduction nor an investment credit may be taken on the asset to the extent that the taxpayer has elected to expense the cost.

Property purchased or acquired by one member of a controlled group from another member of the same controlled group does not qualify for this deduction. (This situation would occur when buyer and seller businesses are both owned by the same person or corporation.)

Other transfers that do not qualify for this first-year expensing include property acquired from a related person whose relationship to the person acquiring it would result in the disallowance of any losses.

The basis of the qualifying property is reduced by the amount of first-year expensing taken under this rule. If the asset is not used predominantly in a trade or business at any time before the close of the second tax year following the year in which it was placed in service, the taxpayer must include as income the amount of the deduction (in the tax year the nonbusiness use occurs).

As noted earlier, this expensing in lieu of depreciation must be made in the first year that the asset is placed in service. If spouses file separate returns, then each may expense only one-half of the maximum amount, i.e., $5000.

Intangible personal property, i.e., stocks, bonds, patents, and copyrights, are not eligible for this treatment. In addition, there is a lower limit allowable for automobiles.

If the property is partially for business use and partially for nonbusiness use and the business use exceeds 50 percent, then this deduction may be used. The taxpayer must, however, allocate the cost of the property to reflect only the business use of the asset. This is accomplished by multiplying the cost of the property by the percentage of business use. From this adjusted cost, the taxpayer may deduct up to the applicable limit.

A taxpayer electing to deduct the cost of qualifying assets is required to specify the items to which the election applies. If, for example, a taxpayer purchases and places in service two assets costing $6000 and $7000, respectively, and the taxpayer wishes to use his or her $10,000 deduction, the taxpayer must state which parts of which assets will be deducted. In this case, the taxpayer might take $5000 from each and thus have a remaining adjusted basis of $1000 and $2000, respectively, or the taxpayer might take all from the higher-priced asset and have an adjusted basis of $3000 left in the other asset. In determining the allocation of the deduction, the taxpayer should consider the depreciation treatment allowable for the remaining adjusted basis. Since different assets are depreciated on different schedules, it is advisable to deduct that asset with the least favorable depreciation schedule.

Depreciation

In computing depreciation, three factors are considered: (1) the asset basis; (2) the date the asset was placed in service, and (3) the method of depreciation the taxpayer is permitted to use.

Depreciation is discussed in detail in Chapter 7. Most business assets are subject to the accelerated cost recovery system (ACRS) or the modified ACRS. For a detailed discussion on ACRS, see the appropriate section of Chapter 7.

The basis of property for depreciation purposes is generally the same as that discussed for first-year expensing. The basis for nonbusiness property that is converted to business property is either the cost (or adjusted basis) of the property or its fair market value on the day of its conversion to business use, whichever is less. For purposes of this rule, property is converted when placed in service for the business.

Depletion

A depletion deduction may be taken for certain types of property: mineral, standing timber, or an oil, gas, or geothermal well.

There are two methods of figuring depletion: cost and percentage. Cost depletion is determined by dividing the adjusted basis of the asset by the number of recoverable units and then multiplying the resulting rate per unit by one of the following. If the taxpayer uses the cash method of accounting, the rate is multiplied by the number of units sold and paid for during that tax year. If the taxpayer uses the accrual method of accounting, the rate is multiplied by the number of units sold that year without regard to payments received. The accrual and cash methods of accounting are discussed in Chapter 8.

The percentage depletion is determined by using a certain percentage, specified for each mineral, multiplied by the gross income from the property. The use of percentage depletion for oil and gas is normally not allowed except for certain domestic production. Any royalties paid for the property is excluded from the gross income from the property when computing the percentage depletion deduction. A net income loss on the property is not deducted from gross income for figuring the percentage depletion.

Amortization

Amortization generally allows a write-off of partial costs each year of certain capital expenditures. Recovery is taken by straight-line deductions over a set number of years. Whereas depreciable property has a determinable life, most amortizable assets have no definable life. Only certain specified expenditures may be amortized.

The three types of expenditures that qualify for amortization are (1) business startup costs, (2) organizational expenses for a corporation, or (3) organizational expenses for a partnership.

Allowable Startup Costs

Startup costs are those that are incurred in establishing or investigating an active trade or business. To be eligible for amortization, the expenses must meet these two tests:

1. They must be deductible as an expense if they were paid or incurred by an ongoing business.
2. They must actually be paid or incurred before the business began operations.

Startup costs include expenses of investigating the feasibility of a prospective business and for getting the business started. They include a survey of potential markets; an analysis of available facilities, labor supply, etc.; advertising for the opening of the business; salaries and wages for employees and their instructors during training; travel and other expenses for securing distributors, customers, and suppliers; and salaries and fees for professional services and consultants.

Startup costs must be paid or incurred before the day on which the active trade or business begins. Startup costs do not include deductible interest or taxes. Startup expenses, also, do not include any organizational expenses for a corporation or a partnership.

If startup costs are not completely amortized when the business is disposed of, any deferred startup costs can be deducted to the extent that they qualify as a loss from a trade or business.

Corporate Organizational Costs

Corporate organizational costs are those costs associated with the creation of the corporation. Included as such costs are the cost for temporary directors; costs for organizational meetings; state-required fees necessary to create the corporation; and legal and accounting fees paid to establish the corporation and prepare the necessary documents.

The cost of selling stock, commissions, and printing costs are not organizational costs and may not be amortized. In addition, any cost associated with the transfer of property to a corporation is not subject to amortization. In most cases the latter costs will be added to the basis of the property in question.

To qualify for amortization, the corporate organizational cost must meet these three tests:

1. The expenditures must be incident to the creation of the corporation and incurred before the end of the first tax year in which the corporation is in business. (A corporation using the cash method of accounting may still amortize organizational costs incurred within or prior to the first year even if the costs are not paid in that year.)
2. The expenditures are costs that are chargeable to a capital account.
3. The expenditures are costs that can be deducted over the life of the corporation, if the corporation has a fixed life.

Partnership Organizational Costs

Partnership organizational costs are those that are incident to the creation of the partnership. To be eligible for amortization, the expenditures must be ones that are chargeable to a capital account and they must be able to be amortized over the life of the partnership if the partnership has a fixed life.

Partnership organizational costs do not include syndication fees or costs associated with issuing and marketing of interests in the partnership, such as sales commissions.

Amortization Period

Costs that may be amortized are normally deductible over a period of not less than 60 months. The business can elect to take a longer, but not shorter, period than 60 months. Once an amortization period is elected, it cannot be changed.

The amount of the tax year amortization deduction is computed by dividing the total costs allowable by the number of months in the amortization period. This establishes the monthly deduction. If the tax year is not a short year (i.e., not less than 12 months), then the monthly amount is multiplied by 12 to obtain the year's deduction. If the tax year is a short one, then the monthly amount is multiplied by the number of months in the tax year. For partial months, 15 or more days is counted as a month and fewer than 15 days is disregarded.

The amortization period must begin in the month that the business begins operations. A partnership or corporation is considered to have begun business when it starts the activities for which it was organized. This can occur before the corporate charter is granted or the partnership agreement is signed.

If a business never begins operations, then the startup and the organizational costs cannot be amortized by the business. In some cases, the costs may qualify as a business expense or loss to the individual taxpayer.

Election to Amortize

The election to amortize is made by attaching Form 4562 to the tax return. A statement must be attached to the form for each type of cost amortized. The statements should contain (1) the total amount of the startup or organizational costs to be amortized; (2) a description of each cost; (3) the date each cost was incurred; (4) the month the business began operations or the month the business was acquired; and (5) the number of months in the amortization period (not less than 60).

The statement must be attached to the tax return for the first year in which the amortization period starts. Both the statement and the form must be filed by the due date for the tax return, including any extensions of time to file.

For partnerships and corporations, the deduction must be taken by the partnership or the corporation, not by individual taxpayers. With a partnership, however, the deduction is taken before determining the profits or losses of the business so that, indirectly, the value of the deduction is passed on to the individual taxpayer.

An individual may elect to amortize the expenses of investigating an interest in an existing business, if the individual actually invests in the business. Any deduction is subject to the passive loss limitation rule established by the Tax Reform Act of 1986. This rule limits the amount of passive losses able to be deducted (see Chapter 9).

Construction Period Interest and Taxes

Corporations are not allowed to amortize construction period interest and taxes for construction begun after March 15, 1984. All corporations are now required to capitalize construction period interest and taxes, i.e., add this cost to the adjusted basis.

If the individual taxpayer does not invest in the new business or a similar business, then the expenses may not be deductible under the Tax Reform Act. The determining factor is whether or not the individual needs to file a Schedule C for business income.

Construction period interest and taxes include (1) interest paid or accrued during the construction period on a debt to acquire, build, or carry real property; and (2) real property taxes paid or accrued during the construction period that are otherwise deductible.

Individuals may to a limited extent amortize construction period interest and taxes. Normally, such amortization is achieved by deducting a fixed percentage of the interest and taxes each year. The normal percentage allowed is 10 percent.

The construction period begins on the date on which construction of the building or other improvement begins and ends on the date the asset is placed in service or is ready for sale.

Amortization of Trademarks and Trade Names

Prior to the Tax Reform Act, trademarks and trade names could be amortized over a 5-year period (60 months). There were, however, substantial problems in determining the cost allocation for trademarks and trade names in the purchase of businesses. In addition, it appears that in most cases the value of a trademark or trade name does not decline. Consequently, Congress repealed the amortization election provision and now requires the cost of trademarks and trade names to be capitalized and thus generally recovered on disposition of the asset. The amortization election provisions continue in those cases where legally binding contracts existed as of March 1, 1986 (subject to certain exceptions).

Uniform Capitalization Rules

The Tax Reform Act established uniform capitalization rules. Under comprehensive uniform capitalization rules, taxpayers are required to capitalize both direct and indirect inventory, construction, and development costs, including interest. Wholesalers and retailers with gross receipts of $5 million or less are exempt from the rules. There is also a transitional rule that allows a continuation of former rules for excess depreciation on plant and equipment used to produce inventory or self-constructed assets that were placed in service prior to March 1, 1986.

The uniform rules should more accurately reflect income of a business and make the income tax system more neutral regarding the capitalization of costs of producing, acquiring, and holding business property. According to congressional staff, the prior rules were deficient in two respects. First, the prior rules allowed costs that were really costs of producing, acquiring, or carrying property to be deducted currently rather than capitalized into the basis of the property and recovered when the property was sold or used in service. Second, different capitalization rules applied depending on the nature of the property and its intended use. The rules do not apply to farming businesses.

Scope and Nature of Rules

The Secretary of the Treasury is tasked with publishing uniform rules to govern the inclusion in inventory or capital accounts all costs incurred in manufacturing, construction, and other types of activities involving the production of real or personal property; or those incurred in acquiring or holding such property for resale. These rules apply to assets held for sale to customers in the ordinary course of business and to assets or improvements to assets constructed by a taxpayer for use in a trade or business or in an activity engaged in for profit. The rules are applicable to both intangible and tangible property.

The rules are not intended as a modification of present rules regarding the determination of whether an expenditure results in a separate and distinct asset that has a useful life in excess of 1 year. The rules will prescribe which costs associated with an asset are required to be included in its basis or otherwise capitalized.

The uniform rules are to be patterned after the rules applicable to extended-period, long-term contracts. Taxpayers subject to the rules will be required to capitalize not only direct costs but also most indirect costs that benefit the assets being produced or acquired for resale. These costs include administrative and overhead costs.

Retailers and Wholesalers

The uniform rules apply to businesses that acquire and hold property for resale just as they apply to producers. Costs that retailers and wholesalers are required to treat as inventory include costs incident to purchasing inventory (e.g., wages or salaries paid to employees responsible for purchasing); repackaging, assembly, and other costs associated with processing goods for sale; costs of storing goods (e.g., rent or depreciation of buildings used and wages of warehouse personnel); and the portion of general and administrative costs allocable to these functions.

The rules relating to capitalization of interest do not apply to real or personal property acquired solely for resale. In retail sales businesses, only off-site storage costs can be inventoried. Off-site storage costs are the costs of storing goods in a facility distinct from the place of business where the retailer conducts retail sales of these goods.

An exception to the capitalization rules is also provided for personal property held for resale by retailers and wholesalers whose average annual gross receipts do not exceed $10 million. Simplified methods of absorbing costs are provided under IRS regulations for personal property held for resale by other retailers and wholesalers. The rules are discussed in IRS publication 544, "Sales and Other Dispositions of Assets."

Pensions

Under the uniform capitalization rules, contributions to a pension, profit-sharing, or stock-bonus plans, as well as other employee benefits, are considered indirect costs that must be capitalized to the same extent as other indirect costs, unless the contributions relate to past-service costs.

Exceptions

The uniform rules do not apply to any costs associated with research and development or experimental expenditures or to certain other costs of oil and gas wells or mineral property. With regard to property held for resale, the rules apply only if the taxpayer's average annual gross receipts for the past 3 years were $5 million or less. Nor do the rules apply to expenditures properly treated as repair costs that do not relate to the manufacture, remanufacture, or production of property. In addition, the rules do not modify the present rules regarding the valuation of inventories on a basis other than costs.

Interest

Capitalization of interest on debt is required if the debt is incurred or continued to finance the construction or production of (1) real property (whether such property is held for sale to customers or is used by the business or taxpayer in a trade or business or activity for profit), or (2) other property with a class life of 20 years or more under the depreciation system if the property is to be used by the taxpayer in its trade or business or in an activity for profit.

Interest incurred in connection with property estimated to have a production period of more than 2 years (or 1 year in case of items costing more than $1 million) is also required to be capitalized. The production period as stated under this rule begins when construction is started and ends when the asset is ready to be placed in service or held for sale. With property such as whiskey that must be aged before selling, the production period includes the aging period. Pre-production period activities such as planning and designing are not considered part of the production period.

Any interest expense that would have been avoided if production or construction expenditures had been used to repay indebtedness of the taxpayer is treated as construction period interest subject to capitalization. Therefore, any debts that can be specifically traced to production or construction expenditures first must be allocated to production or construction. If the production or construction expenditures exceed the amount of the debt, interest on other debts of the taxpayer must be treated, to the extent of this excess, as production or construction period interest.

These rules are designed to prevent avoidance of the rules by use of related parties such as subsidiary corporations. Also, interest capitalization rules are to be applied first at the level of partnership or other flow-through entity, and then at the level of the partners or beneficiaries to the extent that the partnership has insufficient debt to support the production or construction expenditures.

In cases where the production or construction is for a customer who makes progress payments or advance payments for property to be used in a business or profit-making activity, or held for sale, the customer is treated as constructing the property to the extent of such payments. Interest costs attributable, therefore, to payments to the contractor are subject to capitalization by the customer if the property is real property or long-lived property, or if it requires a construction or production period of more than 2 years (1 year if the cost exceeds $1 million). The contractor is required to capitalize interest only with respect to indebtedness relating to the excess of its accumulated contract costs over the accumulated payments received by the contractor during the year.

Long-Term Contracts

As a general rule, interest and other costs attributable to non-extended-period, long-term contracts are required to be capitalized and a percentage of completion method used to deduct general and administrative costs that are clearly identifiable to the contract. This change was made to prevent the mismatching of income and expenses in these contracts.

Now, businesses or taxpayers reporting on long-term contracts who use a method of accounting other than the percentage of completion method are required to capitalize any costs identified by the business or taxpayer as being attributable to the contract. For example, general and administrative expenses identified pursuant to a cost-plus contract or pursuant to a contract with a federal agency must be capitalized regardless of whether such costs may be treated as period costs under prior regulations.

Interest incurred in connection with long-term contracts generally must be allocated under the same rules as interest allocable to property not produced under a long-term contract. For purposes of this rule, the production period normally begins on the contract date or the date the contractor incurs any costs under the contract and ends on the contract completion date.

If the contractor does not use the completed contract method of accounting, the production period begins on the date by which at least 5 percent of the total estimated costs, including design and planning costs, under the contract have been incurred if later than the contract commencement date.

Research and development costs unrelated to a particular contract, marketing, selling and advertising expenses, and unsuccessful bid and proposal costs are exempt from the capitalization method. Bid and proposal costs are considered as unsuccessful for purposes of this rule only when the bidder has withdrawn the bid or has been informed that the bid was awarded to another business or person.

The uniform capitalization rules do not apply to any contract for the construction or improvement of real property if the contract will be completed within 2 years from the contract date; and the work is performed by a taxpayer whose average annual gross receipts for the past 3 tax years do not exceed $10 million.

An improvement to real property includes any building, road, dam, or other similar property. There has been no change in the rules for contracts eligible for this exception or for those contracts being reported under the percentage of completion method.

Capital Gains and Losses

Key concepts regarding the income tax treatment of capital gains and losses are as follows:

- The net capital gain for individuals is taxed at the maximum rate of 28 percent.
- Losses from the sale of capital assets may offset capital gains and a maximum of $3000 of ordinary income.
- The capital gains on the sale of a principal residence may qualify for nonrecognition if reinvested in a new residence.
- There is a one-time exclusion of up to $125,000 of the gain on the sale of a principal residence by a taxpayer age 55 or older.
- Employee stock options may qualify for preferred tax treatment.

In this section, the reporting of capital gains and losses from sales, exchanges, and other dispositions of investment or business property is discussed. Prior to the Tax Reform Act, there was a net capital gain deduction for individuals. That was repealed with the Tax Reform Act, and from 1986 through tax year 1990, capital gains were considered ordinary income in most cases. The Tax Act of 1990, while considering net capital gains as ordinary income, placed a maximum tax rate of 28 percent on net capital gains.

Prior to the Tax Reform Act, long-term capital gains on the sale of assets had been taxed at preferential rates since 1921 as a method to encourage investment. Congress repealed the preferential treatment, arguing that the overall reduction in tax rates eliminated the need for a reduced tax rate for capital gains. An additional justification provided by the tax writers was to eliminate much of the game-playing that occurred as individuals tried to convert ordinary income into capital gains to take advantage of the preferential tax treatment. The preferential tax treatment of net capital gains was restored with the 1990 tax changes.

While the changes provided only a small advantage (maximum tax rate of 28 percent), most experts see this as a window that will be enlarged in the future.

The 1990 changes also reinstated the requirement that capital assets be held by the taxpayer for an extended period of time to receive favorable tax treatment. Congress, reestablishing the 6 months' holding requirement for long-term capital gains, is once more encouraging investments in assets that can be freely traded, e.g., stocks.

From 1987 to 1990, capital gains by an investor were treated as ordinary income. Losses from the sale or exchange of capital assets are still allowed to offset ordinary income to the extent of the gains from the sale or exchange of capital assets plus $3000.

Capital Assets

Capital gains and losses arise from the sale or exchange of capital assets. A capital asset is defined as property held by a taxpayer that is not one of the following:

- Accounts and notes receivable
- Inventories, stock in trade, or property held primarily for sale to customers in the ordinary course of a trade or business
- Depreciable property used in a trade or business
- Certain copyrights, literary material, etc.
- Real property used in the taxpayer's trade or business
- U.S. government publications

Examples of capital assets include:

- Stocks and bonds
- Home owned and occupied by the taxpayer
- Household furnishings
- Coin or stamp collection
- Gems and jewelry
- Motor vehicle used for pleasure or commuting

Property held mainly for sale to customers is not a capital asset. The question as to whether property is held mainly for sale to customers is a question of fact to be judged in each case. Among the factors to be considered are the purpose for which the property was acquired, the number and frequency of sales, and the amount of time the property is held before it is sold.

The most common capital assets held by an individual taxpayer are personal residences, automobiles, and investment property such as real estate. An asset is not a capital asset if it is an integral part of the taxpayer's business.

Goodwill.   Goodwill of a business is a capital asset. When a business is sold, the seller can receive capital gain treatment on the part of the sale price that is attributed to capital gain. The buyer cannot deduct any of the amount paid for goodwill because it is a capital asset with an unknown useful life and thus cannot be depreciated. Accordingly, the amount that the buyer pays for the goodwill becomes its basis.

Because of the tax treatment of goodwill, it is generally to the seller's advantage to have a high value allocated to goodwill and to the buyer's advantage to have a lower value allocated to it. The basis of goodwill may be figured by first allocating the amount paid among the other assets acquired, with the remainder being considered the amount paid for goodwill. For example, a taxpayer buys a going business for $500,000. The assets, not considering any goodwill, are valued at $450,000. Accordingly, the cost of the goodwill would be $50,000 ($500,000 − 450,000).

Contract for Service.   A contract for service is not considered a capital asset. Accordingly, if you assign or sell such a contract, and the assignee or purchaser is entitled to compensation for services only under the terms of the contract for its remaining life, the amount you receive is ordinary income.

Franchises or Trademarks.   Whether or not a franchise or trademark is a capital asset depends on whether the franchisor or seller retains any significant power, right, or continuing interest. If the seller does not retain any significant power, right, or continuing interest, then payment is for the purchase of a capital asset. If any power is retained, the purchase is not a transfer of a capital asset and any gain will be treated as ordinary income.

Capital Gains Distributions

Normally any distributions or dividends paid by regulated investment companies and mutual funds in real estate investment trust from long-term capital gains are taxable. Some mutual funds will keep the long-term capital gains and pay taxes on these amounts. In this case, you must report as a long-term capital gain any amount that the mutual fund allocated to you as a capital gains distribution even though that distribution was a stock distribution and you did not actually receive cash.

Undistributed long-term capital gains are reported on Form 2439, and any capital gains distributions are reported on Form 1099-DIV. Real estate investment trusts (REITs) normally issue Form 1099-DIV or som similar statements indicating the capital gains distribution that you must include in your taxable income. Note that you may report these as long-term capital gains without regard to the period of time that you have held the stock.

Any return of capital in the form of a distribution is considered a nontaxable distribution and thus is not a taxable event. The return of capital, however, reduces the basis of your stock. When the basis of your stock has been reduced to zero, then you have to report the return of any capital funds that you receive as capital gains. Whether the received funds qualify as long-term or short-term distributions depends upon the length of time for which you have held the stock in question.

Liquidated distributions, often called *liquidated dividends,* are distributions you receive during a partial or complete liquidation of a corporation. Often these distributions.are part return of capital and part capital gains distribution. The organization making the distributions will normally issue Form 1099 or some equivalent that indicates what portion of the funds are taxable as capital gains, what part is ordinary income, if any, and what is a return of capital.

Distributions of Stock and Stock Rights

When a corporation distributes its own stock, often referred to as *stock dividends,* generally, the stock dividends are not taxable to you and are not required to be reported on your tax return until the stocks are disposed of. In certain circumstances, however, taxable stock dividends and stock rights can result. The distributions are taxable if:

1. You or any other shareholder has the choice to receive cash or other property instead of the stock dividend.

2. The distribution gives cash or other property to some shareholders and an increase in the percentage interest in the corporation's assets or earning profits to other stockholders.

3. The distribution is convertible preferred stock and has the same result as in item 2.

4. The distribution gives preferred stock to some stockholders and common stock to other stockholders.

5. The distribution is of preferred stock (this requirement does not apply if the distribution is made for convertible preferred stock solely to take into account a stock dividend, stock split, or similar event that would otherwise result in reducing the conversion right).

Dividends on Insurance Policies

Dividends on insurance policies are normally considered a partial return of the premiums paid. Accordingly, they are not included in your gross income until they amount to more than the total of all net premiums you paid on that insurance policy. However, any interest paid or credited on the dividends that are left with the insurance company are considered taxable income and must be reported.

Dividends on veterans insurance and certain other government-sponsored insurance policies are not taxable. However, you must report as taxable income interest on dividends left with the Veterans Administration.

Patronage dividends are dividends that you receive in money from a cooperative organization. They are generally included in your income unless excluded for some specific reasons. Individuals receiving dividends from the Alaskan Permanent Fund are not required to report these amounts as dividends. They are required however to be reported on line 22 of Form 1040, i.e., as other income.

Nonrecognition of Gain

Normally gains or losses on the exchange of like property will not be required to be recognized if the property held for productive use in a taxpayer's trade or business is exchanged for "like-kind property." The term *like-kind property* is broadly defined. Real property, however, must be exchanged for real property. Personal property must be of the same nature. For example, livestock of different sexes is not considered to be like-kind property.

To qualify for nonrecognition there must be an exchange of property or a sale and repurchase. If any boot is paid, any gain realized to the extent of the boot must be recognized and reported as gain. Boot may not be used to cause the recognition of a loss. If the boot is paid in like-kind property, no gain need be recognized. Any liability or debts assumed are treated as boot paid by the person assuming the liability or debts.

The basis of the newly acquired property in a like-kind trade is the basis of the like-kind property given up, plus any boot paid or minus any boot given and gain recognized.

Involuntary Conversions

Normally a taxpayer whose property is subject to an involuntary conversion may postpone the recognition of gain from the conversion. The general rule is that gain is realized to the extent that the amount is not reinvested in replacement property. To qualify as an involuntary conversion, the property must be completely or partially destroyed by fire, flood, etc.; stolen; or sold or exchanged under threat of condemnation or eminence of requisition by a governmental or public entity.

If the conversion is into money, the taxpayer may elect to postpone the gain if the money is reinvested in replacement property within the required time period. If there is a direct replacement, the basis of the converted property is carried over to the new property.

In the condemnation of a personal residence, any loss realized may not be recognized. If the loss of the personal residence is the result of a casualty, the loss may be recognized subject to limitations on casualty losses.

Gain realized includes only that amount received as compensation for the property and does not include any amounts paid as severance damages.

Other exchanges which may qualify for nonrecognition include exchanges of insurance policies; exchanges of stock of the same corporation, e.g., exchange of preferred stock for common stock; repossession of real property (only limited gains may be required to be recognized); and exchanges of stock for property by a corporation. A corporation normally does not recognize a gain when dealing with its own stock.

Selling a Home

Losses on the sale of a personal residence may not be claimed. Gains, however, are taxable unless the gain is deferred by the purchase or construction of a new residence. Under most circumstances, when a taxpayer sells his or her home and purchases a new one, the income tax on the gain from the sale of the old home may be deferred. If the new residence costs less than the sale price of the old home, normally there is a requirement that a portion of the gain be recognized. The rules regarding the deferral of the gain are discussed in this section.

If your spouse dies after you sell your old home and before a new home is purchased, the tax on the gain of the sale of the old home can be postponed if the basic requirements are met and (1) you were married when your spouse died, and (2) you used the new home as your main residence.

The selling of a multifamily apartment building qualifies for a deferment of taxes on that portion of the gain allocated to the apartment that the taxpayer used as principal residence. Likewise, a mobile home, houseboat, etc., may qualify as a principal residence and be subject to the same rules. Sale of land surrounding a personal residence, however, does not qualify, and you cannot defer the gain on the sale of the land.

A taxpayer is not required to reinvest cash received from the sale of the old residence. For example, if other requirements are met, a taxpayer may defer gain on the sale of his or her house for cash when a new residence is bought with nothing down but a mortgage higher than the basis of the old property.

Taxpayers are required to report the sale of a personal residence in the tax year in which the property is sold. If a new residence is not replaced within the required time period, then the taxpayer is required to file an amended return for the tax year in which the sale occurred and recognize the gain from the sale.

Employee Incentive Stock Options

If an employer gives stock to an employee or allows the employee to buy stock at less than the market price, the employee is taxable on the value of the stock minus what he or she paid for the stock. To encourage the use of incentive stock options (ISOs) as a means of attracting and motivating talented employees, an employee is not taxed on the grant or on exercising an incentive stock option if there is a risk that he or she will be required to forfeit the stock.

No expense deduction may be taken by the employer when the option is granted or exercised. The employee is normally taxed on gain received when the stock from a stock option is sold. At this time, he or she would be subject to tax on the gain, that is, the difference between what was actually paid for the stock and its selling price.

To attract or retain executives, companies often give the employees ISOs as part of the compensation package. There is no taxable income when you exercise the option. You are, however, taxed on the gain when you eventually sell the stock.

The Tax Reform Act repealed the restriction that incentive stock options must be exercisable in the order in which the stock options were granted. In addition, the act changed the $100,000 annual limitation to provide that the aggregate fair market value (determined at the time the option is granted) of the stock with respect to which ISOs are exercisable for the first time under the terms of the plan by any employee during any calendar year may not exceed $100,000. This latter change was to assist small and relatively new companies and allow them to offer comprehensive compensation packages to attract and motivate talented employees.

General Utilities Doctrine

One provision of the Tax Reform Act repealed the general utilities doctrine. This was a doctrine that allowed the postponement of gain or losses on the merger of corporations. This doctrine relates back to the 1930s, when a company by the name of General Utilities was involved in a famous U.S. Supreme Court case. The court decision permitted corporate taxes to be avoided when corporate assets are liquidated and the proceeds are distributed to the shareholders. In most mergers and acquisitions, liquidations of assets are involved. Many experts attributed the increase in mergers in recent years to the tax advantages of this doctrine.

The law now requires gain or loss to be recognized by a corporation, upon liquidation and distribution of the corporate assets, as if the corporation had sold the assets at fair market value.

Equipment Leasing

Prior to the Tax Reform Act, equipment leasing was a popular tax shelter since it produced a fairly definite income and tax deduction on the part of the lessor. For the lessee it allowed the use of necessary business assets without the necessity of purchasing them, and thus business debt-asset ratios were not increased. In addition, lease payments are usually lower than payments on equivalent loans.

A complicated set of rules regarding financial leases developed over the years through court decisions and IRS rulings. The general concept was that it was the economic substance of the transaction, not the form, that determined who is the owner of the assets and thus who is entitled to take advantage of the tax savings. In addition, the rules provided that lease transactions could not be used solely for the purposes of transferring tax benefits. The Tax Equity and Fiscal Responsibility Act of

1982 (TEFRA) codified the financial leasing rules and further liberalized them. These rules were further modified in two other tax changes in 1983 and 1984. The Tax Reform Act of 1986 repeals the rules.

The repeal of the investment tax credit, also, which was one of the most important benefits of this type of tax shelter, may change the ground rules for this method of acquiring business assets.

Valuation of Goodwill and Going-Concern Value

The sale of a going business for a lump-sum price is viewed as a sale of each individual asset rather than of a single capital asset. For tax purposes, both the seller and the buyer must allocate the purchase price among the assets. For the seller it is necessary to determine the amount and character of gain or loss, if any, that must be recognized on the sale. For the buyer, it is necessary to determine the basis of each asset purchased.

The parties may agree to a total price for the business. The tax code does not require that the buyer and seller agree to an allocation of the purchase price among the assets. It is to the buyer's advantage to assign higher prices to assets that can be depreciated and lower prices to goodwill and the going-concern value which must be capitalized. It is, likewise, to the seller's advantage to place lower prices on assets to prevent the recapture of depreciation and higher prices on goodwill or the going-concern value.

The valuation of goodwill and the going-concern value of a business are generally considered the most difficult area of pricing. Prior to the Tax Reform Act, there were two methods of determining the value of goodwill, the residual method and the formula method.

Under the formula method, goodwill and going concern are valued by capitalizing the excess earning capacity of the tangible assets of the business based on the performance of the business over some period prior to valuation date. The excess earning capacity is the excess of the average earnings of the business during this period over an assumed rate of return on the value of its tangible assets. The excess earning is then capitalized at an appropriate discount rate.

For example, suppose a business whose tangible assets are valued at $100,000 earns a profit for the prior year of $10,000, or a 10 percent rate of return. If the assumed rate of return on $100,000 is 8 percent, or $8000, then the excess earning capacity is $2000. This amount is then discounted (the excess earning capacity is divided by the assumed rate) to determine value of the goodwill, which would be about $25,000.

(*Note:* For purposes of this example, compounding of interest and earnings was disregarded.)

Under the residual method, the value of goodwill and the going-concern value are the excess of the purchase price over the fair market value of the tangible assets and other identifiable intangible assets such as accounts receivable.

Under the Tax Reform Act, for all transactions involving the sale of a going business, the residual method must be used unless the sale is subject to a binding contract entered into between the parties prior to May 6, 1986. This requirement is intended to reduce some of the present disagreements between taxpayers and the IRS over the value of goodwill.

The Tax Reform Act also authorized the Secretary of the Treasury to publish rules that will require reporting by the parties to the sale of the business and to provide information regarding the sale, including amounts allocated to goodwill and going-concern value and to any other categories of assets or specific assets. This information is to enable the IRS to make an independent determination as to these values.

7

Depreciation of Business Assets

Key concepts regarding depreciation allowances for business assets are as follows:

- Tax changes have reduced the annual depreciation allowances for investments in real estate.

- The depreciation allowances for nonreal property are now more generous to partially offset the repeal of the investment tax credit.

- The Tax Reform Act generally retained the accelerated cost recovery system (ACRS), introduced in 1981, with certain modifications discussed later in this chapter.

- The allowances under the ACRS do not permit any deductions greater than the actual investment in the asset but permits you to recover the cost in a shorter period of time.

- The ACRS may not be used for property first placed in service prior to tax year 1981.

- The modified ACRS applies only to property, whether new or used, first placed in service after December 31, 1986.

- The cost of residential rental property, first placed in service after December 31, 1986, is recovered using the straight-line method of depreciation and a recovery period of 27.5 years.

- The cost of nonresidential real property is recovered using the straight-line method and a recovery period of 31.5 years.

- Under the modified ACRS all property placed in service or disposed of during a tax year is considered as placed in service or disposed of at the midpoint of the year. Therefore, one-half of the depreciation allowance may be taken in the year the property is placed in service and one-half in the year the property is disposed of.

- In some cases a taxpayer may use optional depreciation methods. These are discussed later in this chapter.

- Taxpayers are permitted expenses up to $10,000 of the cost of tangible personal property used in business, subject to a phaseout for an investment that exceeds $200,000 for the year.

- Depreciation deductions are not permitted on property used for personal purposes such as a personal residence or personal automobile. If the property is used for both personal and business purposes, only that portion associated with business use may be deducted.

- You may not use the ACRS for property for cellular telephones and computers whose business use is 50 percent or less.

Depreciable Property

The tax code allows for a depreciation deduction as a means of providing for the exhaustion, wear and tear, and obsolescence of business property and property held for production income. The general limitations on depreciation deductions are:

1. Only tangible property is depreciable. Intangible property (stocks, bonds, etc.) is not depreciable unless it has a definite useful life, such as a patent or copyright.

2. The basis for the property is normally its cost. Personal property converted for business or income-producing use has a depreciable basis of its value at the time of the conversion or its cost, whichever is lower.

3. Property placed in service prior to 1981 may be depreciated using one of four methods: (1) the straight-line method (basis less salvage value divided by the estimated useful life); (2) the declining balance method (using a rate not more than 200 percent of the declining balance without regard to salvage value); (3) sum-of-the-year's digits; or (4) machine-hours or units of production.

4. Property placed in service after January 1, 1981, and before January 1, 1987, is generally subject to the ACRS.

5. Property placed in service after January 1, 1987, is generally subject to the modified ACRS (MACRS).

What Can Be Depreciated

This section discusses special classes of property with regard to depreciation. The discussion is intended to provide the reader with a general framework for how the IRS regards various questions.

Land

Normally land cannot be depreciated. In some cases, cost of preparing the land can be depreciated if the preparation costs are closely associated with a depreciable asset so that it is possible to determine a useful life for the preparation costs. Costs of clearing land, grading, and landscaping are normally not depreciable.

Demolition of Buildings

Any amounts paid or incurred to demolish any structures are normally not deductible but are added to the basis of the land.

Patents and Copyrights

Normally intangible property is not depreciable because of the inability to ascertain its useful life. Two exceptions to this rule are patents and copyrights. Since they normally have a definite life, they can be depreciated over their useful life. The useful life is determined by the period of time that the patent or copyright is granted by the government, not its estimated actual economical life. If the patent or copyright is determined to be valueless, then the remainder of its basis may be deducted in the year that the valueless determination is made.

Agreement Not to Compete

An agreement not to compete is normally associated with the sale of a business. Most are restrictive in time and agreed-upon areas. If the agreement has a definite time period, then it may qualify for a depreciation deduction over that time period. If it is restrictive only in area, then normally it must be capitalized.

Customer Lists

If a business can establish that a customer list that it purchases has a definite useful life that can be predicted with reasonable accuracy, then the lists may be deducted if they meet the other requirements for depreciable property. If the lists are purchased in connection with the purchase of a business, then ascertaining the cost of the lists may be a problem and may limit deductibility of them.

Goodwill

Goodwill is not depreciable because there is no reasonable way to determine its useful life. Normally, cost of goodwill must be capitalized.

Trademarks and Trade Names

Trademarks and trade names are not depreciable. (See Chapter 6 for a discussion of the new tax changes regarding trademarks and trade names.)

Designs, Drawings, and Patterns

Designs, drawings, and patterns are intangible property that normally may be depreciated if a useful life can be established with reasonable accuracy.

Inventory

Inventory may not be depreciated. It is held primarily for sale and thus is recovered in the price of the item sold or as a business expense.

Containers

In most cases, containers are part of inventory and thus are not depreciable. If the containers have a useful life in excess of 1 year and are commonly reused, then they may qualify as depreciable property. Questions that the IRS considers in determining whether containers are depreciable property are:

1. Who retains title of the containers in a sale? If title passes to the buyer, then the containers are considered part of the inventory.
2. Do the invoices treat containers as separate items? If so, they are part of the inventory.
3. Do the business records properly state the basis of the containers? If the basis cannot be ascertained, then they cannot be depreciated.

Professional Libraries

Professional libraries that are maintained by businesses can be depreciated because they become obsolete with time. The Tax Reform Act of 1986 placed restrictions on individual taxpayers depreciating their professional libraries. They still, however, may be deducted by a business or on a Schedule C for an individual taxpayer if the individual has business income.

Idle Assets

If the idle asset is normally used in your trade or business but is temporarily idle for lack of business use, then the asset may be depreciated if otherwise qualified.

Accelerated Depreciation

The Economic Recovery Tax Act of 1981 established the accelerated cost recovery system (ACRS) for most depreciable property placed in service after 1980. Under the ACRS, the cost of the property is recovered by depreciation deductions using an accelerated method of depreciation over a set period. Prior to that act, the property's cost (less salvage value) was recovered over its estimated useful life. The ACRS is designed to encourage capital investments by allowing a rapid recovery of those investments.

A taxpayer could also elect to expense up to $5000 of the cost of personal property in the year that the property was placed in service instead of depreciating it (increased to $10,000 for tax years after 1986 for small businesses). A tax credit was allowed for up to 10 percent of the taxpayer's investment for certain machines, tools, etc. The investment credit was generally required to be claimed in the tax year that the property was placed in service.

Property not covered by the ACRS includes property not depreciated in years, e.g., units of production and intangible personal property such as stocks, bonds, and notes.

Modified Accelerated Cost Recovery System

The Tax Reform Act retained the ACRS, but made substantial modifications to it. Now, tangible personal property (generally all property except land and buildings) is assigned to classes of either 3, 5, 7, 10, 15, or 20 years. The classes are listed below in the section on property classes, which gives a general description of each class and the depreciation method used. *Note:* The modifications apply only to property placed in service after December 31, 1986.

Antichurning Rules

To prevent transfers without an actual change in ownership of property placed in service prior to the effective date of the ACRS or modified ACRS so that the taxpayer can take advantage of the accelerated depreciation rules under ACRS or to increase the basis of the property, the antichurning rules were retained. Under these rules, transfers of property to the same or related taxpayers normally will not be treated as a transfer of property if the transferee of the property will "step into the shoes" of the transferor. Included in this rule are transfers between family members or other related persons and transfers of property that is leased back to the person from whom it was acquired.

The rules will, also, apply in some cases to property converted from personal use to business use. The expanded antichurning rules applies to all ACRS property other than residential rental property and nonresidential real property.

Averaging Conventions

In making depreciation computations under the ACRS and the alternative depreciation system (described subsequently), certain assumptions are used to establish when the recovery period begins.

Half-Year Convention. In general, all property placed in service or disposed of during a tax year is considered to have been placed in service at the midpoint of that tax year regardless of the actual date the property was first used or disposed of. Accordingly, a half-year depreciation is allowed for the year it is placed in service and a half-year when the property is disposed of.

For example, if a taxpayer places in service equipment that is assigned to the 5-year class, the ACRS deductions for each year would be as follows. In the 5-year class, using 200 percent of the declining balance, the computation percentage would be 40 percent. (The 5-year recovery percentage using the straight-line method would be 20 percent each year; therefore, using 200 percent, it equals 40 percent.) Assuming the basis of the asset is $100, depreciation is figured as follows:

First Year: $20 (one-half of the 200 percent declining balance sum)

Second Year: $32 (200 percent of declining balance sum, i.e., $100 minus the $20 deducted for the first year times 40 percent)

Third Year: $19.20 (200 percent of declining balance)

Fourth Year: $11.52 (200 percent of declining balance)

Fifth Year: $11.52 (straight-line using fourth-year amount)

Sixth Year: $5.76 (one-half year convention rule)

If the property was disposed of in the second year, then in lieu of the $32 deduction, the one-half year convention would reduce the deduction to $16.

Mid-Quarter Convention.   A mid-quarter convention must be used in lieu of the half-year convention under the following conditions: you place in service during the last 3 months of the tax year depreciable property other than nonresidential real property and residential real property; and the total basis of the property placed in service during the last 3 months is more than 40 percent of the total basis of all depreciable property placed in service during the year.

Salvage Value Under the ACRS

Under the ACRS, the salvage of the property is disregarded for tangible personal property.

Property Classes

The six classes of property allowed under the MACRS are as follows:

1. *Three-Year Class.*   This class includes personal property with an asset depreciation range (ADR) midpoint of 4 years or less except for au-

tomobiles, light general-purpose trucks, over-the-road tractors, and property used in connection with research and experimentation. The cost of this class is recovered by using the 200 percent declining balance method. The prior law for treatment of horses was retained and included in this class.

2. *Five-Year Class.* This class includes automobiles, light general-purpose trucks, and property used to manufacture semiconductors. Also included in this class is tangible personal property with ADR midpoints of more than 4 years and less than 10 years, qualified technological equipment, computer-based central office switching equipment, renewable energy and biomass properties that are small power production facilities, and research and experimentation property. The cost of this property is recovered using the 200 percent declining balance method.

3. *Seven-Year Class.* This class includes property with the ADR midpoints of 10 years and more and less than 16 years. Also included is single-purpose agricultural or horticultural structures and property with no ADR midpoint and not classified elsewhere. The cost of property included in this class is recovered using the 200 percent declining balance method.

4. *Ten-Year Class.* This class includes property with an ADR midpoint life of 16 or more years and less than 20 years. The cost of property included in this class is recovered during a 10-year period by first using the 200 percent declining balance method.

5. *Fifteen-Year Class.* This class includes property with ADR midpoints of 20 years and more and less than 25 years, including sewage treatment plants, and telephone distribution plant and comparable equipment used for the two-way exchange of voice and data communications. This class is also used for public utility property, which is any property used predominantly in the trade or business of furnishing or selling public utilities. This property is recovering using a 150 percent declining balance method.

6. *Twenty-Year Class.* This class includes property with an ADR of 25 years and more, other than real property with an ADR of 27.5 years and more, and includes sewer pipes.

Real Property

Real property (acquired after January 1987) that has a class life of more than 27.5 years, must in most cases be depreciated using the straight-line method. The recovery periods for residential rental property and nonresidential rental property are different.

Residential rental property is now defined as buildings and structures in which 80 percent of gross income is rental income from dwelling units. A dwelling unit is a house or apartment used to provide living accommodations. Excluded are hotels, motels, and other establishments where more than one-half of the units are used on a transient basis.

The cost of residential rental property is recovered using the straight-line method of depreciation and a recovery period of 27.5 years.

Nonresidential real property is real property that is not within the above definition of residential real property. The cost of this property is recovered using the straight-line method and a recovery period of 31.5 years.

In the case of both residential and nonresidential real property, a mid-month convention is used. Under this convention, real property is considered to have been placed in service in the middle of the month and also disposed of in the middle of the month. A mid-quarter convention may be used by taxpayers who place more than 40 percent of property in service in the last quarter of the tax year.

Optional Depreciation Method

No longer may a taxpayer elect to use the straight-line method over an optional recovery period. The taxpayer may, however, elect to use the straight-line method over the applicable ACRS recovery period. For example, cost of property in the 5-year class may be deducted using the straight-line method, but the taxpayer must use the 5-year recovery period.

A taxpayer may, also, elect to use an alternative depreciation system based on ADR midpoints for property that is otherwise eligible for the ACRS. The alternative depreciation tables can be used to compute annual depreciation under the MACRS. The percentages in Figure 7-1a, b, and c (set forth below) make the change from the declining balance to the straight-line method in the year that the straight-line method will yield a larger deduction.

To figure the depreciation using the tables, use Figure 7-1a for 5-year property, Figure 7-1b for 7-year property, and Figure 7-1c for 15-year property. The percentages for the first 6 years are shown in the figure. The charts take the half-year and mid-quarter conventions into considerations in figuring percentages. Use the percentage in the first column unless you are required to use the mid-quarter convention. Following are some examples using the charts.

Assume you purchase a stove and refrigerator and placed them in

MACRS 5-Year Property

Year	Half-year convention	Mid-quarter convention			
		First quarter	Second quarter	Third quarter	Fourth quarter
1	20.00%	35.00%	25.00%	15.00%	5.00%
2	32.00	26.00	30.00	34.00	38.00
3	19.20	15.60	18.00	20.40	22.80
4	11.52	11.01	11.37	12.24	13.68
5	11.52	11.01	11.37	11.30	10.94
6	5.76	1.38	4.26	7.06	9.58

(a)

MACRS 7-Year Property

Year	Half-year convention	Mid-quarter convention			
		First quarter	Second quarter	Third quarter	Fourth quarter
1	14.29%	25.00%	17.85%	10.71%	3.57%
2	24.49	21.43	23.47	25.51	27.55
3	17.49	15.31	16.76	18.22	19.68
4	12.49	10.93	11.97	13.02	14.06
5	8.93	8.75	8.87	9.30	10.04
6	8.92	8.74	8.87	8.85	8.73

(b)

MACRS 15-Year Property

Year	Half-year convention	Mid-quarter convention			
		First quarter	Second quarter	Third quarter	Fourth quarter
1	5.00%	8.75%	6.25%	3.75%	1.25%
2	9.50	9.13	9.38	9.63	9.88
3	8.55	8.21	8.44	8.66	8.89
4	7.70	7.39	7.59	7.80	8.00
5	6.93	6.65	6.83	7.02	7.20
6	6.23	5.99	6.15	6.31	6.48

(c)

Residential Rental Property (27.5-year)

Year	Use the column for the month of taxable year placed in service											
	1	2	3	4	5	6	7	8	9	10	11	12
1	3.485%	3.182%	2.879%	2.576%	2.273%	1.970%	1.667%	1.364%	1.061%	0.758%	0.455%	0.152%
2	3.636	3.636	3.636	3.636	3.636	3.636	3.636	3.636	3.636	3.636	3.636	3.636
3	3.636	3.636	3.636	3.636	3.636	3.636	3.636	3.636	3.636	3.636	3.636	3.636
4	3.636	3.636	3.636	3.636	3.636	3.636	3.636	3.636	3.636	3.636	3.636	3.636
5	3.636	3.636	3.636	3.636	3.636	3.636	3.636	3.636	3.636	3.636	3.636	3.636
6	3.636	3.636	3.636	3.636	3.636	3.636	3.636	3.636	3.636	3.636	3.636	3.636

(d)

Nonresidential Real Property (31.5-year)

Year	Use the column for the month of taxable year placed in service											
	1	2	3	4	5	6	7	8	9	10	11	12
1	3.042%	2.778%	2.513%	2.249%	1.984%	1.720%	1.455%	1.190%	0.926%	0.661%	0.397%	0.132%
2	3.175	3.175	3.175	3.175	3.175	3.175	3.175	3.175	3.175	3.175	3.175	3.175
3	3.175	3.175	3.175	3.175	3.175	3.175	3.175	3.175	3.175	3.175	3.175	3.175
4	3.175	3.175	3.175	3.175	3.175	3.175	3.175	3.175	3.175	3.175	3.175	3.175
5	3.175	3.175	3.175	3.175	3.175	3.175	3.175	3.175	3.175	3.175	3.175	3.175
6	3.175	3.175	3.175	3.175	3.175	3.175	3.175	3.175	3.175	3.175	3.175	3.175

(e)

Additional tax on preference items. If you use accelerated depreciation, you may have to file Form 6251, *Alternative Minimum Tax—Individuals*. Accelerated depreciation includes MACRS and ACRS and any other method that allows you to deduct more depreciation than you could deduct using a straight line method.

Figure 7-1. Property depreciated for various number of years using the MACRS.

service on February 1 of this tax year. Your basis in the stove is $300 and your basis in the refrigerator is $500. Since these are classed as 7-year properties, you would use Figure 7-1*b*. Your depreciation deduction would be $43 for the stove ($300 × 14.29%) and $71 for the refrigerator ($500 × 14.29%).

Assume that you purchased the refrigerator in October instead of February (fourth quarter) and you cannot use the half-year convention. Your deduction for the refrigerator would be $18 ($500 × 3.57%). The depreciation for the stove (purchased in February, i.e., the first quarter) would be $75 ($300 × 25%).

Changes in Classifications

The Secretary of the Treasury is authorized to monitor and analyze actual experience with all tangible depreciable assets and to establish new classes for any property or class of property that does not have a class life.

Expensing an Investment

The 1986 Tax Reform Act continued with some modifications the first-year expensing option first started in 1981. Under this option, the taxpayer may elect to treat all or part of an investment as a current expense, and thus it is deductible in the current tax year. This deduction is commonly referred to as a "Section 179 Deduction." The requirements for expensing are as follows:

1. After 1986, the maximum dollar limitation on the amount that can be expensed is $10,000 a year ($5000 per married individual filing separate returns). This was an increase from the previous limitation of $5000.

2. This election is unavailable to any taxpayer for any tax year in which the aggregate cost of the investment for that year exceeds $210,000. In addition, there is a phaseout of the option for those cases where the investment exceeds $200,000. The phaseout schedule is $1 for each dollar that the aggregate total exceeds $200,000.

3. To be eligible to be expensed under this rule, the property must be used in the active trade or business of the taxpayer. The Secretary of the Treasury is authorized to prescribe regulations for the allocation of income or expense to a trade or business.

4. If the property is converted to nonbusiness use at any time, the difference between the amount expensed and the ACRS deduction that

would have been allowed for the period of business use is recaptured as ordinary income.

5. For passenger automobiles placed in service after January 1, 1990, the total deduction for each automobile (by both Section 179 and depreciation) is limited to approximately $2660 (adjusted for inflation).

6. No Section 179 deduction may be taken for computers and cellular telephones that are not used more than 50 percent for business use.

Alternative Depreciation System

The ACRS is modified for foreign-use property, tax-exempt use property, tax-exempt bond-financed property, luxury automobiles, mixed-use property, and certain imported property. In addition, the taxpayer may elect to use the alternative depreciation system for any class of property.

The recovery period under the alternative system generally is equal to the property's ADR midpoint life, 12 years for personal property with no ADR midpoint life, and 40 years for real property. Under this system, you use the straight-line method of depreciation.

Foreign-Use Property

Subject to several exceptions, if the property is to be used outside the United States more than half of a tax year, it is considered as foreign-use property and the ACRS cannot be used. One exception to this is for satellites or other spacecraft held by a U.S. citizen if such property is launched from within the United States.

Tax-Exempt Use Property

The Tax Reform Act retained the rules for tax-exempt use property and requires the recovery period for purpose of computing depreciation to be at least 125 percent of the lease term in case of leased property. Qualified technological equipment considered as tax-exempt use property with a lease term that exceeds 5 years may be considered as having a recovery period of 5 years.

Tax-Exempt Bond-Financed Property

The definition of tax-exempt bond-financed property was changed to include any property if part or all of such property is financed either directly or indirectly by tax-exempt bonds. Solid-waste disposal facilities and hazardous waste facilities are considered as having an ADR midpoint of 8 years, and low-income residential rental property is treated as having a recovery period of 27.5 years.

Luxury Automobiles

To limit taxpayers' deductions for luxury automobiles, depreciation deductions are limited. The fixed limitations on luxury automobiles apply to all deductions claimed for depreciation of automobiles, not just those under the ACRS.

Mixed-Use Property

Generally for property that is used 50 percent or more for personal or nonbusiness purposes, the depreciation deductions must be computed under the alternative depreciation system.

Certain Imported Property

The president is authorized to require by executive order the use of the alternative depreciation system to certain imported property from countries maintaining trade restrictions or engaging in discriminatory acts against the United States that unjustifiably restrict U.S. commerce. The alternative depreciation system delays the recovery of the investment by establishing a longer life for the items for tax purposes. Therefore, this should discourage business persons from buying from these countries.

For the purpose of this limitation, "imported property" means any property that is completed outside the United States or any property in which less than 50 percent of its cost is attributable to value added within the United States. Note that the United States includes Puerto Rico and other U.S. possessions.

Voluntary Election

A taxpayer may irrevocably elect to apply the alternative system in lieu of the ACRS to any class of property. If an election is made, it applies to all property in the ACRS class placed in service during that tax year. In the case of residential rental property and nonresidential real property, however, this election may be made on a property-by-property basis. The right to use the alternative system is in addition to the earlier discussed right to use the optional depreciation method.

Improvements to Property

The tax law continues to prohibit the use of the component method of depreciation. The recovery period for any addition or improvement to real or personal property begins either on the date on which the improvement is placed in service or the date on which the improved property is placed in service, whichever is later.

Any ACRS deduction for improvement to real or personal property is computed in the same manner as the deduction for the underlying property would be if such property were placed in service at the same time. For example, any improvement to nonresidential real property is recovered over 31.5 years using the straight-line method. In many cases, expensing of the improvement may be appropriate.

Recapture of Depreciation

A taxpayer who uses the ACRS to recover the investment costs of tangible personal property must treat the gain on the disposition of the property as ordinary income. There is no recapture of previously allowed depreciation deductions in the case of residential rental property and nonresidential real property. For the purpose of this recapture rule, the expensing of the costs of removing certain architectural and transportation barriers for disabled persons and the annual expensing of up to $10,000 are treated as depreciation deductions.

8

Tax Accounting and Receivables

In this chapter, the income tax aspects of accounting and accounts receivables (bad debts and installment sales) are discussed. Also included in this chapter is a discussion of IRS record keeping requirements.

Tax Accounting

This section is intended as a general review of IRS rules with regard to tax accounting.

Taxpayer Identification Numbers

The individual taxpayer generally uses his or her social security number as the taxpayer identification number. This number must appear on each of your individual income tax forms, such as Form 1040 and its schedules. However, every partnership and corporation (including S corporations) must have an employer identification number (EIN) to use as a taxpayer identification number. Sole proprietors must also have EINs, if they (1) pay wages to one or more employees, or (2) must file any pension or excise tax returns, including those for alcohol, tobacco, or firearms.

If you are required to have an EIN, include it along with your social security number on your Schedule C (Form 1040). Otherwise, sole proprietors can use their social security numbers as their business taxpayer identification numbers.

To apply for an EIN, use Form SS-4, "Application for Employer Identification Number." This form is available from the IRS and Social Security Administration offices.

Payments to Others.   If you make payments that require an information return, you must include the payee's taxpayer identification number on the information return. To get the payee's number, use Form W-9, "Request for Taxpayer Identification Number and Certification." This form is available from the IRS. A payee who does not provide you with an identification number may be subject to backup withholding of 20 percent on the payments you make.

Penalties.   A $50 penalty applies for each failure to comply by the required due date with certain specified information reporting requirements, up to a maximum of $100,000 for all such failures. Most of these requirements concern furnishing and including taxpayer identification numbers on returns, statements, and other documents.

New EIN.   You may need to get a new EIN if either the form or the ownership of your business changes. A new EIN is required for the following changes:

1. A sole proprietorship incorporates.
2. A sole proprietorship takes in partners and operates as a partnership.
3. A partnership incorporates.
4. A partnership is taken over by one of the partners and is operated as a sole proprietorship.
5. A corporation changes to a partnership or to a sole proprietorship.

If a corporation chooses to be taxed as an S corporation, it does not need a new EIN.

Change in Ownership.   A new EIN is required for the following changes:

1. You purchase or inherit an existing business that you will operate as a sole proprietorship (you cannot use the EIN of the former owner, even if he or she is your spouse).
2. You represent an estate that operates a business after the owner's death.
3. You terminate an old partnership and begin a new one.

Records of Employers

An employer must keep all records on employment taxes (income tax withholding, social security, and federal unemployment tax) for at least 4 years after the due date of the return or after the date the tax is paid, whichever is later. In addition to the following items required for each specific kind of employment tax, the records should also contain your employer identification number, copies of the returns you have filed, and the dates and amounts of deposits made.

Income Tax Withholding.   The specific records you must keep for income tax withholding are as follows:

1. Each employee's name, address, and social security number.
2. The total amount and date of each wage payment and the period of time the payment covers.
3. For each wage payment, the amount subject to withholding.
4. The amount of withholding tax collected on each payment and the date it was collected.
5. If the taxable amount is less than the total payment, the reason why it is less.
6. Copies of any statements furnished by employees relating to nonresident alien status, residence in Puerto Rico or the Virgin Islands, or residence or physical presence in a foreign country.
7. The fair market value and date of each payment of noncash compensation made to a retail commission salesperson, if no income tax was withheld.
8. For accident or health plans, information about the amount of each payment.
9. The withholding allowance certificate (Form W-4) filed by each employee.
10. Any agreement between you and the employee for the voluntary withholding of additional amounts of tax.
11. The dates in each calendar quarter on which any employee worked for you, not in the course of your trade or business, and the amount paid for that work.
12. Copies of statements given to you by employees reporting tips received in their work, unless the information shown on the statements appears in another item on this list.

13. Requests by employees to have their withheld tax figured on the basis of their individual cumulative wages.

14. Form W-5, "Earned Income Credit Advance Payment Certificate," for each of your employees eligible for the earned income credit who wish to receive their payment in advance rather than when they file their income tax returns.

An employee's earnings ledger, which you can buy at most office supply stores, normally has space for the information required in items 1 to 4.

Social Security Taxes.   An employer must also maintain the following information in his or her records on the social security (FICA) taxes of the employees: (1) the amount of each wage payment subject to FICA tax; (2) the amount of FICA tax collected for each payment and the date collected; and (3) the reason for the difference, if one exists, between the total wage payment and the taxable amount.

Federal Unemployment Tax Act.   The Federal Unemployment Tax Act (FUTA) requires employers to maintain the following information in their records: (1) the total amount paid to employees during the calendar year; (2) the amount of compensation subject to unemployment tax; (3) the amount paid into the state unemployment fund; and (4) any other information required to be shown on Form 940 (or Form 940-EZ), "Employer's Annual Federal Unemployment (FUTA) Tax Return."

Accounting Periods

Every taxpayer (business or individual) must figure taxable income and file a tax return on the basis of an annual accounting period. The term *tax year* is the annual accounting period you use for keeping your records and reporting your income and expenses. The accounting period you may use is either a calendar year or a fiscal year. You adopt a tax year when you file your first income tax return. You must adopt your first tax year by the due date (not including extensions) for filing a return for that year.

The due date for individuals and partnerships is the fifteenth day of the fourth month after the end of the tax year. Individuals include sole proprietors, partners, and S corporation shareholders. The due date for filing returns for corporations and S corporations is the fifteenth day of the third month after the end of the tax year. If the fifteenth day of the month falls on a Saturday, Sunday, or legal holiday, the due date is the next day that is not a Saturday, Sunday, or legal holiday. *Note:* Employment taxes are figured on a calendar year basis. You must use the calendar quarter for withheld income tax and social security tax. You must also use the calendar year for federal unemployment tax.

Calendar Tax Year

If you adopt the calendar year for your annual accounting period, you must maintain your books and records and report your income and expenses for the period from January 1 through December 31 of each year.

If you filed your first return using the calendar tax year, and you later begin business as a sole proprietor, or you become a partner in a partnership or a shareholder in an S corporation, you must continue to use the calendar tax year unless you get permission from the IRS to change (see the section entitled "Change in Tax Year"). You must report your income from all sources, including your sole proprietorship, salaries, partnership income, and dividends, using the same tax year.

You must adopt the calendar tax year if you do not keep adequate records, you have no annual accounting period, or your present tax year does not qualify as a fiscal year.

Fiscal Tax Year

A regular fiscal tax year is 12 consecutive months ending on the last day of any month except December. A 52–53 week year is a fiscal tax year that varies from 52 to 53 weeks.

If you adopt a fiscal tax year, you must maintain your books and records and report your income and expenses using the same tax year.

52–53 Week Tax Year. You can use a 52–53 week tax year if you keep your own books and records and report your income on that basis. This is a fiscal year that varies from 52 to 53 weeks, always ends on the same day of the week, and always ends on the date that day last falls in a particular calendar month or the date the day falls nearest to the last day of the particular calendar month. For example, if you elect a tax year that always ends on the last Monday in March, then for the year ending in 1991, your tax year will end on March 25, 1991. If you elected a tax year ending on the Monday nearest to the end of March, then for the tax year ending in 1991, your tax year will end on April 1, 1991.

You make the election by filing your tax return for the 52–53 week year and attaching to it a statement showing (1) the day of the week on which the tax year will always end, (2) whether it will end on the last such day of the week in the calendar month or on the date such day of the week occurs nearest the end of the month, and (3) the month in which or with reference to which the tax year will end.

You may change to a 52–53 week year that ends with reference to the end of the same month with which your parent tax year ends, without first getting permission from the IRS. You must attach the statement, discussed earlier, to the tax return for the year for which the election is made. For example, if you now use a calendar year and want to change to a 52–53 week year ending on the Friday closest to December 31, prior approval is not needed. You make the election to change by filing the statement described above with your return.

Approval Required.   If you change to a 52–53 week tax year that ends with reference to the end of a month that is not the same month in which your old tax year ended, you must first get approval from the IRS, as explained later.

For example, if you use a calendar year and want to change to a 52–53 week year ending on the Saturday nearest to the end of November, you must first get approval from the IRS.

To change from a 52–53 week year to any other tax year, including another 52–53 week year, you must first get approval from the IRS.

Short Tax Year

A short tax year is a tax year of less than 12 months. There are two situations that can result in a short tax year. The first occurs where you (as a taxable entity) are not in existence for an entire tax year. The second occurs when you change your accounting period. Each situation results in a different way of figuring tax for the short tax year.

If your business was not in existence the entire year, a tax return is required for the short period during which you were in existence. Requirements for filing the return and paying the tax generally are the same as if the return were for a full tax year of 12 months that ended on the last day of the short tax year.

Example 1.   Corporation X came into existence on July 2, 1990. It elected the calendar year for its accounting period. Corporation X must file its return by March 15, 1991. The return covers the period July 2, 1990, through December 31, 1990.

Example 2. A calendar year corporation dissolved on July 26, 1991. It must file its final return by October 15, 1991, for the period January 1 through July 26, 1991.

Corporations

A new corporation establishes its tax year when it files its first income tax return. An S corporation or a personal service corporation must use the required tax year rules, discussed earlier, to establish its tax year. A newly reactivated corporation, which has been inactive for a number of years, is treated as a new taxpayer for the purpose of adopting a tax year.

A corporation (other than an S corporation or a personal service corporation) may change its tax year without first getting the approval of the IRS if the following conditions are met:

1. It must not have changed its tax year within the 10 calendar years ending with the calendar year in which the short tax year resulting from the change begins.

2. Its short tax year must not be a tax year in which it has a net operating loss.

3. Its taxable income for the short tax year must be (when annualized) 80 percent or more of its taxable income for the tax year before the short tax year.

4. It must not try to become an S corporation for the tax year that would immediately follow the short tax year required to effect the change.

Accounting Methods

An accounting method is a set of rules used to determine when and how income and expenses are reported. The term *accounting method* includes not only the overall method of accounting you use but also the accounting treatment you use for any item.

You choose your accounting method when you file your first tax return. After that, if you want to change your accounting method, you must first get permission from the IRS.

No single accounting method is required of all taxpayers. You must use a system that clearly shows your income and expenses and you must maintain records that will enable you to file a correct return. In addition to your permanent books of account, you must keep any other records necessary to support the entries on your books and tax returns.

You must use the same method from year to year and figure your taxable income following the accounting method you use to keep your books. This method must clearly show your income and expenses. Any accounting method that shows the consistent use of generally accepted accounting principles for your trade or business generally is considered to clearly show income. An accounting method clearly shows income only if all items of gross income and all expenses are treated the same from year to year.

If you do not regularly use an accounting method that clearly shows your income, your income will be figured under the method that, in the opinion of the IRS, clearly shows your income.

Methods You May Use

Generally, you may figure your taxable income under any of the following accounting methods: (1) cash method; (2) accrual method; (3) special methods of accounting for certain items of income and expenses, such as depreciation, amortization and depletion, deduction for bad debts, and installment sales; and (4) a combination (hybrid) method using elements of methods 1, 2, or 3.

Combination (Hybrid) Method

Any combination of cash, accrual, and special methods of accounting can be used if the combination clearly shows income and is consistently used. You may specifically use the accrual method for purchases and sales, and the cash method for all items of income and expenses. The following restrictions, however, apply:

1. If you use the cash method for figuring your income, you must use the cash method for reporting your expenses.
2. If you use the accrual method for reporting your expenses, you must use the accrual method for figuring your income.

Any combination that includes the cash method is treated as the cash method, subject to the limitations applied to this method.

Business and Personal Items

You may account for business and personal items under different accounting methods. Thus, you may figure the income from your business under an accrual method even though you use the cash method to figure personal items.

Two or More Businesses

If you operate more than one business, you may use a different accounting method for each separate and distinct business if the method you use for each clearly shows your income. For example, if you operate a personal service business and a manufacturing business, you may use the cash method for the personal service business, but you must use the accrual method for the manufacturing business.

No business will be considered separate and distinct if you do not keep a complete and separable set of books and records for that business.

Cash Method

The cash method of accounting is used by most individuals and many small businesses with no inventories. However, if inventories are necessary in accounting for your income, you must use the accrual method for your sales and purchases. If you are not required to keep inventories, you usually will use the cash method. However, see below for a discussion of limits on the use of the cash method.

Income. With the cash method, you include in your gross income all items of income you actually or constructively receive during the year. You must include property and services you receive in your income at their fair market value.

Constructive Receipt. You have constructive receipt of income when an amount is credited to your account or made available to you without restriction. You do not need to have possession of it. If you authorize someone to be your agent and receive income for you, you are treated as having received it when your agent receives it.

For example, suppose you have interest credited to your bank account in December 1990. You must include it in your gross income for 1990 and not for 1991 when you withdraw it or enter it in your passbook.

As another example, suppose you have interest coupons that mature and are payable in 1990, but you do not cash them until 1991. You must include them in income for 1990. You must include this matured interest in your gross income even though you later exchange the coupons for other property instead of cashing them.

Delaying Receipt of Income. You cannot hold checks or postpone taking possession of similar property from one tax year to another to avoid paying the tax on the income. You must report the income in the year the property is made available to you without restriction.

Expenses. Usually, you must deduct expenses in the tax year in which you actually pay them. However, expenses you pay in advance can be deducted only in the year to which they apply. In addition, if the uniform capitalization rules apply, you may have to capitalize certain costs.

For example, suppose you are a calendar year taxpayer and you pay $1000 for a business insurance policy that is effective on July 1, 1990, for a 1-year period. You may deduct $500 in 1990 and $500 in 1991.

Limits of Use of Cash Method. The cash method, including any combination of methods that include the cash method, cannot be used by the following entities: (1) corporations (other than S corporations), (2) partnerships having a corporation (other than an S corporation) as a partner, and (3) tax shelters.

Exceptions

An exception allows farming businesses (including the raising, harvesting, or growing of trees), qualified personal service corporations, and entities with average annual gross receipts of $5 million or less to continue using the cash method. However, these exceptions do not apply to tax shelters. See IRS Publication 538, "Accounting Periods and Methods," for more information.

Bad Debts

In general, bad debts may be deducted from your adjusted gross income for tax purposes. To qualify as a bad debt, (1) there must be a true creditor-debtor relationship between the parties involved; (2) there must be a legal obligation to pay a fixed sum of money; (3) there must either be an actual loss of money or the debt as already been reported as income; and (4) there must be a practical inability to collect the debt.

The deduction normally may be taken only in the tax year that the debt becomes worthless and is written off the books of the taxpayer as worthless. A debt for write-off purposes becomes worthless when there is no longer any practical possibility of it being paid. In some cases, a debt may become worthless before it is due. For example, if the debtor goes bankrupt, the debt may be written off even though it is not due.

Payment of someone else's obligation by a person who guarantees payment of it may qualify the payor for treatment of the amount paid as a bad debt. This is based on the concept that when someone pays a debt that he or she has guaranteed, then a debt exists between the person who pays the debt and the person who was primarily liable on the debt.

There are two basic types of bad debts: nonbusiness debts and business debts. The rules regarding the treatment of each differ.

Worthless corporate securities do not qualify as bad debts and are therefore normally deductible as a loss of capital. Corporate securities include stock rights, bonds, debentures, or notes and certificates issued by a corporation with interest coupons or in registered form.

Nonbusiness Bad Debts

Nonbusiness bad debts are those incurred not in the normal course of a trade or business. For example, an architect made several loans to his clients. Since the architect is not normally in the trade or business of loaning money, these debts are considered as nonbusiness debts. Note that, as in this example, a business may have a nonbusiness debt.

For a nonbusiness debt to be deductible, it must be totally worthless. Taxpayers are not allowed to deduct partially worthless nonbusiness bad debts. In addition, the Tax Reform Act restricted the deductibility of nonbusiness bad debts.

Business Bad Debts

Business bad debts are normally deducted directly from the business's gross income. To qualify as a business bad debt, the debt must be closely related to the activity of the business. There must, also, have been a dominant business reason for the business or the individual to have entered into the transaction as the creditor. Credit transactions normally qualify as business bad debts.

Partially bad business debts may qualify for tax deduction in the amount of the partial loss. Accounts or notes receivable are valued at fair market value at the time of the transaction, and only the fair market value is deductible even though that value may be less than the face value of the accounts or notes.

There are two methods to deduct business bad debts: by the specific charge-off method and by the reserve method. The Tax Reform Act limited the use of the reserve method to certain financial institutions, small business investment companies, thrift institutions, and farm credit institutions. Therefore, for tax years beginning after December 31, 1986, most businesses must use the specific charge-off method.

The specific charge-off method allows a taxpayer to deduct specific business bad debts that become totally or partially worthless in that tax year. The reserve method permits taxpayers to deduct a reasonable addition of a reserve for bad debts.

The deduction is available only for the amount in question that has been included as income for the current or an earlier tax year. This rule applies to amounts owed from all sources of taxable income, such as sales, services, rents, or interest.

Taxpayers and businesses using an accrual method of accounting normally report income that is due as soon as it is earned. Accordingly, they may take a bad debt deduction when the amount proves to be uncollectible, provided it has been reported as income. Businesses and taxpayers using the cash method of accounting normally do not report income from bills due them until the bills are paid. Accordingly, they may not take a bad debt deduction on payments they have not received or cannot collect, since this situation does not meet the reported income requirement.

The bad debt may be deducted, if otherwise qualified, even after the business ceases operation as an active business. An individual taxpayer may also deduct a business bad debt even after the taxpayer has ceased the active trade or business involved.

Thrift institutions are allowed to continue to use the reserve method, but the percentage of taxable income that may be reserved for bad debts has been reduced to 8 percent. Commercial banks with gross assets of $500 million or less may continue to use the reserve method.

Guarantees of Payment

A person or business who is required to pay a debt for someone else because that person or business guaranteed payment of the debt may in some cases qualify for a bad debt deduction. The guarantee must have been entered into for a profit motive or be related to the trade or business of the person giving the guarantee. It does not matter what capacity the taxpayer has, as long as there is a legal obligation to pay the debt when the primary debtor does not.

Guarantees made to protect or improve employment opportunities of the person making the guarantee is considered as being closely related to a person's trade or business. If the guarantee is made as a favor to someone and not related to trade or business or for profit motive, then the payment required by the guarantee is not deductible.

Determination of Worthlessness

The determination of worthlessness is a question of fact and thus determined by all the evidence. Matters considered include the value of any collateral, financial condition of the debtor, whether or not the debtor has filed for bankruptcy, and the value of other property owned by the debtor. A debt is not worthless merely because there may be problems in collecting it.

Write-off Year

Prior to the Tax Reform Act, the bad debt deduction could be charged off only in the year that the debt became worthless. The period that the debt is actually charged off the books was immaterial. Many times a taxpayer would be required to file an amended tax return when it was discovered in a later year that a debt actually became worthless in an earlier year.

Now, not only must the debt be worthless to be deducted, but it should also be recognized for other purposes by the taxpayer (written off the books). This change was to resolve the difficulty that arises when the taxpayer discovers that the debt was worthless in an earlier year. A taxpayer cannot delay to a later year the write-off in order to take maximum advantage of it. Where it is demonstrated that a taxpayer is actually aware of the fact that the debt is worthless, then the deduction must be taken that tax year. If the debt is wholly worthless, then it need not be written off to be deductible.

For example, suppose a business filed a tax return in April of one year for the prior year. Then the business finds out that a debtor had declared bankruptcy in the prior year. In this case, prior to the code modification, the business would have been required to file an amended return in order to take the bad debt deduction. Now, by writing off the debt in the year it discovered the bankruptcy, the business could also take the bad debt in the year of the write-off and thus would not need to amend a prior return. Under the new law, the business in most cases may deduct the loss in the year of discovery of its worthless status.

Reporting Bad Debts

Bad debt deductions included on an income tax return are required to be fully explained. A statement must be attached to the return that contains the following information:

1. Description of the debt, including amount

2. Name of the debtor

3. The business or family relationship between the taxpayer and the debtor, if any

4. The date the debt is due

5. Statement of efforts made to collect the debt

6. Facts that establish the inability to collect the debt

Nonbusiness bad debts are required to be deducted as short-term capital losses. Recovery of bad debts previously deducted must be reported as income.

Bad Debt Reserves for Guarantees

The Tax Reform Act repealed the reserve method for dealers who guarantee, endorse, or provide indemnity agreements with respect to debts owed to others. Now, expenses associated with bad debts for such dealers are not deductible until the dealer suffers a loss.

Installment Sales

An installment sale is a sale of property in which one or more payments on the sale are to be received after the end of the tax year. Use of the installment method has been limited by the Tax Reform Act and other recent tax changes. The key concepts in the tax treatment of installment sales are as follows:

- Gain or loss on the sale of property is generally required to be recognized in the tax year that the property is sold.

- Under the installment method, the taxpayer recognizes income and return on investment equal to the amount that bears the ratio of profit or return to the basis.

- Time shares and residential lots may elect to use the installment method in certain situations.

- Sellers using revolving credit plans may not use the installment method.

- Sellers of publicly traded property may not use the installment method.

- If you use an installment obligation to secure any debt, the net proceeds from the debt may be treated as payment of the installment obligation. This rule applies if the sale price of the property was more than $150,000 and was not the sale of farm property.

Price gain or loss on the sale of property is generally required to be recognized in the tax year in which the property was sold. The gain from certain sales of property in exchange for which the seller receives deferred payments, however, may be in some cases reported on the installment method. The installment method may not be used for a sale resulting in a loss.

The rationale for allowing the reporting of gain on the installment method for federal income tax purposes is that the seller may be unable to pay tax currently because no cash may be available until payments are received under the obligation; the ability to defer taxation would eliminate this problem. In general, you report gain from an installment sale only when you actually receive payment.

Each payment you receive on an installment sale usually consists of three parts: (1) return of your investment (basis), (2) gain on the sale, and (3) interest.

Under the installment method, in any tax year, the taxpayer recognizes income resulting from the disposition of property equal to the amount that bears the same ratio to the payments received in that year if the gross profit under the contract bears to the contract price. For example, assume that the taxpayer sold property that had an adjusted basis of $100,000. The selling price is $200,000. Therefore, 50 percent of all money received by the seller will be considered gross profit. If the seller receives $40,000 immediately and will receive the remaining $140,000 plus interest over the next 2 tax years, then, under the installment method, the seller need recognize only 50 percent of the gain since 50 percent would be a return of the basis. The same ratio would apply each time the seller receives a payment.

Installment Payments

A buyer's note, if payable on demand, may be considered payment in full. If the note is not payable on demand, it is not considered payment on the sale. Its full face value is included in figuring both the selling price and contract price. The payments you receive on the note may be reported on the installment method.

If you receive property rather than money from the buyer, it is still considered payment. The value of the payment is the property's fair market value on the date you receive it.

If the property the buyer gives you is a third-party note or obligation, you are considered to have received a payment equal to the note's fair market value. Because the note is itself a payment on your installment sale, any payments you later receive on the note from the third party are not considered payments on the sale.

Proportionate Disallowance Rule

The Tax Reform Act limits the availability of the installment method of accounting in three circumstances. First, the act disallowed the use of the installment method with respect to a portion of certain installment receivables based on the amount of the outstanding indebtedness of the taxpayer. Second, the act prohibited taxpayers from using the installment method for sales pursuant to a revolving credit plan. Third, the act provided that the installment method may not be used for sale of certain publicly traded property.

Under the code, the use of the installment method for certain sales by persons who regularly sell real estate or personal property and for certain sales of business or rental property is limited, based on the amount of the outstanding indebtedness of the taxpayer. The limitation generally is applied by determining the amount of the taxpayer's "allocable installment indebtedness" (AII) for each tax year and treating such amount as a payment immediately before the close of the tax year on applicable installment obligations of the taxpayer that arose in that tax year and were still outstanding as of the end of the year.

Time Shares and Residential Lots.   The Tax Reform Act provided an election under which the proportionate disallowance rule would not apply to installment obligations that arise from the sale of certain types of property by a dealer to an individual, but only if the individual's obligation is not guaranteed or insured by any third person other than an individual. The obligation must arise from the sale of a time share or of unimproved land, the development of which will not be undertaken by the seller of the land or any affiliate of the seller.

A parcel of land is not to be considered to have been improved or developed if it merely has been provided with the benefits of common infrastructure items such as roads and sewers. For purposes of this rule, a time share is a right to use a specified parcel of residential real property for a period not exceeding 6 weeks per year. Where an individual or any related person owns more than one time share in a single parcel of residential real property, then all the time shares of the individual and the related parties are aggregated for purposes of determining whether the 6-week test is met. A time share may include a right to use campground sites in designated locations over ascertainable periods of time for recreational (not residential) purposes.

Subject to the above conditions, the seller of the property may elect not to have the general rules relating to installment sales apply, provided that the seller pays interest on the deferral of his or her tax liability attributable to the use of the installment method.

Revolving Credit Plans.   Sellers are not permitted to use the installment method to account for certain revolving credit plan sales on the basis of the concept that such sales more closely resemble the provisions of the flexible line of credit accompanied by cash sales of the seller. Therefore, it is not considered appropriate to use the installment method for these sales.

Publicly Traded Property.   Taxpayers who sell stock, or securities that are traded on the established security market or property of a kind regularly traded on an established market are not permitted to use the installment method to account for such sales. The rationale behind this restriction is apparently that publicly traded property is considered to be a sufficiently liquid asset to be treated the same as payment for cash for purposes of applying the installment method. Also, the taxpayer can easily sell such property for cash to the public market, and, therefore, it does not present the same liquidity problem that the installment method is intended to alleviate.

Guarantees

If a third party or government agency guarantees the buyer's payments to you on an installment obligation, the guarantee itself is not considered to be a payment.

Imputed Interest

Both the buyer and the seller must treat a part of each installment sale payment as interest. If a fair interest rate is stated in the agreement, that rate will be used. A *fair rate* is defined as at least that rate at which the government borrows money. If no rate is stated in the agreement, the parties must treat a portion of the payment, usually the fair interest rate, as interest. That portion of the payment that is considered as interest must be treated as current income in the year that the payment is received.

Depreciation Recapture

As discussed in Chapter 7, when property is depreciated, your basis in the property is reduced. If you use an accelerated depreciation method rather than a straight-line method, you must "recapture" the extra depreciation in the year that the asset is sold. That part of the profit that results from the extra depreciation is taxed as ordinary income rather than as capital gains.

All depreciation recapture must be taxed in the year of the sale, regardless of when the payments are received. Accordingly, for installment sales, consider the fact that unless the first-year payment exceeds the amount of the depreciation recapture, you may have a negative cash flow for the first year.

Single Sale of Several Assets

If you sell two or more assets in a single sale to one buyer, you may be required to allocate the down payment for the assets in proportion to their respective selling price. The IRS will normally accept an arm's-length allocation of the selling price, and the payments received in the year of sale will be accepted if substantiated by all the facts and circumstances. However, an allocation that is not based on the respective selling prices of the assets sold is not acceptable. The sale at a gain of separate and unrelated assets of the same class under a single contract is reported as a single asset.

Dispositions of Installment Obligations

If you dispose of an installment obligation (usually the buyer's note, mortgage, etc.), you will usually have a gain or loss to report. The gain or loss is considered to result from the sale of the property for which the installment obligation was received. If the original installment sale of the property produced ordinary income, the disposition of the obligation will result in ordinary income or loss. If the original sale resulted in a capital gain, the disposition of the obligation will result in a capital gain or loss.

The following rules are used to figure your gain or loss from the disposition of an installment obligation:

- If you sell or exchange the obligation, or if you accept less than face value in satisfaction of the obligation, the gain or loss is the difference between your basis in the obligation and the amount you receive for it.

- If you dispose of the obligation in any other way, the gain or loss is the difference between the basis in the obligation and its fair market value at the time of the disposition.

An example of the disposal of the obligation in "another way" is the cancellation of the obligation. In this case, the gain or loss is the difference between the basis of the obligation and its fair market value.

If you reduce the selling price or accept partial payment in a later year and cancel the balance of the buyer's debt on an installment sale, you treat the settlement as a disposition of the obligation. Accordingly, you must report the gain or loss on the difference between your basis in the obligation and the amount that you realize.

If the buyer defaults on the contract and you repossess the property, you may have a gain, a loss, or a bad debt. The rules used to figure the gain or loss from repossessions of personal property are different from those used to figure the gain or loss from repossessions of most real property. For a detailed treatment on how to compute gains or losses from repossessions, see IRS Publication 537.

Electing Out

You may choose not to have the installment sales rules apply to your sale. If you make this decision, then the entire gain on the property must be reported in the year of sale even though you will not be paid until later. This election must be made by reporting the gain on Schedule D for the year in which the sale was made. Once made, the election generally cannot be changed.

Reduction in Selling Price

If the selling price is later reduced, the gross profit on the sale will also change. You must refigure the gross profit percentage for the remaining payments. You cannot go back and refigure the gain you have reported in earlier years.

Sales to Related Persons

Special rules apply to sales to related persons, if that person then sells or otherwise disposes of the property before you receive all the payments from the first sale. Spouses, parents, children, brothers, sisters, grandchildren, and grandparents are considered as related persons. A partnership or corporation in which you own an interest in can also be considered as a related party. For more information on installment sales to related parties, see IRS Publication 537.

Keeping Records

The tax code and IRS regulations require the taxpayer to keep adequate records. Some key concepts in keeping records are as follows:

- The burden of proof to establish income, deductions, adjustments, etc., is on the taxpayer.
- Failure to keep adequate records may result in the taxpayer being required to pay more tax than necessary.
- Certain types of records are required to support certain tax transactions.
- Tax records should be retained for a minimum of 6 years.
- Missing copies of tax returns may be obtained from the IRS service center where the returns were filed.
- Most taxpayers are required to use the cash method of accounting.

Good record keeping offers the best means of substantiating the claims on your tax return. Records are necessary when your returns are audited. The burden is on the taxpayer to establish the correctness of his or her return. Usually, an examination of a taxpayer's return does not occur until 1 to 3 years after the return is filed. Without good records it is almost impossible to establish the correctness of a return filed by a taxpayer.

Types of Records Required

IRS regulations require the taxpayer to keep sufficient and adequate records to determine the proper tax due. Records must be kept accurately. No particular form is required. As a rule, the nonbusiness taxpayer should keep at least the following records:

- Invoices and sales slips pertaining to tax-deductible purchases
- Canceled checks
- Stock brokerage statements
- Form W-2 for wage and tax statements
- Form W-2P, "Statement for Recipients of Annuities, Pensions, Retired Pay, or IRA Payments"
- Forms 1099 on interests, dividends, distributions, etc.
- Pay statements
- Automobile logs to establish business use of automobile

- Copies of tax returns from prior years
- Any other documents that establish either income or tax adjustments transactions

The use of running records (kept daily) are more acceptable to the IRS and in many cases can be the difference between a successful and an unsuccessful audit. In addition, keeping good records helps prevent the taxpayer from overlooking deductions or adjustments.

At one time, IRS regulations attempted to require the keeping of contemporaneous records to support travel, transportation, entertainment, and business gift expenses. This requirement was rejected by Congress before it became effective. The requirement now is that the taxpayer must establish the deductions or credits by adequate records or by sufficient evidence corroborating the taxpayer's statements. In one case, the courts held that entries on a desk calendar not supported by other evidence was not sufficient proof to support claimed deductions.

The courts and the IRS will examine a taxpayer's records closely to determine whether or not to accept them as sufficient to uphold a claimed deduction or credit. Advice on keeping good records follows:

- Record an expense item in an account book at or near the time of the expense. Late entries are considered suspect.

- Keep copies of any expense records or travel claims presented to your employer. Statements the taxpayer gives to his or her employer, client, or customer are considered an adequate record of the expenses. In most cases, the statement may be a copy of your account book or other record.

- Bear in mind that deductions are not allowed for approximations or estimates, or for expenses that are lavish or extravagant.

- As the taxpayer, you must establish not only the cost of the expense but also that the expense is deductible.

- Separate your expenses; each separate payment is normally considered as a separate expense. The IRS requires that expenses be recorded separately. However, you are not required to keep separate records regarding expenses of a similar nature occurring during the course of a single event. For example, you may record your meal expenses for 1 day in a single entry.

- Keep all receipts; they are considered as the best item of evidence.

- Support through documentary evidence all lodging expenses while traveling away from home. Evidence is also required for any expense of $25 or more.

- A canceled check does not by itself support a business expense; keep both your check and a bill or invoice, which are normally sufficient.

Travel

To deduct or credit travel expenses, the taxpayer must show and corroborate:

- Each separate amount that was spent for travel away from home, such as the cost of your transportation or lodging. The taxpayer may total the daily cost of breakfast, lunch, and dinner and other incidental elements of such travel if they are listed in reasonable categories, such as meals, gas and oil, and taxi fares.
- The dates the taxpayer left and returned home for each trip, and the number of days spent on business away from home.
- The destination or locality of the travel, described by name of city, town, or similar designation.
- The business reason for the travel or the business benefit gained from the travel.

Entertainment

To deduct entertainment expenses, the taxpayer must show and be able to prove these items:

- The amount of each separate expense for entertainment, except for incidental items, such as taxi fares and telephone calls, which may be totaled on a daily basis.
- The date the entertainment took place.
- The name, address or location, and the type of entertainment, such as dinner or theater, if the information is not apparent from the name or designation of the place.
- The reason for the entertainment or the business benefit gained or expected to be gained from entertaining and, except for business meals, the nature of any activity that took place.
- The occupation or other information about the person or persons entertained, including name, title, or other designation sufficient to establish the business relationship to the taxpayer; in addition, information regarding whether or not the taxpayer or his/her representative or agent was present.

Deduction for an Office in the Home

The records necessary to establish a deduction for an office in the home must show that part of the home used for business and that you use this part of the home exclusively and regularly for business as either your principal place of business as a direct seller or as the place where you meet or deal with clients or customers in the normal course of your business. In addition, you must show the amount of depreciation and other expenses for keeping up the part of the home that is for business.

Automobile Expenses

Whether or not the taxpayer uses the standard mileage rates, the taxpayer must keep records to show when the taxpayer started using the automobile for business and the cost or other basis of the car. The records must also show the business miles and the total miles the car was used during the tax year. In most cases, a log of trips is essential to establish business use of the automobile.

If the actual expenses are claimed, in addition to the above expenses, the records must also show the cost of operating the car, including insurance, personal property, etc. (receipts will be needed), and the extent the car expenses reflect travel away from home.

Gifts

To deduct gift expenses, the taxpayer must show the cost of each gift; the date each gift was given; a description of each gift; the reason for giving the gift, or any business benefit gained or expected to be gained from giving it; and the occupation or other information about the person receiving the gift, including name, title, or other designation to establish the business relationship to the taxpayer.

Additional Information

The IRS may require additional information to clarify or to establish the accuracy or reliability of information contained in the taxpayer's records, statements, testimony, or documentary evidence before a deduction is allowed.

Inadequate Records

As noted, the Internal Revenue Code requires every person to keep such records as the Secretary of the Treasury may require. IRS regulations require taxpayers to maintain such accounting records as will enable them to file correct returns. The tax code, also, requires taxpayers to maintain records sufficient to clearly reflect income. In addition, taxpayers are required to maintain sufficient records to establish their right to any deductions and adjustments to gross income.

If the IRS determines that a taxpayer's records are "inadequate," then it can use certain methods to arrive at the taxable income of a taxpayer, including net worth and bank deposits. The IRS's methods of arriving at the taxable income of a taxpayer are discussed in Chapter 5.

The IRS has defined *inadequate records* as either the lack of records or records so incomplete that correctness of taxable income cannot be determined. The IRS has determined that a taxpayer's records were inadequate where they were adequate in all respects except for one area. If the IRS determines that the lack of adequate records was intentional, then the taxpayer may be prosecuted for civil or criminal fraud.

In most cases, the lack of adequate records causes the IRS to examine more thoroughly a taxpayer's status. Accordingly, the examiners may look at areas that normally would not be examined. In one recent case, the lack of adequate records was used by the IRS as primary reason to obtain a search warrant to examine the contents of a taxpayer's safe deposit box.

Notice of Inadequate Records. In addition to assessing additional taxes, the IRS can issue a Notice of Inadequate Records. This is accomplished by IRS's Standard Letter 978 (DO). This letter directs the taxpayer to keep certain records in the future. The required records include:

- The date and description of each transaction that the taxpayer engages in
- The date and amount of each payment made by the taxpayer
- The date and amount of each item of gross income received
- The date and amount of each payment made
- The name and address of each payee
- A description of the nature of each payment

Reconstruction of Records. If the taxpayer's records are inadequate, there is nothing illegal in reconstructing them. Reconstructing records is not the same as back-dating records, which may be a crime.

If the records are reconstructed, the examiner should be advised of this fact. In addition, the methods used to reconstruct the records should be explained to the examiner. For example, in a case involving the business use of an automobile by a public school teacher, the use of attendance records at various schools may be used to construct an automobile use log. Often, the use of third-party records will assist in reconstructing tax records.

If the taxpayer claims that the records have been stolen or destroyed, then the examiner will expect a police or file report to back up the claim. If the report of the loss to fire or police is dated after notice of audit is received by the taxpayer, the examiner may be suspicious. In most cases, it will be better for the taxpayer to admit the inadequacy of his or her records rather than attempt to falsify receipts.

IRS regulations provide that if a taxpayer does not have adequate records to support an element of an expense, then to support the element, the taxpayer may submit a statement containing specific information in detail as to the element, and provide other supporting evidence sufficient to establish the element.

How Long to Keep Records

Generally, the taxpayer should keep records as long as they are important for any federal tax law. Most records are important for at least 3 years following the filing of the return.

In some cases, the government can question a return 6 years after it is filed, for example, if the IRS contends that you underreported your income by more than 25 percent or that fraud was committed. Taxpayers may feel that the 6-year period does not apply to them, but the essential fact is to prove that to the IRS. Accordingly, taxpayers should as a minimum keep their records for 6 years after the last date the return was filed or due to be filed (whichever is later).

In some cases, as with receipts for home improvements, a taxpayer may need to establish many years later the cost of certain property. The taxpayer should retain those types of records for at least 3 years after the property is disposed of. For example, a taxpayer who owned a home for 20 years and decided to retire and move to a warmer climate would be required to establish the amount of monetary gain made on the sale of the house. In this regard, all receipts for home improvements, the addition of a pool, etc., will be needed regardless of the date of the expenditure.

Recommended Record-Keeping Procedures

Joseph Narun, a management consultant, recommends the keeping of a four-part system that integrates daily recording, single-item tracking of expenses, filing of receipts, and regular reviews of your tax position. The system uses a daily general diary in which to keep most of the itemized deductions. Separate special diaries are recommended for the recording of single activities such as automobile logs and sideline business activities.

He recommends the use of color-coded entries. This requires the taxpayer to keep different color pens for each type of entry. For example, one color should be used for medical expenses and a different color for taxes paid. A handy reference code is needed to simply the color codings.

Receipts for expenses should be filed in separate envelopes. It is helpful to make notes on the receipts as to date and possible tax consequences. Narun also recommends totaling up at least quarterly each expense category.

Other useful hints include completing the memo line on checks to help explain expenses, making notations on the front and back of charge receipts, making copies of diary pages and storing them in a different location from other records, and using the same color-code system for all your records and checkbook statements.

If a taxpayer has lost or destroyed his or her copies of tax forms that were previously filed, replacement copies may be obtained from the service center where the forms were originally filed. The taxpayer should file a Form 4506, "Request for Copy of Tax Form," with the service center to obtain the copies. It normally takes about 6 weeks to get replacement copies.

9

Income and Loss Problems

In this chapter special tax problems that relate to net income and losses are discussed. These include the dividends-received deductions, net income or loss reporting including net operating loss carry-forwards, and accumulated earnings tax.

Dividends-Received Deduction

A corporation is allowed a deduction for a percentage of certain dividends the corporation received during its tax year. The purpose of the deduction is to remove some of the effects of multiple taxation. For example, the dividend-paying corporation pays a tax on profits that constitute the dividend; then the receiving corporation must claim the dividend as income and thus it is subject once again to income tax liability. Finally, when the receiving corporation pays dividends, the taxpayer who receives the dividend is subject to tax liability on it.

A corporation may deduct, subject to certain limitations, 70 percent of the dividends it receives from taxable domestic corporations (other than dividends on certain preferred stock of public utility companies, which will be discussed later). If the dividends are from a corporation in which the corporation receiving the dividends owns more than 20 percent of the dividend-paying corporation, the deduction may be 80 percent.

The 70 percent deduction applies to certain dividends of the Federal Home Loan banks paid out of earnings and also to profits of the Federal Home Loan Mortgage Corporation. The dividends must be distributions from the earnings and profits of the paying corporation. Prior to the Tax Reform Act of 1986, the normal deduction was 85 percent.

Companies that qualify as small business investment companies may deduct 100 percent of the dividends received from a taxable domestic corporation. Members of an affiliated group of corporations may elect, if certain conditions are met, to deduct 100 percent of the dividends received from a member of the same affiliated group. An affiliated group is one or more chains of includable corporations connected through stock ownership with a common parent corporation. The parent corporation is an includable corporation if (1) one or more of the includable corporations directly own stock possessing at least 80 percent of the total combined voting power of the stock entitled to vote and that stock has a value of at least 80 percent of the total value of the stock of each of the includable corporations except the common parent corporation; and (2) the common parent corporation directly owns stock possessing at least 80 percent of the voting power of stock entitled to vote, and that has a value of at least 80 percent of the total value of the stock of at least one other includable corporation.

The term *includable corporation* refers to any corporation except corporations exempt from income tax, foreign corporations, regulated investment companies, real estate trusts, and interest-charged domestic international sales corporations (DISCs) or former DISCs.

A corporation may deduct a percentage of dividends it receives from certain foreign corporations if the distributing corporation is not a foreign personal holding company, is not exempt from federal income tax, and is engaged in trade or business within the United States for a 36-month period ending with the close of the foreign corporation's tax year in which the dividends were paid. In addition, the distributing corporation must have 50 percent or more of its gross income from all sources that is effectively connected with the conduct of a trade or business within the United States for a 36-month period.

If the foreign corporation has not existed for 36 months, then the entire period of its existence may be used to satisfy the 36-month period. Normally, the deduction in this case is 70 percent of the portion of dividends of the foreign corporation attributable to its income effectively connected with the conduct of trade or business within the United States during the qualifying time period.

No deductions are allowed for dividends received from the following sources:

1. A real estate investment trust

2. A corporation that is exempt from tax for either the tax year of the distribution or the preceding year

3. A corporation whose stock has been held by your corporation for 45 days or less

4. Any corporation to the extent your corporation is under an obligation to make related payments with respect to provisions in any similar situated property

5. A former DISC

If the receiving corporation sustains a net operating loss for the tax year, the limitation of 70 percent of taxable income does not apply. To determine whether or not the corporation has a net operating loss, the dividends-received deduction is figured without regard to the limitation of 70 percent of taxable income.

When a corporation receives a dividend from another domestic corporation in form of property other than cash, the dividend is included in an amount equal to either the lesser of the property's fair market value or the adjusted basis of the property in the hands of the distributing corporation increased by the amount of any gain recognized by the distributing corporation on the distribution.

Net Income or Loss

The net income or loss from a sole proprietorship is reported on the individual's income tax return for that year using Schedule C (Form 1040). For a partnership, a partnership figures its net income or loss on Form 1065. The partnership then distributes its net income or loss to its partners. If the partnership has net income, each partner's share is added to the partner's gross income. If the partnership has a net loss, the partner's share is deducted in computing the partner's gross income.

An S corporation figures net income or loss on Form 1120-S. It then distributes its net income or loss to the stockholders. If the S corporation has net income, each stockholder's share becomes a part of that stockholder's gross income to be reported on Form 1040. If it has a loss, each shareholder's share is deducted in figuring gross income.

A corporation figures its net income or loss on Form 1120. Being a separate tax entity, the corporation must pay a tax on its own earnings. It figures its net income and loss for the year in much the same way as an individual, with the exception that certain deductions are not allowed for a corporation.

At-Risk Loss

There are special at-risk rules that apply to most business or income-producing activities. At-risk rules limit the amount of loss that a person or business may deduct to the amount that person or business is considered to have net risk in an activity. Generally, you are considered at risk up to the amount of money and the adjusted basis of property that you had contributed to the activity plus certain amounts borrowed for use of the activity. You are considered at risk for amounts borrowed for use of the activity if you are personally liable for repayment of the amounts or if the amounts borrowed are secured by your property that is not used in the activity.

Net Operating Loss

If your authorized deductions for the year are more than your adjusted gross income, then a net operating loss (NOL) results. An NOL may be used to reduce taxable income in other years. It may be carried back and deducted from income from an earlier tax year. In this case, an amended income tax form for the previous year must be filed. To carry back an NOL, you must first refigure the tax for the year you carry it to, and then if you owe less tax than you paid for that year, the business files for a refund.

Normally, an NOL is caused by business losses. However, casualty and theft losses can also cause an NOL. There are limitations, however, on the amount of deductions a person can take regarding a casualty or theft loss.

An NOL is computed in much the same way as a person's gross income. You generally can carry an NOL back 3 years before the NOL, i.e., the year in which the loss occurred, or carry it over up to 15 years after the NOL. If you elect to carry back the loss, you must first carry your NOL back 3 years to the third taxable year before the NOL. If it takes only part of the NOL to reduce the income tax in that year, you carry the unused part back to the next year—the second year before the NOL loss. If the NOL is not used up in the second year, then you carry it, the unused part, to the next tax year, the year before the NOL.

If the NOL is not totally used up in the 3-year carryback, then what remains of it can carry over 15 years following the NOL year. It is started by carrying it over to the first tax year after the NOL. If it is not used after deducting it from the taxable income for that year, carry it to the unused part over to the next year. Continue to carry over any unused part of the NOL from year to year until the 15-year carryover period expires or the NOL is used up.

A business can choose not to carry the NOL to a carryback period, in which case it may be used only in a 15-year carryover period. In making this choice, a statement must be attached to the tax return for the NOL year. The statement must indicate that you are choosing to forgo the carryback period. This statement must be filed by the due date, including extensions of time for filing your return, for the NOL year. If it is not filed at that time, a person cannot forgo the carryback period. Once this choice is made, it cannot be changed.

Partnerships and S corporations are not allowed to take NOL deductions, but the individual partners or shareholders may use their separate shares of the partnership or S corporation loss to figure their own individual NOLs.

Corporations, for the most part, figure and deduct an NOL the same way an individual does. The same carryback and carryover periods apply. A corporation NOL differs from an individual in two ways: first, the corporation is allowed to take different deductions when figuring an NOL; and second, a corporation must make different modifications to its taxable income in the carryback or carryover years when figuring how much of the NOL to deduct.

A corporation's NOL is figured the same way as its taxable income. The corporation starts with its gross income and subtracts its deductions. If the deductions are more than its gross income, the corporation has an NOL. However, there are rules that limit what can be deducted or that permit deductions which are not ordinarily allowed:

1. You cannot deduct any NOL carryback or carryover from other years.

2. You can take the deduction for dividends received without limiting it by 70 percent of the corporation's taxable income.

3. You can figure the deductions for dividends paid on certain preferred stock of public utilities without limiting it to the taxable income for the year.

For a corporation to carry back an NOL, the corporation can either file a Form 1120-X, "Amended U.S. Corporate Income Tax Return," or Form 1139, "Corporate Application for Tentative Refund." To get a refund of taxes, the forms must be filed within 3 years of the due date, plus the extension for filing the return the year the corporation has the NOL.

The Tax Reform Act restricted the amount of a corporation's NOL that could be picked up by a successor corporation. This was to prevent corporations from buying other corporations to take advantage of the selling corporation's unused NOLs. The act modifies the rules for corporate NOLs when there is a 50 percent or greater change in ownership of the selling corporation. The restriction of NOL carryovers for those corporations that have a 50 percent change in ownership is in the form of an annual limitation on their use after the change. The total amount of the NOL is not reduced.

Special NOL rules are provided for financial institutions. In general, the 10-year carryback is retained for commercial banks for portions of NOLs attributable to bad debts for losses incurred in tax years beginning after December 31, 1986; and an additional 3-year carry-forward is provided for losses of thrift institutions incurred after 1981 and before 1986.

Accumulated Earnings Taxes

The Internal Revenue Code imposes in addition to the corporate tax a graduated tax on accumulated taxable income. Presently, the accumulated earnings tax is 28 percent of the undistributed current earnings of a corporation.

The accumulated earnings tax applies to any domestic or foreign corporation not specifically exempted that was formed or availed of to avoid or prevent the imposition of individual income tax on its shareholders or the shareholders of any other corporation by permitting earnings and profits to accumulate instead of distributing them. Accumulated earnings tax does not apply to personal holding companies.

In order for the tax to be imposed, there must be a determination by the IRS that the corporation was formed or availed of for the purpose of avoiding income tax with respect to shareholders. There is a presumption that if earnings and profits of the corporation are permitted to accumulate beyond those reasonably necessary for operation of the business of the corporation, then the accumulated earnings was for the purpose to avoid income tax with respect to the shareholders. The corporation, however, may by admissible evidence prove to the contrary. The burden of proving that earnings and profits have been permitted to accumulate beyond the reasonable needs of the corporation is on the IRS. However, once the IRS has established an accumulation of profits beyond that reasonably necessary to operate the corporation, then the corporation or stockholders must establish a legitimate business reason for the accumulation of the profits.

Some of the circumstances that will be considered in determining whether or not there was an attempt to avoid taxes are:

1. Any dealings between the corporation and its shareholders, such as personal loans or expenditures of funds for the corporation, that personally benefit the shareholders

2. The investment by the corporation of the undistributed earnings and assets having no legitimate connection with the business of the corporation

3. The extent to which the corporation has in the past distributed its earnings and profits

In any action to determine whether or not the corporation has accumulated excessive profits, the corporation may be required by the IRS to furnish a statement of its accumulated earnings and profits, a record of payment of dividends, the names and addresses of and the number of shares held by each shareholder, and the amounts that would be payable to each shareholder if the income of the corporation were distributed.

The term *reasonable needs of the business* includes the reasonably anticipated needs of the business plus a reasonable reserve.

In order for the corporation to justify an accumulation of earnings and profits for reasonably anticipated future needs, there must be some evidence that the future needs require such accumulation; however, the accumulation need not be for immediate use nor must it plan to be consumed within a short period after the close of the tax year. If the future needs of the business are vague and uncertain and the plans for use of the accumulation are not definite, then normally the accumulation of earnings will be considered by the IRS as unreasonable.

Accumulation of earnings profits were held to be reasonable in cases where they were used to provide for bona fide plant expansion; to provide for the retirement of bona fide indebtedness of the corporation; to provide for additional working capital where necessary for procurement of inventories, business equipment, etc.; to acquire another business enterprise through purchasing of stock or assets; or to provide for investments or loans to suppliers or customers where such investments or loans would benefit directly the corporation. The business of the corporation is interpreted very broadly. It includes not only the line of business presently carried on by the corporation, but also any lines of business that the corporation may undertake in the reasonably foreseeable future.

10
Employees

Introduction

This chapter discusses the many tax aspects of employee salaries and benefits, including withholding schedules and pension plans. Also discussed are employee fringe benefits. Certain employer-provided benefits may be excluded from the gross income of employees. Permissible tax-free benefits include health benefit plans, group term life insurance, group legal services plans, dependent care assistance programs, and cafeteria plans (benefit selection plans). Nondiscrimination rules require employers to cover a substantial number of employees on a broad basis rather than a selected class of employees.

Finally, business expenses, including the types of expenses that may be deducted, are discussed.

Withholding Schedules

The Tax Reform Act substantially modified the employee withholding schedules. In addition, the act provides that those employees who do not submit new W-4 forms (revised by the tax change) are to be considered for tax withholding purposes as single employees with one allowance or, if married, married with two allowances.

The act also directs the IRS to modify the withholding schedules to "better approximate tax liability." Accordingly, both Form W-4 and withholding schedules were modified. The goal of the modifications is to design withholding of wages to approximate as closely as possible the taxpayer's ultimate tax liability. The act also eliminates that provision of the code that permitted the employees to request decreases in withholding. Accordingly, employees may request withholding from wages in excess of but not less than the amount established by the schedules.

Pensions and Deferred Compensation

Employee benefit plans are used either to provide retirement benefits or to defer compensation to some future date. Among the types of plans available to employees are pension plans, deferred-salary plans and the 401(k) plan, the simplified employee pension plan, certain salary reduction plans, and individual retirement arrangements (IRAs). Key concepts involving the income tax treatment of pensions and deferred compensation are:

- The deductions for IRA contributions are limited to individuals not covered by a tax-favored retirement plan and individuals with limited adjusted gross incomes.

- Individuals in the 28 percent tax bracket who are eligible to purchase a fully deductible IRA can immediately save $560 in taxes by purchasing an IRA.

- Individuals covered by tax-favored retirement plans may make nondeductible contributions to IRAs within certain limitations.

- Earnings on amounts allowed to be contributed to an IRA, whether or not the contribution is deductible, are tax-exempt until withdrawn.

- Simplified employee pension plans (SEPs) maintained by small employers may include cash or deferred arrangements.

- A 10 percent early distribution penalty is imposed on early withdrawals from qualified plans or IRAs unless the payments are made in the form of a life annuity or substantially level distributions over the individual's life. There are certain hardship exceptions to the penalty rules.

- There is a 10 percent nondeductible excise tax imposed on reversions of surplus assets from terminated plans except for surplus assets transferred from a terminated plan to an employee stock option plan (ESOP).

- The 3-year basis recovery rule for certain government annuities has been eliminated.

Prior to the Tax Reform Act, deferred compensation and pension plans were methods used by highly paid executives to enable them to keep a larger share of their income. For example, a company executive earning over \$350,000 per year would normally be taxed at the highest tax rate (50 percent) for a portion of his or her income. If a large portion of that income (normally about 30 percent) could be deferred from taxes by using deferred compensation or pension plans and thus taxed after the individual has retired, it would be taxed at a lower tax rate (assuming the individual has a lower adjusted income after retirement). This arrangement would keep a larger portion of the executive's income from the IRS. In 1985, of the top 500 companies (determined by capital worth), over two-thirds paid their top executives partially with deferred compensation and attractive pension plans.

The Tax Reform Act has changed this scenario in several respects. First, the act placed significant restrictions on the use of 401(k) plans (discussed subsequently), set limits on the maximum pension benefits that a company may pay out of a funded pension plan to employees who retire prior to the age of 65, and put income ceilings on the deductibility of contributions to IRAs for those employees covered by qualified pension plans.

Second, the act lowered the benefits of deferring taxes by lowering the tax rates. In addition, most executives feel that because of the nation's budget problems tax rates will probably be higher in 5 years than they are now. Thus, it appears that the differences between taxes that would be paid if the income were not deferred and the taxes paid if a large portion of the income were deferred have been reduced or eliminated as the result of the tax changes.

The consensus is that the tax rates will certainly not be lower when the individual retires than they are now. Where in the past, many highly compensated individuals were lured to different companies by attractive employee benefits such as deferred compensation and pension plans, it now appears that most executives are more interested in cash (salary) than in benefits.

The tax change also shortens the maximum length of employment service that an employer may require before employees become vested in company pension plans from 10 years. Now companies can choose between two vesting plans. The "cliff" plan provides that the employees will be 100 percent vested after 5 years. Under this plan, the employee is either not vested or completely vested, i.e., a cliff of 0 to 100 percent. Under the second plan, the employee is vested over a 7-year plan. Under the latter plan, you are 20 percent vested after 2 years and an additional 20 percent each year until you are 100 percent vested, i.e., in 7 years. Prior to the tax change, employees who took their pensions in one lump sum were given special tax benefits. They could forward-average the payout for 10 years. This benefit was retained, but the forward averaging period was reduced to 5 years. However, taxpayers born prior to 1936 may still use the 10-year forward averaging period. The full taxes are required to be paid in the year of distribution (yet the tax is computed as if the payments were spread out over 5 years).

The special rule that allowed many federal government employees to withdraw their own contributions to a pension plan within 3 years after retiring without paying taxes on that amount was canceled.

The tax act also places a 10 percent early withdrawal penalty in addition to taxes owed on all early withdrawals. An exception to this is that an employee may withdraw excess contributions without being subject to the additional tax.

Pension Plans

Contributions to qualified pension and deferred compensation plans receive preferred tax treatment in that income tax is normally not required to be paid on the contributions until the taxpayer withdraws the funds. There are three basic types of plans: pension plans, profit-sharing plans, and stock bonus plans.

A pension plan is a deferred compensation arrangement generally made from an employer-fund retirement plan for past services rendered. The plan provides for systematic payments of the retirement benefits normally based on employer contributions that are computed on an actuarial basis to be adequate to provide benefits for the required time (normally the remainder of the pensioner's life).

A profit-sharing plan is an arrangement whereby the employer provides the employees with company stock as a share of the company's profits. In a stock bonus plan, the employer contributes stocks to a plan that is used to provide benefits for the employees.

Deferred-Salary and 401(k) Plans

The deferred salary or 401(k) plans allow an employer to make contributions to the profit-sharing or stock bonus plan in either one of two ways:

1. The employer contributes an amount for the employee's benefit to a trust account. The employee is not taxed on the employer's contribution.

2. The employee agrees to take a reduced salary or to forgo a salary increase. The reduction is placed in a trust account for the employee. The income earned on the trust account is tax-free until withdrawn.

The employer may take an immediate business expense deduction for the contribution.

A 401(k) plan is one that allows participants to elect to receive cash or invest in a profit-sharing or stock bonus plan. The plan can also be a salary reduction arrangement. The contributions made by employees to a plan are 100 percent vested. The employer contributions and their earnings are tax-deferred.

Limits on Elective Deferrals. The maximum amount that an employee can elect to defer for any tax year under all cash or deferred arrangements is limited without regard to community property laws. The per-year limitation is based on the employee's tax year, the plan's year. The limitation is also subject to indexing for inflation by reference to percentage increases in the social security wage base.

The limit, however, applies only to elective deferrals made by an employee. The cap applies to the sum of all deferrals made, even with other employers. Employers may make additional contributions on behalf of any employee as long as the total of elective and nonelective deferrals for any given year does not exceed an adjusted overall limit. The elective limitation may be increased by an additional amount in the case of investments in the employer's securities.

Other Restrictions. Hardship withdrawals on qualified cash or deferred arrangements are limited to the amount of the employee's elective deferrals. A qualified cash or deferred arrangement cannot require, as a condition of participation in the arrangement, that an employee complete a period of service with the employer maintaining the plan in excess of 1 year.

An employer generally may not condition, either directly or indirectly, contributions and benefits except matching contributions upon an employee's elective deferrals. Qualified or deferred arrangements are not available to employees of state or local governments.

Simplified Employee Pension Plans

Simplified employee pension plans (SEPs) are available to employers with 25 or fewer employees as of the beginning of the year. SEPs are designed to encourage small businesses to offer pension plans for their employees without the administrative burdens and costs that are associated with other qualified plans.

Special rules for SEPs include the following:

- The election to have amounts contributed to a SEP or received in cash is available only if at least 50 percent of the employees of the employer elect to have amounts contributed to the SEP.

- The amount eligible to be deferred as a percentage of each highly compensated employee's compensation is limited by the average deferral percentage for all other employees.

- The deferral percentage for each highly compensated employee cannot exceed the deferral percentage for all other participating employees by more than 150 percent. If the 150 percent test is not satisfied, rules similar to the rules applicable to excess contributions to a cash or deferred arrangement shall apply.

Amounts contributed to a SEP by an employer on behalf of an employee and the elective deferral under a SEP are excludable from gross income. Contributions to a SEP may be made by the due date of the employer's tax return for the tax year (April 15 of the preceding year in most cases).

Participation requirements for SEPs require that an employer make contributions for a year on behalf of each employee who has attained the age of 21, has performed services for the employer during at least 3 of the preceding 5 years, and has received at least $300 in compensation from the employer for the year.

The 100 percent participant requirement applies separately to elective arrangements, and, for purposes of such elective arrangements, an individual who is eligible is deemed to receive an employer contribution. If nonelective SEP contributions are made for any employees, then nonelective contributions must be made for all eligible employees satisfying the participant requirements.

Salary Reduction Plans

Employees who participate in Section 501(c)(18) pension (salary reduction) plans may elect to make deductible contributions if certain requirements are met. Nondiscrimination requirements similar to those imposed on qualified cash or deferred arrangements are imposed on salary reduction plans.

Individual Retirement Arrangements

In 1981, the tax code was changed to allow individual retirement arrangements (IRAs) for employees without regard to whether they were covered by a pension plan. The 1981 amendment was made in an effort to increase retirement savings of taxpayers. The change as noted below was one of the most controversial elements of the Tax Reform Act of 1986. It represents a compromise among members of Congress.

Amounts contributed to IRAs are deductible (after December 31, 1986) only for those individuals who are not active participants in an employer-maintained retirement plan for any part of the tax year and for low-income employees. For the purposes of this limitation, an employer-maintained retirement plan means (1) a qualified pension, profit-sharing, or stock bonus plan; (2) a qualified annuity plan; (3) a simplified employee pension (SEP); (4) a tax-sheltered annuity to which amounts are contributed, on an elective or nonelective basis, by an employer; (5) a plan established by any governmental agency or political subdivision for their employees; or (6) employee plans described in Section 501(c)(18) of the tax code.

Active Participant.   As noted earlier, prior to 1981, IRAs were available only to taxpayers who were not "active participants" in a qualified plan. The Economic Recovery Act of 1981 (ERTA) eliminated the active participant restriction and extended the IRA availability to all taxpayers. The Tax Reform Act, however, reinstated the active participant restriction for the deductibility of IRA contributions.

The determination as to whether or not an individual is an active participant or whether amounts are contributed on the individual's behalf is made without regard to whether the individual's rights to benefits under a plan are nonforfeitable. The determination of active participant status is dependent upon the type of plan in which the individual participates or is eligible to participate in.

If the individual is covered by a defined-benefit pension plan, that individual is considered an active participant if he or she is not otherwise excluded under the eligibility requirements of the plan for any part of the plan year ending with the individual's tax year. Even if the individual chooses not to participate in the defined-benefit pension plan, the individual is still considered an active participant and thus contributions to an IRA are not deductible.

An individual is considered an active participant in a profit-sharing or stock bonus plan if any employer contributions are added to the individual's account during the year. A contribution is considered to be added to an individual's account on the later of the date the contribution is made or is allocated to the account.

An individual is treated as an active participant for any tax year in which the individual makes a voluntary or mandatory employee contribution. The individual is not treated as an active participant if earnings, rather than contributions or forfeitures, are allocated to the individual's account.

Limits of Contributions.   Except as noted below, if otherwise qualified, the individual may make contributions of 100 percent of compensation or $2000, whichever is the lesser amount, if invested in an IRA. In the case of married taxpayers, 100 percent of each spouse's compensation not to exceed $2000 per spouse may be invested in IRAs and thus deducted from income. If one spouse does not have any income or has an income of less than $250, then the total spousal IRAs may not exceed $2250 for the year.

Within the $2250 limit for spousal IRAs, the annual contribution may be divided as the spouses choose, as long as the contribution for either spouse does not exceed $2000. If both spouses are employed and only one is an active participant in a qualified plan, the other may make a spousal contribution of $2250 that is deductible.

Contributions to Nondeductible IRAs.   Individuals not qualified for deductible contributions to IRAs may still make nondeductible contributions in the amounts listed above. Earnings on the amounts contributed to IRAs under this provision will normally qualify for tax-exempt status.

Any contributions to a nondeductible IRA will normally be designated as such when the contribution is made. The designation of nondeductibility may be revoked up to the due date of the individual's tax return for that year (in most cases, April 15 of the preceding year).

Financial institutions are required to report to the IRS all contributions to IRAs and to indicate those designated as nondeductible. The report will reflect the status as of the date of the annual filing by the institution.

Normally any amounts paid or distributed that represent a return of a nondeductible contribution are treated as a nontaxable return of original investment.

Excess Contributions.   Any IRA contributions which exceed the limits discussed are subject to an excise tax. This excise tax applies to both nondeductible and deductible IRAs. If contributions in a later tax year are less than the limit for that year, then the excess contributions of earlier years may be applied against the limit for that year. This applies for both deductible and nondeductible contributions. In addition, excess nondeductible contributions in one tax year may be applied against the deductible limit for a later tax year. Also, excess deductible contributions may be recharacterized as nondeductible contributions for a later tax year.

Interest on IRA Loans.   No interest deduction is available for loans taken to fund either deductible or nondeductible IRAs.

Penalty for Early Withdrawals.   An additional income tax on early withdrawals is increased from 10 to 15 percent in the case of withdrawals attributable to *deductible* contributions and income therefrom. Early withdrawals are withdrawals prior to age 59.5.

Changes in Excludable Income for Employees

The Tax Reform Act made two significant changes regarding what income is excludable from adjusted gross income. The two changes involved unemployment compensation benefits and the treatment of prizes and awards.

Unemployment Compensation Benefits

Prior to the Tax Reform Act, unemployment compensation benefits were excluded if the taxpayer's adjusted gross income and benefits totaled less than a certain base amount ($18,000 in the case of married individuals filing joint returns). After the taxpayer exceeded the base amount, there was still a partial exclusion of the benefits in many cases. Now, any amounts received as unemployment compensation benefits must be included in gross income.

In practical effects, this loss of an exclusion amounts to a 15 percent reduction (after taxes) for unemployment compensation. If a state replaces the loss in income, it will amount to an indirect shift in funds from the state to the federal government.

Prizes and Awards

Prior to the recent Tax Reform Act, most prizes and awards were not taxable as income. Now most are required to be included in gross income, except as noted below.

Scientific awards and awards for charitable, artistic, scientific, and like achievements are required to be included in the recipient's gross income unless the recipient designates that the prize or award is to be transferred to a governmental unit or a tax-exempt charitable, educational, or religious organization. The designation must be made by the taxpayer and must be carried out by the organization making the award. Uses by the taxpayer of the property or by one associated with the taxpayer (member of taxpayer's family) will disqualify the transfer and dictate that the award be included in the gross income of the individual.

Employee achievement awards are not included in the gross income of the employee if all these conditions are met:

1. The award is one for length of service or for safety achievement.

2. The award is awarded as part of a meaningful presentation.

3. The award is awarded under circumstances that do not create a significant likelihood of the payment of disguised compensation.

4. The award is of tangible personal property and not cash, gift certificates, or equivalent items.

5. If the award is for length of service, the service cannot be for less than 5 years of employment.

6. If the award is for safety achievement, awards must not be made to more than 10 percent of the employer's eligible employees.

7. The value of the award shall not exceed $400 per award. In case of one or more qualified plan awards for safety and/or length of service, the aggregate total per employee is $1600 per year.

An example of how the award limitations apply is the case of an employee who receives an award that cost the company $625 and has a fair market value of $700. In this case, the higher of cost or fair market value will be used for taxation purposes. Accordingly, the individual will be taxed on $300 ($700 − $400), the excess over the allowable deduction. The $400 and $1600 cannot be added together to allow awards in excess of $1600 per year.

Payroll Deposits

Since the tax code does not specify the mode or time for collecting payroll taxes, IRS regulations determine the mode and time for collecting the taxes. Under present IRS regulations, if the aggregate amount of undeposited taxes reaches $500 or more in any calendar month, the employer must deposit that amount in a Federal Reserve bank or authorized financial institution within 15 days from the end of the month.

A different rule applies if the amount of undeposited taxes reaches $5000 or more at the end of any one eight-month period. In this case, the employer must deposit the taxes within 3 banking days of the close of the eight-month period.

Employee Fringe Benefits

Fringe benefits are extra benefits received by an employee (or spouse or other dependent) in connection with employment. Unless exempt by a specific code provision, fringe benefits are generally taxable to the employee as compensation for personal service, regardless of the form of the benefits. Certain employer-provided benefits, however, may be excluded from the gross income of employees.

A fringe benefit is taxable to the person employed, not necessarily the person receiving the benefit. Accordingly, if the benefit is received by someone other than the employee, i.e., a child, the employee may still be required to pay taxes on it. If the fringe benefit is received in a noncash form, the reasonable value of the benefit may be required to be included in the employee's compensation.

A *de minimis* fringe benefit, or one whose value is so small that accounting for it is unreasonable or administratively impractical, is normally excludable from taxable gross income. An example of such a benefit would be using the company telephone for personal telephone calls.

Certain employer-provided employee benefits are excluded from the gross income of employees if those benefits are provided under prescribed statutory conditions. The most common of these employee benefit provisions are health benefit plans, group term life insurance plans, group legal service plans, educational assistance programs, dependent care assistance programs, welfare benefit plans, and cafeteria plans. For example, employer-provided health insurance and life insurance coverage is available to more than 80 percent of the employees in the United States. The exclusion from income of such employee benefits is conditional on their being nondiscriminatory. In general, the nondiscrimination rules require employers to cover a substantial number of employees over a broad cross section rather than a selected class of employees. Under the code, the penalty for plans determined to be discriminatory toward highly compensated employees is that the fair market value of those benefits must be included as income in that tax year for those highly compensated employees. The Tax Reform Act established complicated rules for determining whether benefits were nondiscriminatory. The rules were revoked in 1990 and the rules prior to 1986 were basically reestablished.

Permissible Employee Benefits

Permissible employee benefits, if qualified under the nondiscrimination test discussed later in this chapter, may be provided to employees without the requirement of reporting their fair market value as compensation under certain conditions. The list of statutory fringe benefits that are generally excludable from the taxable income of an employee include:

- Athletic facilities located on employer's property
- Cafeteria plans
- Educational assistance benefits (see also Chapter 1)
- Group-term life insurance
- Meals and lodging
- Moving expenses
- Stock options (see Chapter 10)
- *De minimis* fringe benefits
- Retirement plans (see Chapter 9)

Who May Claim the Benefit

Certain fringe benefits are furnished to an employee in a manner that primarily benefits the employer. If the benefit is provided primarily to serve a legitimate business purpose of the employer, the benefit may be excluded from the gross income of the employee. For example, the employer provides meals to employees in order to keep them available and on call during the meal periods. In this case, the value of the meals would probably be excluded from the employee's gross income because the benefit is primarily to serve a legitimate business purpose of the employer. If, however, the benefit is made primarily for the benefit of the employee, then it should be included in the employee's gross income. For example, the payment of convention expenses to Hawaii for spouses of salespersons where the employee had to meet a higher quota in order to have the spouse's expenses paid was considered as primarily for the benefit of the spouse and therefore taxable to the employee.

Personal Expenses

The payment by the employer of personal expenses of an employee is considered as taxable compensation. For example, if the employer pays the employee's portion of the FICA taxes (social security taxes), then amount paid is additional taxable compensation to the employee.

Cafeteria Plans

Under a cafeteria plan, a participant is offered a choice between cash or one or more employee benefits. The mere availability of cash or certain taxable benefits under a cafeteria plan does not cause an employee to be taxed as having received the available cash or taxable benefits for income purposes if certain conditions are met.

Until recently, cafeteria plans were restricted to employers with more than 1000 employees. Because of the flexible benefit plans available, it was impractical for small companies to use this approach for employee benefit plans. Many companies are now in a position to offer to each employee a "core" plan consisting of limited benefits, plus a benefit budget that the employee can use to obtain medical insurance, dental coverage, dependent care, or cash. In some cases, approved plans have allowed employees to trade a week's vacation for extra health benefits.

The following benefits are not qualified benefits for purposes of cafeteria plans: van pooling, educational assistance programs, and meals and lodging.

Educational Benefits

At least until tax year 1992, an employee will not be taxed on educational benefits provided by the employer (not to exceed $5250 per employee). The benefits may be paid to the educational institution or may be reimbursements to the employee for educational costs. Approved educational benefits include any form of instruction or training that improves or develops an individual's capabilities, whether or not job-related. Benefits may include tuition, fees, books, and supplies. Meals, lodging, transportation, tools, or supplies that are retained by the employee after the instruction ends, and courses involving sports or games, are not excludable from the employee's gross income.

Employer-Operated Eating Facilities

Generally the value of meals provided at an employer-operated eating facility are excludable by the employee if the facility's annual revenues exceed its direct operating cost. Accordingly, if meals are cheaper in the employer's eating facilities, the money saved by the employee in eating there is normally not considered taxable income if the facility's annual revenues exceed its direct operating cost. If the meals do not qualify under the above tests, then the value of the meals less the price paid by the employee generally is required to be included in the employee's gross income.

Working Condition Fringe Benefits

A *working condition fringe benefit* is a benefit that would have been deductible by the employee if the employee had paid for it. Examples of working condition fringe benefits include employer-paid business travel, employer-provided vehicles for business purposes, employer-paid subscriptions to business periodicals, and the use of company-owned aircraft for business travel. A working condition fringe benefit is excluded from the employee's gross income.

Dependent Care Assistance

Dependent care assistance payments are excluded from an employee's gross income under a qualified program for dependent care. The qualified care program must be pursuant to a written plan by the employer, not be discriminatory against non-highly compensated employees, comply with the reporting requirements, provide employees with dependent care assistance, be provided for the exclusive benefit of employees, and comply with certain code requirements set forth in Section 129(d) of the tax code.

An employee for purposes of this benefit includes those persons who are self-employed. A partner for purposes of this section is considered an employee of the other partners.

The expenses paid under this program must be for payment for household and dependent care services necessary for gainful employment. Payments to sons, daughters, etc., are not deductible.

Employee Loans

Generally if an employee receives a loan from his or her employer which is interest-free or below market rates, the value of that benefit is included in the gross income of the employee. A below-market loan is one in which the interest is payable at a rate less than a specified "federal" rate and was obtained directly or indirectly from an employer or an independent contractor under an arrangement made between the employer and the contractor. These rules do not apply to loans that do not exceed $10,000 on the theory that these small loans are a *de minimis* exception. In addition, employee relocation loans are also exempt if the relocation was work-related.

Moving Expenses

In general, employer-paid moving expenses are included in the employee's gross income. The moving expenses can generally be deducted as a personal tax deduction if the employee itemizes. Any employer reimbursement for an employee's loss of the sale of a home in conjunction with a work-related relocation is income to the employee.

Employer-Provided Automobiles

Employees must include in their gross income the value of the personal use of an employer-provided automobile. There are three methods that may be used to valuate the benefit: cents-per-mile, annual lease value, and commuting value. The cents-per-mile and the commuting value methods may be used for all employer-provided vehicles. The annual lease value may be used only to value employer-provided automobiles.

The annual lease value method is based on the fair market value of the vehicle and what it would cost the employee to lease an automobile with a similar fair market value. Under the cents-per-mile method the value to the employee is determined by determining the total cost per mile to operate the vehicle, including both business and nonbusiness mileage. The mileage rate obtained is then applied to personal mileage. The commuting value method is computed as $1.50 per one-way commute to work or return. The commuting value method can be used only if the employer allows the employee to commute in the vehicle for noncompensatory business reasons and prohibits by written policy other personal use of the vehicle.

Valuation of Taxable Fringe Benefits

Taxable fringe benefits must be included in the employee's gross income as compensation for employment. If the benefit is not paid in cash, then the fair market value of the benefit must be included. The fair market value is determined on the basis of the surrounding circumstances and objective facts. It is the amount that the employee would be required to pay for the benefit if the employee had purchased the benefit in an arm's-length transaction. Fair market value is *not* determined by the cost of the benefit to the employer or by what the employee thinks that the benefit is worth.

Employee Death Benefits and Life Insurance

In most cases, employee death benefits are tax-exempt to a maximum of $5000. There is no exclusion, however, if the employee had a "nonforfeitable" right to payment. The exclusion can also be used for death benefits paid on behalf of a self-employed individual.

The cost of employer-provided life insurance for the employee's benefit is generally taxable. An exception to this rule is employer-paid premiums for group life insurance coverage for employees; they are excludable for up to $50,000 coverage per employee.

Nondiscrimination Rules

For qualified benefits to be excludable from the gross income of highly compensated employees, the plans under which the benefits are established must not be discriminatory in favor of highly compensated employees. Below are some of the general guidelines.

A plan meets the reasonable classification test if it benefits a reasonably broad spectrum of employees and does not allow more than a reasonable difference in favor of highly compensated employees between their coverage percentage and the coverage percentage of other employees.

Benefits can be allocated on the basis of seniority, if the benefits available to the non-highly compensated employees have an average value per employee of at least 75 percent of that provided per highly compensated employees of the employer, and if notice of the terms of availability is provided to all employees.

The average benefit provided to employees under a plan is to be determined by secretarial regulation. The benefits include all amounts excludable under a plan, including elective contributions.

Business Expenses

Key concepts involved in business expense write-offs are:

1. No tax deductions are allowed for personal, family, or living expenses.

2. The taxpayer has the burden of proving both the eligibility of an expenditure as a tax deduction and the amount of any such eligible expenditure.

3. Entertainment expenses are not deductible unless the taxpayer establishes that the item is directly related to the active conduct of the taxpayer's trade or business.

4. Normally only 80 percent of business meal expenses and business entertainment expenses are deductible. Exceptions to the 80 percent rule are discussed later in this chapter.

5. Requirements for deducting meal expenses were tightened by recent legislation. Meal expenses are not deductible unless there is a substantial and bona fide business purpose. In addition, meal expenses are not deductible unless there is a substantial and bona fide business discussion during, directly preceding, or directly following the meal. An exception to this requirement is for the taxpayer who is away from home in the pursuit of a trade or business.

6. The cost of a meal is not deductible if it serves a nontrade or nonbusiness purpose e.g., investment, rather than an active trade or business purpose.

7. No deductions are allowed for costs of attending investment seminars or for educational travel.

8. Unreimbursed employee expenses are limited to only itemizers and are subject to a floor of 2 percent of adjusted gross income.

9. Deductions for hobby losses and home office expenses are limited.

10. Documentary evidence is required to substantiate all business expense deductions, except in those cases where the standard meal allowance can be used.

11. Deductions for luxury box seats in sports stadiums have been phased out over a 3-year period. Presently only 80 percent of the cost of the highest-priced nonluxury seats are deductible. There is an exception to this rule for sky-box seats if the box is rented only once a year. In this case, 80 percent of the cost of the sky-box may be deductible.

12. Itemized deductions for union dues and the like are deductible only to the extent they exceed 2 percent of adjusted gross income.

Ending deductions for the three-martini lunches and other abuses in business expense write-offs was one of the goals of the congressional committees that drafted the recent tax changes. It appears that they were successful in eliminating only 20 percent of such claims. With certain exceptions, only 80 percent of business meal and entertainment expenses may be deducted. The tax changes did not, however, eliminate the vast majority of business expense write-offs.

In this section deductions or adjustments allowable as ordinary and necessary expenses paid and incurred in carrying on a trade or business are discussed. Also discussed are strategies to increase business deductions by shifting normal and ordinary expenses from nondeductible to deductible items.

Both above-the-line and below-the-line business deductions and adjustments are covered. A deduction or adjustment is considered an above-the-line deduction if it used as a deduction from adjusted gross income. It is considered a below-the-line deduction if it must be claimed as an itemized deduction on Schedule A. Since the Tax Reform Act of 1986, most business expenses are required to be below-the-line deductions and thus listed on Schedule A. The disadvantage of this is that many of the expenses are not available to nonitemizers and the expenses are also subject to the 2-percent-of-gross-income floor.

The tax changes have not, however, modified the above-the-line deductions for most reimbursable expenses of an employee under a reimbursement plan or other expense allowance with his or her employer. If the employee has a reimbursement or other expense arrangement with his or her employer but under the arrangement the employer does not reimburse the full amount of such expenses, the unreimbursed portion paid by the employee may be allowable as an itemized deduction.

Tests for Deductibility

If audited, a taxpayer must establish first that the expenditure qualifies as a deduction or adjustment and, second, the monetary amount of the eligible expense. A taxpayer is subject to penalties if an audit determines that there is an underpayment of taxes as a result of improperly claimed deductions or adjustments and the payment deficiencies are due to negligence or the intentional disregard of the rules or regulations or fraud on the taxpayer's part.

No deductions are allowed for any expenses that are illegal under federal or state law. An exception to this rule is that the restriction does not apply to any payment that is illegal under state law if the state law is generally not enforced. For example, if it is illegal to pay more for the face value of a certain deductible item, such as a ticket to a sports or entertainment event, the code, would disallow any deduction for such payment as a business entertainment expense unless the state law against scalping is not generally enforced, in which case only the face value would be allowed..

The basic rule to determine whether or not an item is deductible is that the expense in question must meet the "ordinary and necessary" requirement for the act of carrying on a taxpayer's active trade or business. *Note:* Legislative changes added the "active" requirement to eliminate many of the previously allowable deductions relating to passive investments.

Entertainment Expenses

In order for entertainment expenses to be deductible, not only must the expenses meet the requirements that they be ordinary and necessary and related to active trade or business; in addition, such expenses either must be "directly related" to the active conduct of the taxpayers' business, or must be incurred directly preceding or following a bona fide business discussion regarding the active conduct of the taxpayer's business. The "directly-related" and "associated-with" requirements for entertainment activities have been added to the tax code in an attempt to eliminate the deduction of personal entertainment expenses as business expenses. In addition to these two tests, there are several other statutory exceptions that will be discussed later, such as the limitation on luxury water travel.

Directly-Related Test. The directly-related test was designed to require the taxpayer to show a clear business purpose for the deduction and a reasonable expectation of business benefit.

The directly-related test may be met if there was active business discussion during the entertainment period and the active business discussion is for a direct business benefit. The general expectation of deriving some income or other business benefit at some indefinite future time is not sufficient to meet this test. The regulations, also, presume that active business circumstances do not exist if there is little or no possibility of engaging in meaningful business discussion during the entertainment period, i.e., because the entertainment took place at a night club or cocktail party or if the taxpayer had met with a group which included non-business-related individuals at vacation resorts. There is an indication that the IRS will take a closer look at business expenses that occur at vacation resorts in the future.

The recent tax changes are designed to severely limit entertainment expense deductions. However, if properly planned and documented, a significant portion of your entertainment expenses may be transferred to deductible business items. The key to this is proper planning and record keeping. In order to maximize your deduction in this regard, seek professional tax advice during the planning phase of any entertainment activity that may result in a significant tax deduction or adjustment to gross income. Minor adjustments in plans may make a significant difference in whether the expense is legally deductible as a business expense. Since each situation is different, advice as to specific aspects of your situation is necessary.

Associated-with Test.   The second group of deductible entertainment expenses are those associated with the taxpayer's business that are incurred directly preceding or following a substantial or bona fide business discussion. The latest tax changes place certain restrictions on this test.

This test has in the past generally permitted deduction of items or costs intended to encourage goodwill where the taxpayer established a clear business purpose for the expenditure. Now, expenditures to encourage goodwill are generally not considered as deductible business expenses unless they meet either the directly-related or associated-with tests.

Like the directly-related test, the associated-with test requires that business actually be transacted or discussed during the entertainment.

Exceptions to Test Requirements.   There are statutory exceptions to the requirement that an expenditure for an entertainment, recreation, or amusement activity must satisfy either the directly-related or associated-with test. Expenses associated with these statutory exceptions are deductible if they are ordinary and necessary for the conduct of business. The exceptions are:

1. Business meals (discussed later in this chapter)

2. Food and beverage furnished to employees on the taxpayer's business premises

3. Entertainment expenses considered by the employer and the employee as wages to the employee

4. Expenses paid by the taxpayer under a reimbursement or expense allowance

5. Expenses for recreation, social, or similar activities for the benefit of all employees generally

6. Entertainment expense directly related to bona fide meetings of taxpayers, employees, stockholders, or directors

7. Entertainment expense directly related to and necessary for the attendance at a business meeting or convention of a tax-exempt trade association

8. Expenditures for entertainment made available by the taxpayer to the general public

9. Expenses for entertainment sold by the taxpayer to the public

10. Expense that may be included in the income of persons who are not employees

If your entertainment expense can be fitted within one of the above-listed exceptions, then there is no requirement that it be directly related or associated with the conduct of a taxpayer's active business or trade. The regulations state that entertainment expenses under the above exceptions are not deductible to the extent that they are lavish or extravagant. The IRS has not interpreted this provision to disallow any deductions merely because the entertainment expenses exceeded a fixed dollar amount or were incurred at expensive restaurants, hotels, night clubs, or resorts or because they involved first-class accommodations or service, with the exception of luxury water travel, which is discussed under travel expenses.

Tickets to Entertainment Events.   Deductions, if otherwise permitted, for the cost of a ticket to an entertainment activity or sporting event are limited to the face value of the ticket. In addition, there may be an 80 percent limitation, which is discussed later in this chapter. The face value of the ticket includes any amount of tax on the ticket. It does not, however, include any payment to a scalper. Payment to a ticket agency for a ticket also is limited to the face value of the ticket, and any fee added by the ticket agent is not normally deductible (unless modified by IRS regulations).

Meal Expenses

As noted earlier, meal expenses are an exception to the directly-related and associated-with requirements generally applicable to entertainment expenses. To be deductible, expenditures for the meals or drinks must take place in an atmosphere favorable to business discussions. In this regard, the deduction covers both the expenses of the taxpayer's business guests and of the taxpayer. Under present requirements, for a business meal expense to be deductible other than those associated with overnight travel, it is required that a substantial, bona fide business discussion directly related to the taxpayer's active business or trade takes place either during, directly preceding, or directly following the meal.

An active-business-discussion test is deemed not to have been met if neither the taxpayer, employee, nor agent of the taxpayer is present at the meal. For example, a taxpayer reserves a table at a business dinner, but if neither the taxpayer, the agent, nor the employee of the taxpayer attends, then no deduction will be allowed. A similar situation exists if one party to contract negotiations buys dinner for the other parties involved in the negotiations but does not attend the dinner; in this case, the deduction is denied the taxpayer even if the other parties engage in active business discussion. There may be an exception to the attendance requirement if the taxpayer intends to be there but is prevented from attending because of an emergency.

For the purposes of attendance at meals, an attorney who attends on behalf of a taxpayer is considered an agent of the taxpayer, and, therefore, the taxpayer may deduct the meal expenses.

The requirement that the meal have a clear business purpose directly related to the active conduct of the trade or business of the taxpayer is normally not satisfied in the case of a meal at which business discussions do not concern business transactions or arrangements. The cost of the meal also is not deductible if it serves a nonbusiness or active trade purpose of the taxpayer, for example, investment, rather than the trade or business in which the taxpayer is actively engaged.

To reduce abuses of meal deductions, the regulations contain a special penalty rule which applies if meal deductions are determined to be in error and the error is a result of negligence or fraud on the part of the taxpayer. If the erroneous deduction was due to negligence or disregard of rules and regulations, a negligence penalty of not less than 50 percent of the underpayment of taxes resulting from the improperly claimed deduction will be imposed. If the error is due to fraud, the penalty must equal 100 percent of the amount of taxes due.

Present regulations, also, have eliminated the practice of allowing approximations of the expense amount of any business meal or other entertainment. Required is documentary evidence such as restaurant receipts substantiating business meal expenses unless the taxpayer can use the standard meal allowance. If you are traveling away from home for business, you can deduct a standard amount for your daily meals instead of deducting the actual cost. You can use the standard meal allowance even if your expenses are not reimbursed by your employer. You may not use the allowance if you are related to your employer. If you use the allowance, it may be subject to the 80 percent limit discussed below. The standard meal allowance is published each year by the IRS and is approximately $30 with greater amounts allowed for certain high-cost locations.

Percentage Reduction Rule

The amount of allowable business deductions for meal or entertainment expenses is 80 percent. Thus, if a taxpayer business meal costs $100, and $40 of that amount is considered lavish and extravagant while $60 is considered reasonable, then the taxpayer could deduct only 80 percent of $60, or $48. Likewise, when a taxpayer buys a ticket to an entertainment event and pays more than the face value of the ticket, only 80 percent of the ticket's face value may be deducted. There are several exceptions to the percentage reduction rule. Those exceptions are as follows:

1. The full cost of a meal is deductible if the full value is taxed as compensation to the recipient or is excludable under an authorized fringe benefit.

2. A taxpayer who is reimbursed for the cost of a meal or entertainment by an employer may deduct for purposes of reimbursement 100 percent of the cost. The percentage reduction rule would, however, apply to the employer who is making the reimbursement.

3. The percentage reduction rule does not apply in the case of traditional recreational expenses for employees who are paid by employers the reasonable cost of a Christmas party or summer outing for employees and their spouses.

4. The reduction requirement does not apply in the case of an item, such as one related to sample and promotional activities, made available to the general public.

5. Expenses for a sports event, if otherwise allowable, are not subject to

the reduction rule if event is for charitable fund raising. In order to meet the charitable fund-raising requirement and therefore be totally deductible as business expenses, the event must be organized for the primary purpose of benefiting a charitable organization, 100 percent of the net proceeds must be contributed to the organization, and volunteers must do substantially all the work. An example of such a charity event would be a golf tournament that donates all the proceeds from the event to charity even though prize money is offered to golfers who participated in the event. The golfers, however, must pay taxes on the prizes that they receive.

6. The deduction rule does not apply in those cases where the taxpayer sells meals in a bona fide transaction. For example, a restaurant may deduct the full amount of its ordinary and necessary expenses of providing meals to paying customers.

Figure 10-1 is a chart that may be used by employees, including outside salespersons, to determine if the 80 percent limitation applies to you.

Travel Expenses

Travel expenses are your ordinary and necessary expenses while traveling away from home for your business, profession, or job. You cannot deduct expenses that are for personal or vacation purposes or expenses that are lavish or extravagant. Travel expenses do not include expenses for entertainment during the travel.

Educational Travel. No deduction is allowed for travel as a form of education. Thus, a teacher of French literature who travels to Paris in order to become acquainted with French language and culture would not be allowed to deduct the cost of the travel.

A taxpayer may still deduct the cost of travel for business purposes or for educational purposes directly related to an active business or trade. For example, the travel by a businessperson to a distant city in order to attend a seminar on office management would normally be considered deductible if the taxpayer's active business or trade required him or her to exercise some degree of expertise in office management.

Business Conventions. A taxpayer may deduct expenses for attending business conventions that are directly related to his or her active trade or business. However, deductions for attending conventions for investment purposes or other activities not directly related to the taxpayer's or employer's active trade or business are no longer deductible.

Meal expenses during travel for business purposes, including travel

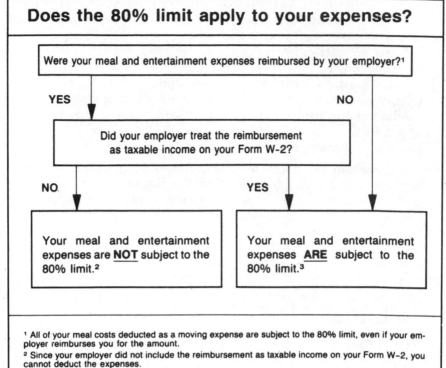

Does the 80% limit apply to your expenses?

Were your meal and entertainment expenses reimbursed by your employer?¹

YES   **NO**

Did your employer treat the reimbursement
as taxable income on your Form W-2?

NO   **YES**

Your meal and entertainment expenses are **NOT** subject to the 80% limit.²

Your meal and entertainment expenses **ARE** subject to the 80% limit.³

¹ All of your meal costs deducted as a moving expense are subject to the 80% limit, even if your employer reimburses you for the amount.

² Since your employer did not include the reimbursement as taxable income on your Form W-2, you cannot deduct the expenses.

³ There are exceptions to this rule. For example, you are not subject to the 80% limit on meals and entertainment if:
- A) You incur the expenses as a means of advertising to, or promoting goodwill in, the general community, or
- B) You pay the expenses as part of a package deal which includes a ticket to a charitable sports event.

Figure 10-1. Does the 80 percent limit apply to your expenses?

to business conventions and at business conventions, are fully deductible and are not subject to the 80 percent limitation referred to earlier. In addition, there is no requirement of an active business discussion for the deductibility of meals during travel or at a business convention.

Travel for Charitable Reasons.   The prior restrictions on travel for medical reasons for lodging away from home are extended to deductions claimed for transportation and other travel expenses incurred in performing services away from home for charitable organizations. Accordingly, deductions are not allowed if there is a significant element of personal pleasure, recreation, or vacation in the travel away from home.

Luxury Water Travel.   In an attempt to reduce some abuses for luxury water travel, the amount of deduction a taxpayer may take for business travel by ocean liner, cruise ship, or other form of luxury water transport has been limited. The deduction allowable in the case of luxury water travel cannot exceed twice the highest amount generally allowed to employees of the executive branch of the U.S. government for a day of travel away from home but in the United States, multiplied by the number of days the taxpayer is engaged in the water travel. For example, if the federal per diem rate is $125, and the taxpayer takes a 6-day business trip via cruise ship, the deduction cannot exceed $250 per day for 6 days, or $1500.

If the expenses for the luxury water travel include separately stated amounts for meals and entertainments, then the costs of meals and entertainments must also be reduced by 20 percent under the percentage reduction rule prior to the application of the per diem limitation. If the meals and entertainment charges are not separately stated, then the taxpayer will not be required to allocate a portion of the total amount to meals and entertainment unless they are clearly and otherwise identifiable.

The per diem rule also does not apply in the case of any expense allowable for a convention, seminar, or other meeting which is held on any cruise ship. And it does not alter the application of the present rule for which deductions for conventions held aboard cruise ships are either denied or not limited to not in excess of $2000 per individual.

Hobby Losses

Expenses arising from hobbies are allowed only as itemized deductions and only to the extent of the gross income of the hobby. If the taxpayer can establish that the activity is engaged in for profit, not as a hobby, then otherwise qualified expenses may be deducted. There is a statutory presumption that the activity is being engaged in for profit if the activity is profitable in 3 out of 5 consecutive years. In the case of horse breeding, training, showing, and racing activities, the presumption is that it is engaged in for profit if in 2 out of 7 consecutive years the activity is profitable.

The amount of profit appears to be immaterial as long as the business shows a profit in 2 of 7 consecutive years. On those years when the second business of a taxpayer has either a small loss or breaks even and the taxpayer is concerned with the 2 of 7 rule, it may be to the taxpayer's advantage to forgo some of the allowable deductions to indicate a small profit. While it is illegal to claim deductions that a person is not entitled to, there is no requirement to claim all the deductions that a person is entitled to.

If you have engaged in the activity for less than 3 years, you can postpone the determination that the activity is not for profit by filing Form 5213, "Election to Postpone Determination." See IRS Publication 535 for additional information regarding this question.

Home Office Expenses

The deduction of home office expenses continues to be unfavorable with the IRS. Recent legislation has added additional restrictions and limitations to such deductions.

To overcome the adverse decision of a 1985 tax court case, *Feldman v. Comm'r.*, which upheld a deduction where the employer nominally rents a portion of the employee's home that is then used by the employee in performing services for the employer, the tax code now provides that no home office deduction is allowable for business use where an employee leases a portion of his or her home to an employer. For purposes of this rule, an independent contractor is treated as an employee, and the party for whom the contractor is performing services is treated as an employer.

Home office deductions are limited to the gross income from the activity, reduced by all other deductible expenses attributable to the activity but not allocable to the use of the office. Accordingly, a home office deduction is not allowed to the extent that it creates or increases a net loss from the business activity to which it relates. Excluded from this limitation are expenses that are deductible without regard to business use, e.g., property taxes and mortgage interests.

Home office deductions that are disallowed solely because of the income limitation on the amount of an otherwise deductible expense may be carried forward to subsequent tax years, although with the same limitations on the deduction.

One chief advantage of having an office in your home is that a portion of the home expenses may be deducted from your gross income for income tax purposes. However, individuals who claim deductions for business use of their residences are subject to tough rules limiting the deductions. In addition, they are more likely to be audited by the IRS.

The tax court has stated that where the office is on the same lot as the residence, and all the expenses for property taxes, utilities, interest, and insurance are included in common bills, then the office building would be considered as an office in the home and not a separate structure.

The deductible expenses include rent, heat, insurance, painting, repairs pertaining to the business part of the home, and similar expenses.

If the home is owned by you, a depreciation and cost recovery method may be used to determine that portion of the property that can be deducted as a business expense. For example, Ms. Holly owns a home valued at $100,000. The land is valued at $25,000 and the house at $75,000. The total area of the house used for business is 30 percent. Accordingly, the basis she uses for determining the depreciation that she may deduct as a business expense is 30 percent of $75,000, or $22,500. The allocation of costs and expenses is generally based on a comparison of space used for business and personal purposes. In the above example, it is assumed that Ms. Holly used 30 percent of the space for business and 70 percent for her personal residence. If audited, you may be required to establish what portion of the home is used for business and what portion is for personal use.

Home office expenses in excess of the income derived from that activity are not deductible. For example, Barbara conducted a business in her home that had a gross income of $10,000. Her business expenses unrelated to the home were $8000. Her business expenses related to the office in the home were $4000. Only $2000 of her business expenses related to the office in the home may be deducted ($10,000 − $8000 = $2000). However, the remaining $2000 may be carried forward to the next tax year. The limitation regarding the deductions applies only to those business expenses directly related to the cost of the business in the home, i.e., rent, heat, etc. If her business expenses not related to the home exceeded her income, normally she could claim a loss on her tax return for those excess non-home-related business expenses.

If a businessperson has more than one trade or business, he or she could have a distinct principal place of business for each separate trade or business.

The records that are necessary to claim deductions for an office in the home must establish:

- The part of your home that is used for the business.

- That you used this part of the home exclusively and regularly for business as either your principal place of business or as the place where you meet or deal with clients or customers in the normal course of your business.

- The amount of depreciation and other expenses for keeping up the part of the home that is used for business.

Selected tax cases on deductions for an office at home include the following:

- A taxpayer who ran a hot dog and food stand was denied a business deduction for that portion of her home where she cooked and prepared the food and kept her records. The court stated that the stand was her principal place of business.

- One tax court allowed home office deductions for a college professor who spends 80 percent of her time writing and researching and does not have an office on the campus. However, in a similar case, another tax court disallowed the deduction.

- Artists whose studios are attached to the dwelling are normally permitted to deduct the expenses associated with the studios.

- A physician who was employed full time in a hospital and who used one bedroom of his two-bedroom condominium exclusively for managing his six rental properties was allowed to deduct the prorated cost of the one bedroom.

Employee Personal Business Expenses

Most of the miscellaneous deductions previously allowed under Schedule A, lines 20 to 23, are no longer deductible. In addition, the code now provides that employee travel and transportation expenses deductible under prior law as adjustments to gross income can now be deducted only as below-the-line deductions under miscellaneous expenses on Schedule A.

One category of expenses that are no longer considered deductible are those associated with investment income. Memberships in professional associations and subscriptions to publications that, in addition to helping the taxpayer conduct a profession also convey personal and recreational benefits, are no longer deductible. This limitation has an impact on investments in mutual funds.

Deductions unreimbursed employee travel and transportation expenses and outside expenses for salespersons were retained. However, as noted earlier, they are now required to be listed on Schedule A rather than as adjustments to gross income. Included in travel and transportation expenses is the expense of going from one job to a second job in those cases where taxpayers hold more than one job. Daily commuting expenses still are not deductible.

Home Computers

Normally, when a taxpayer uses equipment for both business and personal use, an allocation must be made between that portion for business use and that portion for personal use; only the cost allocated to the business use may be depreciated or expensed. An amendment to the Internal Revenue Code placed additional limitations on the deductions for business use of home computers. If the computer is used less than 50 percent for business, the computer may not be expensed in lieu of depreciation, and the computer must be depreciated on a straight-line basis over 12 years. In addition, the employees may not receive a depreciation deduction for a home computer acquired for the convenience of their employer unless it is a condition of employment. In addition, extra record-keeping rules are required to substantiate the business use test.

In two private-letter rulings, the IRS demonstrated the general trend of tightening the requirements for deduction of home computers and home computer expenses. In one case, a registered nurse who purchased a home computer for grant development work did not meet IRS requirements. The registered nurse had purchased the personal computer to help her get required grants and support solicitations. She was working at a state university where the development of external grants was a significant portion of her job requirement. This work required substantial documentation and assembly. According to her, manual typing would not produce the necessary speed; therefore, her workload considerations required after-hours work with only a limited number of support staff available. She kept a contemporaneous log of her computer time which established a 100 percent business usage. In addition, her monitor was not suitable for video games.

In order to assist her in the use of her home computer, the university provided her with a modem to communicate with the university's computer. The IRS, in denying her deduction, stated that in order to satisfy the employer-convenience test, the employees must be required to purchase computers to properly perform the duties of their employment; and that while the computer use was work-related, it was not inextricably related to the performance of her job. In addition, the IRS noted that there was no evidence that persons in a similar position who did not purchase a computer were professionally disadvantaged.

In a similar case, the individual had participated in an employer's subsidized program which had assisted selected employees in purchasing personal computers to increase employee production by facilitating computer literacy. In this case, the taxpayer kept a contemporaneous log indicating that 95 percent of the computer use was business-related. The IRS, as in the earlier case, held that the employee had not satisfied the employer-convenience test and disallowed the deduction. While a private-letter ruling is not binding on other parties, it does reflect the approach that the IRS will take in similar situations.

Type of Reimbursement or Other Expense Allowance Arrangement	Employer Reports on Form W-2	Employee Shows on Form 2106	Employee Claims on Schedule A
Accountable			
Adequate accounting and excess returned	Not reported	Not shown	Not claimed
Adequate accounting and return of excess both required but excess not returned	Excess reported as wages in Box 10 and, if applicable, in Box 12. Amount adequately accounted for is reported only in Box 17—it is *not* reported in Box 10 or in Box 12.	All expenses, and reimbursements reported on Form W-2, Box 17, *only* if some or all of the unreturned excess expenses are claimed.¹ Otherwise, form is not filed.	Expenses the employee can prove and which exceed the reimbursements received and reported on Form W-2, Box 17.²
Per diem or mileage allowance (up to government rate) Adequate accounting and excess returned	Not reported	All expenses and reimbursements *only* if excess expenses are claimed.¹ Otherwise, form is not filed.	Expenses the employee can prove and which exceed the reimbursements received.²
Per diem or mileage allowance (exceeds government rate) Adequate accounting up to the government rate only and excess not returned	Excess reported as wages in Box 10 and, if applicable, in Box 12. Amount up to the government rate is reported only in Box 17—it is *not* reported in Box 10 or in Box 12.	All expenses, and reimbursements equal to the government rate, *only* if expenses in excess of the government rate are claimed.¹ Otherwise, form is not filed.	Expenses the employee can prove and which exceed the government rate.²
Nonaccountable			
Either adequate accounting or return of excess, or both, not required	Entire amount is reported as wages in Box 10 and, if applicable, in Box 12.	All expenses¹	Expenses the employee can prove.²
No reimbursement	Normal reporting of wages, etc.	All expenses¹	Expenses the employee can prove.²

¹ Any allowable expense is carried to line 20 of Schedule A and deducted as a miscellaneous itemized deduction.

² These amounts are subject to the applicable limits including the 80% limit on meals and entertainment expenses and the 2% of adjusted gross income limit on the total miscellaneous itemized deductions.

Figure 10-2. Reporting travel, transportation, meal, and entertainment expenses and reimbursements.

The above limitations and rules do not apply to a computer that is located at a regular business establishment of an employer and used exclusively at that place of business.

Figure 10-2 summarizes the reporting of travel, transportation, meal, and entertainment expenses, and reimbursements.

11
Employment Taxes and Research Credits

In this chapter, employment taxes paid by a business on employees and self-employment taxes are discussed. In addition, tax credits for research and development are covered.

Employment Taxes

The general rule is that employers are required to withhold income taxes on employees that make more than the amount indicated for their withholding allowances. In addition to wages, other payments may be subject to income taxes and thus should be treated as income.

Definition of Employees

In order for the withholding requirements to apply, the workers must be employees. There is no requirement to withhold tax on non-employees such as independent contractors. To determine if a worker is an employee, the courts will look at the substance of the transaction not the labeling by the parties as to the nature of the relationship.

The general test for determining employee status is if the individual is subject to the will and control of the employer as to what shall be done and how it shall be done the individual is considered an employee. It does not matter that the employee has considerable discretion

163

and freedom of action as long as the employer has the legal right to control both the method and the results of the work.

Normal characteristics of an employer-employee relationship are that the employer has the right to discharge the employee and the employer supplies the tools, equipment, and a place of work. No distinction is made between classes of employees; i.e., superintendents as well as janitorial workers are subject to withholding.

Determinations by the IRS

If an employer fails to withhold required taxes from an employee, the employer may be required to pay the taxes anyway. In doubtful cases, withhold. The IRS will make a determination for you in such cases. To receive an IRS determination, file Form SS-8 with the IRS director of the district in which the business is located.

Social Security Taxes

The definition of employees is broader for purposes of social security taxes than for the withholding of income taxes. In addition to the employee-employer relationships discussed above, the law requires employee treatment for social security purposes for the following individuals:

1. A driver who distributes a business's products, even if the driver is an agent or is paid on a commission
2. A full-time life insurance salesperson
3. An individual who works at home on materials or goods which the business supplies and must be returned to the business
4. A full-time traveling or city salesperson who works on the business's behalf and turns in orders to the business

The employer is required to withhold social security taxes from employees' pay. The rate of withholding for 1986 is 7.15 percent. The employer must also pay an additional 7.15 percent.

Employee Tips

An employee is required to report tips and gratuities received if they exceed $20 per month. The employee is required to report them not later than the tenth day of each month for the prior month. The employee may use Form 4070, "Employee's Report of Tips to Employer," which is available from IRS service centers, or may issue a statement containing the name, address, and social security number of the employee; the name and address of the employer; the calendar month or period covered by the statement; and the total amount of tips received during the period covered by the statement.

Gratuities collected by the employer through mandatory charges added to the customer's bill are not considered tips for federal employment tax purposes. The employer is required to consider these as wages subject to both employer and employee social security taxes. *Note:* Employers operating a large food or beverage establishment may be required to comply with the tip reporting requirements based on a percentage of customer bills. IRS Publication 539 contains a detailed discussion of these rules.

Employers are required to collect both social security taxes and income tax withholding on tips reported by employees. The employer may withhold these from other wages due the employee or from other funds the employee makes available. An employer is not required to pay employee social security taxes on tips unless the wages paid to the employee are less than the federal minimum wage.

Withholding on tips may be computed either by treating the tips as part of the employee's current or preceding wage payment and using the regular graduated withholding rates; or if income tax has already been withheld from the regular wage payment, by using a flat 20 percent tax rate.

If employees pool their tips, only the tips actually received by the employees should be reported by them. Employers are required to report on Form W-2 an employee's compensation including tips that are reported by the employee to the employer.

For federal unemployment tax purposes, tips received by an employee are considered as wages up to the amount that they are taken into account in determining the employee's compensation under the federal minimum wage law.

If wages are less than the federal minimum wage, the employer must pay social security taxes on that portion of the employee's tips that are used to constitute the minimum wage level.

Liability for Tax

Employers who are required to withhold taxes, either income or social security, are liable to the federal government whether or not the taxes are collected from the employee. Thus, if the employer deducts less tax than he or she should, the employer is still liable to the IRS for the taxes that should have been collected.

Returns

Social security taxes (FICA) and withheld income tax are reported on the same form, Form 941 or 941E. Form 941E is to be used where the employees are not covered by social security taxes. Form 942 is used for household workers and Form 943 for agricultural employees. All other employers should use Form 941.

Due Dates

Form 943, for agricultural employees, is an annual return and due 1 month after the end of the calendar year. The other forms are quarterly forms and are due 1 month after the end of each calendar quarter. The periods covered by the forms are the same whether the business uses a calendar or fiscal year.

Deposits may be required prior to the time the form must be filed. As noted in Chapter 1, when the amount is $5000 or more at the end of any one eight-month period, the employer must deposit the amount in a federal reserve bank or other authorized institution within 3 banking days. If the amount owed is $500 or more at the end of the month, then it must be deposited by the fifteenth of the next month. In addition, all amounts owed must be deposited by the end of the return period.

In making a deposit, the following information should be written on the check or money order: employer identification number, type of tax being paid, and period covered by the payment.

Self-Employment Taxes

Individuals who are self-employed must pay self-employment taxes in lieu of social security taxes. Sole proprietors and partners normally must pay self-employment taxes on their earnings from the business.

The rules for self-employment taxes are very similar to the rules regarding social security taxes. In addition, similar social security benefits are available to the individual who pays self-employment taxes.

A taxpayer must pay self-employment taxes on net earnings of $400 or more per year. An employee of a church or qualified church-controlled organization that is exempt from social security taxes must pay self-employment taxes on wages of $100 or more.

A salaried taxpayer whose wages are subject to social security taxes may also be subject to self-employment taxes if the taxpayer earns additional money from part-time work that is not subject to withholding for social security taxes. For example, suppose a salaried taxpayer earns $40,000 a year from a job where social security taxes are withheld and $5000 per year from a part-time business venture. The taxpayer would be subject to withholding of social security taxes and self-employment taxes on the first $42,000 of earnings. Therefore, since social security taxes were withheld on $40,000, the taxpayer must pay self-employment taxes on $2000 of the earnings from the part-time business.

Schedule SE (Form 1040)

Schedule SE (Form 1040) is used to report and compute self-employment taxes. The form is attached to the taxpayer's Form 1040 for the year. Taxpayers filing joint returns may not file a joint Schedule SE. If both spouses have earnings subject to self-employment taxes, then both must file separate schedules and attach both to the tax return.

Computing the Tax

To determine the amount of self-employment taxes that an individual must pay:

1. Determine the net earning from self-employment.
2. Determine how much of the earnings are subject to the tax.
3. Multiply the amount by the current self-employment tax.

There are three methods to determine net earnings from self-employment: the regular method, the farm optional method, and the nonfarm optional method. The nonfarm optional method is intended to allow social security coverage even when the taxpayer has little or no profit for the tax year. This method is used only for computing self-employment taxes; it cannot be used to compute income tax. Only farmers may use the farm optional method.

Any person subject to self-employment taxes may use the regular method. Most taxpayers use this method. The taxpayer computes his or her net earnings by subtracting all allowable business expenses and deductions from gross business income. If a taxpayer has more than one trade or business, the net income from each is added together to determine total earnings subject to the tax. A loss from one business is used to reduce or eliminate earnings from a different business.

Exclusions

Certain types of earnings are exempt from self-employment taxes. The most common exclusions are:

1. Rental income (payments received for the use or occupancy of hotels, motels, boarding houses, etc., are not rental income since services are provided)
2. Interest (unless received in the trade or business, such as interest on accounts receivable)
3. Dividends (except for a dealer in securities)
4. Gains and losses on the disposal of assets

Deductions and Exemptions

In computing net earnings for the purpose of the self-employment tax, certain deductions and exemptions are not permitted to be used to reduce the net earnings. They are deductions for personal exemptions, nonbusiness deductions, foreign expropriation loss deductions.

Research and Development Credit

To promote research and development, Congress, in the Economic Recovery Act of 1981, established a nonrefundable 25 percent income tax credit for certain research expenditures paid or incurred in carrying on an existing trade or business. The credit applies only to the extent that the taxpayer's qualified research expenditures for the tax year exceed the average amount of the taxpayer's yearly qualified research expenditures in the specified base period. The base period is normally the preceding 3 tax years.

The tax credit was due to expire on December 31, 1985. The Tax Reform Act of 1986 extended the incremental research tax credit at a lower rate of 20 percent for 3 additional years, until December 31, 1988. The credit was later extended through tax year 1991. It appears that it may be extended beyond tax year 1991. Prior to the 1986 tax changes, a tax credit was not subject to the general limitation on use of business credits (85 percent of tax liability over $25,000). For tax year 1986 and after, the general limitation on the use of business credits applies to the incremental research credit, and the general limitation has been changed to 75 percent of tax liability over $25,000.

Definition of Research

Prior to the Tax Reform Act, the definition of research, in the opinion of Congress, had been applied too broadly in practice, and it was thought that many businesses were claiming the credit for any expenses relating to product development. The basic purpose of the credit was to enhance research that is technological in nature.

Now, the research tax credit is available only if the research is undertaken for the purpose of discovering information (1) that is technological in nature and (2) the application of which is intended to be useful in the development of a new or improved business component of the taxpayer. An additional restriction is that research is eligible for the tax credit only if substantially all the activities or the research constitute elements of a process of experimentation for a functional purpose. In addition, certain research activity expenses are not eligible for this tax credit.

Technological Nature. To be technological in nature, the process of experimentation utilized in the research must rely fundamentally on principles of the physical or biological sciences, engineering, or computer science. If the process relies on other principles, such as economics, then it is not technological in nature.

Process of Experimentation. The term *process of experimentation* means a process of scientific experimentation or engineering activity to design a business component where the design of the component as a whole is uncertain at the outset, but instead must be determined by developing one or more hypotheses for specific design decisions, testing and analyzing those hypotheses, and refining or discarding the hypotheses as part of a sequential design process.

Under the above rules, the costs of developing new or improved business components are not eligible for the credit if the method of reaching the objective is readily discernible and applicable as of the beginning of the research activities. In this example, no true experimentation in the scientific or laboratory sense is undertaken to develop, test, and choose among viable alternatives.

The expenses associated with experiments undertaken by chemists or physicians in developing and testing a new drug are eligible for the tax credit because the researchers are engaged in scientific experimentation. Also, engineers who design or improve integrated circuits for use in computers are engaged in qualified research since the design of the items are uncertain at the outset and must be determined through a process of experimentation relating to specific design hypotheses and decisions.

Functional Purposes. Research relating to a new or improved function, performance, reliability, quality, or reduced cost is considered as conducted for a functional purpose. However, activities undertaken to assure achievement of the intended function, performance, etc., of a business component are not conducted for a functional purpose. Research relating to style, taste, cosmetic, or seasonal design factors is not considered as conducted for a functional purpose.

Application of Tests

For purposes of this tax credit, the term *business component* means a product, process, computer software, technique, or invention that is to be held for sale, lease, or license, or is to be used by the taxpayer in a trade or business. If the requirements are not met but are met by one or more elements thereof, the business component means the most significant set of elements of such product with respect to which all the requirements are met.

The requirements are tested first at the level of the entire product to be offered for sale by the taxpayer. If the product does not meet all the requirements, then it is tested at the most significant subset of elements. This process is continued as to each level until one meets all the requirements or the most basic element fails to qualify.

Internal-Use Computer Software

The Tax Reform Act of 1986 established special rules for computer software that is developed by or for the benefit of the taxpayer primarily for the taxpayer's own internal use. To qualify for the tax credit, the software must be used in (1) qualified research undertaken by the taxpayer (excluding the development of the internal-use software itself), or (2) a production process that involves a component that qualifies for the credit. All other research activities with respect to internal-use software is not eligible for the tax credit.

Included ineligible software includes that developed for payroll, bookkeeping, banking, word processing, etc. Normally, internal-use software is eligible only if the taxpayer can also establish that (1) the software is innovative, (2) the software development involved significant economic risk, and (3) the software is not commercially available. If the software meets these requirements, then the eligibility of expenditures is determined in the same manner as the eligibility of other business expenses.

12
Tax Compliance

This chapter discusses tax-exempt organizations, minimum tax provisions, tax penalties, interest payments, and reporting requirements, including those for real estate transactions, royalties, and federal contracts. Also discussed are legal considerations, such as the Equal Access to Justice Act, the tax court practice fee, and tax amnesty; tax information, including IRS sources and methods of presentation; and IRS search and seizure.

Tax-Exempt Organizations

Certain organizations are generally exempt from federal income tax because of their charitable, educational, religious, or nonprofit purposes and functions. However, a tax is imposed on the unrelated trade or business income of the otherwise tax-exempt organizations. The tax applies to gross income derived by an exempt organization from any unrelated trade or business regularly carried on by it, less allowable deductions directly connected with carrying on such trade or business. Both are subject to certain modifications.

For purposes of this section of the tax code, an unrelated trade or business is defined as any trade or business of a tax-exempt organization, the conduct of which is not substantially related (aside from the need of such organization for income of funds or the use it makes of profits derived) to the exercise or performance of such organization of the charitable, educational, religious or other nonprofitable purpose and function constituting the basis for its exemption.

The Tax Reform Act modified this restriction by providing that the tax on the unrelated trade or business is not to be imposed on income from the exchange or rental of donor or member lists among tax-exempt organizations eligible to receive charitable contributions. In addition, the tax act provided that smaller, unrelated tax-exempt organizations can pool funds for purposes of investing in real estate through a title holding company with the same tax treatment available under present law for larger tax-exempt organizations having a subsidiary title holding company that is tax-exempt.

The Tax Reform Act also added a new category of tax-exempt organizations. It consists of certain corporations or trusts that are organized for the exclusive purpose of acquiring and holding title to property, collecting income from property, and remitting the income to certain tax-exempt organizations. The tax-exempt status in this category applies only if the corporation or trust has no more than 35 shareholders or beneficiaries, has only one class of stock or beneficial interest, and is organized for the exclusive purpose of acquiring property and holding title to and collecting income from such property and remitting the entire amount of the income from such property, less the expenses, to one or more eligible tax-exempt organizations that are shareholders or beneficiaries of such a corporation or trust.

A corporation or trust that meets these requirements is also entitled to use the exception to the tax on unrelated business income under the debt finance property rules for all real property. In order to qualify for this exemption, a title holding company must permit shareholders or beneficiaries to dismiss after reasonable notice the corporation's or trust's investment adviser by majority vote of the shareholders or beneficiaries and to terminate their interest by selling or exchanging their stock or beneficial interest to any other eligible organization as long as such sale or exchange would not increase the number of shareholders or beneficiaries to more than 35 or redeem their stock or beneficial interest after providing 90 days' notice to the corporation.

Tax-exempt organizations eligible to hold interest in title holding companies under the plan are qualified pension, profit-sharing, and stock bonus plans; government pension plans; United States, state, or political subdivisions thereunder, governmental agencies, or instrumentalities; and tax-exempt charitable, educational, religious, or other organizations.

Alternative Minimum Tax

The alternative minimum tax (AMT), also referred to as "another magic tax," was enacted by Congress to ensure that individuals and tax entities with high gross incomes pay at least a minimum tax. Prior to establishing the AMT, there were cases involving taxpayers with gross incomes in excess of $1 million who were paying no income taxes. Now, the individual who uses tax breaks and tax preference items is required in some cases to compute his or her tax liability under the regular tax system and also under the minimum tax schedule and then pay whichever tax is higher. The Tax Reform Act was designed to prevent wealthy persons from avoiding the paying of any taxes at all. The alternative minimum tax that is now imposed on individuals and corporations is at a 24 percent rate. Normally, only taxpayers with high gross incomes need worry about the AMT. In 1988, only 90,000 taxpayers were required to pay under the AMT regulations.

How can the 24 percent tax rate cause problems when the highest tax rate is 31 percent? The problems are caused by the fact that a number of deductions and tax breaks that are subtracted from the adjusted gross income are readded in computing the AMT.

The 24 percent rate is applied to the regular adjusted gross income as increased by certain tax preferences and decreased by itemized deductions. Credits other than foreign tax credits are not allowed against the minimum tax. The foreign tax credit could offset no more than 90 percent of the minimum tax liability. As stated earlier, the goal of the minimum tax is to ensure that no taxpayer with significant income can avoid tax liability by using exclusions, deductions, and credits.

See Chapter 1 for a discussion of the changes in minimum tax law as a result of the recent legislation.

Tax Penalties

The IRS code requires information returns to be filed with the IRS and requires employers to give a copy of each information return to the taxpayer detailing all wages and most other types of income and some deductions. These requirements apply to a variety of specific payments that are described in a number of code provisions. The code also provides civil penalties for failure to file an information return with the IRS. The general penalty for failure to supply the information return is separate from the penalty for failure to give a copy to the taxpayer.

Generally, the penalties are $50 for each failure, with a maximum under each provision of $100,000 per year. The code also provides a penalty of $15 to $50, depending upon the nature of the failure, for failure to furnish a correct taxpayer identification number (for individuals, their social security number).

The Tax Reform Act also provided a new penalty for failure to include correct information either on the information return filed with the IRS or a copy of that information return supplied to the taxpayer. This new penalty applies to both an omission of information or an inclusion of incorrect information. The amount of penalty is $15 for each return or copy, per taxpayer, up to a maximum of $20,000 in any calendar year. This maximum does not apply in the case of intentional disregard of the requirement to file accurate information returns.

The new penalty does not apply to an information return if a penalty for failure to supply a correct taxpayer identification number has been imposed with respect to that information return. Accordingly, if a person filing an information return is subject to a penalty under Section 6676 for including an incorrect social security number on the information return, the newer penalty is not imposed with respect to that same information on the return.

The new penalty was designed to provide persons filing information returns an incentive both to file accurate and complete returns initially and to correct as rapidly as possible any incorrect information that may have been filed. If a person files what purports to be an information return but which contains so many inaccuracies or omissions that the utility of the document is minimized or eliminated, the IRS may under such circumstances impose the penalty for failure to file an information return rather than the new penalty for filing an information return that includes inaccurate or incomplete information. If the IRS imposes a penalty for failure to file an information return, it may not in addition impose a penalty for filing incorrect information with respect to the same return.

There is an exception to all these penalties if the failure to file the information return with the IRS or to provide a copy to the taxpayer or to include correct information on either return is due to reasonable cause and not to willful neglect. Under this standard, if a person is required to file and fails to do so because of negligence or without reasonable cause, that person would be subject to the penalty.

The code also provides that a taxpayer who fails to pay taxes when due must pay a penalty. The penalty applies to the taxpayer who fails to pay taxes shown on the tax return. It also applies to a taxpayer who fails to pay taxes not shown on the tax return within 10 days of notice of demand by the IRS. The penalty may be in addition to any interest. The penalty may amount to 1 percent per month.

While the IRS has the authority in certain situations to impose a 1 percent per month penalty, the normal penalty is ½ of 1 percent of the tax for the first month not paid and increases by ½ of 1 percent for each month the failure to pay continues, up to a maximum of 25 percent. This penalty can be abated if the failure is due to reasonable cause and not willful neglect. Any penalty paid is not deductible for tax purposes.

Taxpayers are subject to a penalty if any part of the underpayment of tax is due to negligence or intentional disregard of the rules or regulations. There are two components to this penalty. The first component is 5 percent of the total underpayment where any portion of the underpayment is attributable to negligence or the intentional disregard of rules or regulations. Thus, if a taxpayer has underpaid $1000 of taxes and the portion due to negligence is $200, the amount of penalty is 5 percent of $1000 or $50. The second component is the amount equal to one-half of the interest rate the taxpayer must pay on underpayment of taxes multiplied by the portion of the underpayment attributable to negligence or intentional disregard for the period beginning on the last date prescribed for payment of the underpayment and ending on the date of assessment of the tax or the date of payment of the tax if that date is earlier.

The Tax Reform Act expanded the scope of the negligence penalty by making it applicable to all taxes under the code. The act also modified the negligence penalty by increasing the rate of penalty but at the same time narrowing its scope. First, the act increased the rate of negligence penalty from 5 to 10 percent. Second, the scope of the negligence penalty is reduced so that in effect it applies only to the amount of underpayment attributable to the negligence. The negligence penalty is determined at the top marginal rate applicable to the taxpayer.

In addition, the Tax Reform Act broadens the scope of the negligence in that now any behavior that is considered negligent by the courts but not specifically included within the definition is also subject to the penalty. If a taxpayer fails to show properly on his or her tax return any amount that is shown on the information return, the taxpayer's failure is treated as negligence in the absence of clear and convincing evidence to the contrary.

The Tax Reform Act also increased the rate of the basic broad penalty from 50 to 75 percent. In addition, it has shifted the burden to establish that any portion of the underpayment is not attributable to fraud by the taxpayer. Once the IRS has initially established that fraud occurred, the burden of proof shifts to the taxpayer to establish that portion of the underpayment that is not attributable to fraud.

If a taxpayer substantially understates income tax for any tax year, the taxpayer must pay an additional tax equal to 20 percent of the underpayment of tax attributable to the understatement. An understatement is substantial if it exceeds the greater of 10 percent of the required tax to be shown on the tax return or $5000 ($10,000 for most corporations). An understatement is generally the excess of the amount of tax required to be shown on a tax return over the amount of tax actually shown on a tax return. The penalty generally does not apply to amounts with respect to which there was substantial authority for the taxpayer's treatment of the amount or the taxpayer discloses irrelevant facts with respect to that amount on the tax return.

Interest Payments

Taxpayers must pay interest to the IRS on underpayment of taxes. Interest generally accrues from the due date of the tax return determined without regard to any extensions. The Treasury must pay interest on taxpayers' overpayment of taxes.

The interest rate that the Treasury must pay to taxpayers on overpayment is the federal short-term rate plus 2 percentage points. The interest rate that the taxpayers pay to the Treasury on underpayment is the federal short-term rate plus 3 percent. These rates are rounded to the nearest full percentage point.

Interest rates are adjusted quarterly. The rates are determined during the first month of the calendar quarter and become effective for the following calendar quarter. Thus, for example, the rates that are determined during January are effective the following April through June. The interest rates are determined by the Secretary of the Treasury on the basis of the average market yield on outstanding marketable obligations of the United States with the remaining periods to maturity to 3 years or less. This is the mechanism used for determining short-term federal rates.

The Tax Reform Act also changed the method of computing interest on accumulated earnings tax. The interest that is imposed on the underpayment of accumulated earnings tax is computed from the due date of the income tax return, without regard to extensions, for the year that the tax is initially imposed.

Reporting Requirements

Real Estate Transactions

The Tax Reform Act broadened the reporting requirements for real estate transactions. Basically, the code requires that real estate transactions be reported. The seller's real estate broker is the first person responsible for reporting the necessary information. If there is no seller's real estate broker, then the reporting is to be done by the buyer's real estate broker. If there is no buyer's real estate broker, then the reporting is to be done by the mortgage lender. If there is more than one mortgage lender, the reporting is to be done by the primary mortgage lender. If there is no mortgage lender, then the reporting is to be done by the title company. If there is no title company, the reporting is to be done by the settlement attorney or other persons responsible for closing the transaction. If there is no settlement attorney, the reporting is to be done in accordance with regulations prescribed by the Treasury.

The reporting will be accomplished by submitting a 1099 form similar to that required for other transactions effected by a broker. The reporting requirements for real estate transactions are added to the general information reporting requirements related to brokers. Therefore, the penalties and related provisions that apply to general brokers also apply to persons required to report real estate transactions. The code provides that real estate transactions will be subject to backup withholding only to the extent required by Treasury regulations.

The regulations on reporting of real estate transactions are effective with respect to any closing on contracts that occur on or after January 1, 1987. Real estate transactions closed on or after that date must be reported without regard to whether or not the Treasury Department has issued regulations requiring that the return be filed.

Federal Contracts

The Tax Reform Act now requires the heads of federal executive agencies to file information returns indicating the name, address, and taxpayer identification number of each person with which the agency enters into a contract. The purpose of this requirement is to provide the IRS with a source of information for collection purposes.

Royalties

The Tax Reform Act requires that persons who make payments of royalties of $10 or more to any other person in a calendar year must provide an information report on the royalty payment to the IRS. A copy of this information report must also be supplied to the taxpayer. If the taxpayer reports to a nominee, the nominee must report the information to the taxpayer and to the IRS as required by secretarial Treasury regulations. Examples of royalty payments required to be reported under this provision include royalty payments with respect to the right to exploit natural resources such as gas, oil, coal, timber, sand, gravel, and mineral interests, as well as royalty payments for the right to exploit intangible property such as copyrights, trademarks, trade names, books, and other literary compositions, musical compositions, artistic works, and secret processes or formulas.

The general applicable rules for information returns for payment of interest and dividends apply also to this provision. Thus, the information report to taxpayers must be provided by the end of January and the report to the IRS must be provided by the end of February. Payers filing a large number of these reports with the IRS are subject to the magnetic media filing requirement. If the payee does not furnish the payor with the payee's taxpayer's identification number (for individuals, the social security number), the royalty payments are generally subject to backup withholding.

Legal Considerations

Equal Access to Justice Act

In 1980, as part of Public Law 96-481, Congress enacted the Equal Access to Justice Act, which in part authorizes awards to prevailing parties other than the United States for attorney's fees and other expenses unless the court finds that the decision of the United States was substantially justified or that special circumstances make the award unjust. The Tax Reform Act modified the tax code to conform more closely to the Equal Access to Justice Act. Therefore, under the new law, the burden of proof is on the government that its position was substantially justified or that the special circumstances exist that make award of the attorney's fees and court costs unjust.

The act provides that, unless the government proves this, attorney's fees may be awarded. The burden of proof replaces the former standard, which required the taxpayer to prove that the government's position was unreasonable before the taxpayer could be awarded attorney's fees. The act, however, did not modify the present legal requirement that in order to be eligible to be awarded attorney's fees, the taxpayer must substantially prevail either with respect to the amount in controversy or with respect to the most significant issue or set of issues presented. The act also did not modify the provision that only the taxpayer and not the government may be awarded attorney's fees.

The act eliminated the $25,000 cap on the award of attorney's fees and substituted a $75-an-hour limitation on attorney's fees unless the court determines that a higher rate is justified. To make this determination, the court may look to an increase in the cost of living or a special factor such as the limited availability of qualified attorneys to deal with particular issues involved in the case. As previously, the act provides that only reasonable litigation costs are recoverable by the taxpayer. In no event are expert witnesses to be compensated at a rate in excess of the highest rate of compensation for such witnesses paid by the United

States. The act also denies any award of attorney's fees to a prevailing party who unreasonably delays the proceedings.

Tax Court Practice Fee

The Tax Reform Act authorized the tax court to impose a periodic registration fee on practitioners admitted to practice before the tax court. The tax court is to establish the level of the fee and the frequency of its collection, but the fee may not exceed $30 per year. The funds are then to be made available to the tax court to pay independent counsel engaged by the court in the pursuit of disciplinary matters. In addition, the Tax Reform Act provided that the tax court did have additional jurisdiction to provide additions to taxes for failure to pay an amount shown on the return where the tax court had jurisdiction to redetermine a deficiency in tax with respect to that issue.

Tax Amnesty

Prior to the Tax Reform Act, the fact that a taxpayer voluntarily disclosed income tax law violations was used as one of many factors in determining whether the IRS would prosecute the violator under criminal statutes. In order to encourage voluntary disclosure by taxpayers of prior tax law violations, the recent tax change provided assurance that taxpayers would avoid all criminal penalties for such disclosures under certain circumstances.

To qualify for amnesty, taxpayers must fully disclose previous violations of income tax law; they must do so before they or a related party is given notice of an inquiry or investigation into their tax affairs by the IRS, another law enforcement agency, or another tax administration agency; and their activities must not be illegal under any law other than the tax code, such as dealing with illegal drugs or guns.

The tax act gave the Secretary of the Treasury broad authority to formulate regulations regarding an amnesty program, including the authority to exclude certain categories of taxpayers from participating in the program. The secretary must also publicize the scope and availability of this program. Required publicity must include press releases, notices in IRS publications, and notices in other material sent to taxpayers.

Tax Information

IRS Sources of Information

The IRS publishes many publications that are of interest to the taxpayer. A list of these may be obtained from the nearest IRS service center. Several other services of the IRS include telephone assistance, the unresolved tax problems program, and private-letter ruling services.

Publications.   The three most useful publications that the IRS publishes are (1) Publication 17, "Your Federal Income Tax," (2) Publication 334, "Tax Guide for Small Business," and (3) Publication X (contains one copy of each standard IRS tax form). These publications are revised annually.

Telephone Assistance.   The IRS has a telephone service called Tele-Tax. This service provides information on over 100 topics covering such areas as filing requirements, employment taxes, and many more. Tele-Tax is available 24 hours a day, 7 days a week, to taxpayers using touch-tone telephones. Brochures listing the topics and containing the local telephone numbers may be obtained from any IRS service center or most major libraries.

During tax season, the IRS also provides a telephone assistance service. There has, however, been a lot of criticism regarding the accuracy of this advice in past tax years. In a 1986 report by the General Accounting Office of the federal government, the IRS was accused of giving wrong advice regarding the tax law 13 percent of the time to callers. The 13 percent figure was down from the 1985 estimate of a 20 percent error rate. The questions that were answered incorrectly most frequently, according to the GAO, pertained to gift taxes, charitable contributions, and use of the short form. Bear in mind that the taxpayer is still held accountable in following erroneous advice by the IRS.

Private-Letter Rulings.   Private-letter rulings may be requested from the IRS if you have a special problem. Private-letter rulings are not binding as precedents, but they reveal IRS's position on the subject.

To obtain a private-letter ruling, send your request to Associate Chief Counsel (Technical), Attn.: CC:IND:S, Internal Revenue Service, 1111 Constitution Avenue N.W., Washington, D.C. 20224.

The request should contain the following:

1. All facts involved, including the names and addresses of all parties.

2. A full and precise statement of the reason for the transaction in question.

3. Copies of supporting documents (do not send originals).

4. A statement regarding previous letter-ruling requests, whether this problem has been submitted to the district director also for resolution, and whether it pertains to a past year's return or a future return.

Unresolved Tax Problems Program. The IRS has an unresolved tax problem program for taxpayers who have been unable to resolve their problems with the IRS. To utilize this program, the taxpayer needs to write or call the district director's office and ask for problem resolution assistance.

Disclosure of Tax Information

The Tax Reform Act provides that, in addition to sharing information with state tax administrators, certain confidential information on a taxpayer's return may be shared with tax administrators of any city with a population in excess of 2 million. Cities that receive this information must reimburse the IRS for the cost of providing the information. The tax law change places the city administrators on the same footing as state tax administrators.

Disclosures under this provision of the tax code are required to be in the same manner and with the same safeguards as any disclosures made to a state agency. The Secretary of the Treasury has sole discretion to issue regulations implementing this program.

Unauthorized disclosure of tax information is a felony punishable by a fine not exceeding $5000 or imprisonment of not more than 5 years or both.

Matching Program

The Internal Revenue Service has developed a matching program that matches individual tax returns against other sources of information such as W-2 wage statements and 1099 forms for interest and dividend reporting. If the income reported does not match with the other information reports, then a letter will be sent asking the taxpayer to explain the difference. For example, in an attempt to find nonfilers, the IRS in one year mailed 3.24 million letters to people who filed tax returns in previous years but not in that year.

IRS Alternatives to Regulations

The IRS is considering alternatives to the presentation and use of current regulations for tax guidance. The present system is cumbersome and awkward, especially since many regulations are obsolete because of legislative changes.

The IRS commissioner has indicated that IRS guidance on the code changes will be provided by:

1. Regulations in the form of questions and answers.
2. Shorter regulations, amplified by rulings rather than written in the traditional comprehensive form.
3. A reduction of the number of clearances needed in order to publish new or modify old regulations.
4. Letter rulings which respond to situations that are not covered by regulations.
5. New releases.
6. Notices in the Internal Revenue Bulletin.
7. Instructions contained on new forms.
8. Interim announcements followed by more permanent guidance.

In addition, the IRS no longer distributes tax forms in bulk as it has in the past. This should save the IRS at least $6 million a year.

Search and Seizure by the IRS

In this section the rights of the IRS to search and seize taxpayer records will be discussed. While searches by the IRS are unusual, when they do occur, taxpayers need to have a basic understanding of their rights.

Recently, the IRS has shown an increased tendency to use the search warrant to obtain necessary records, especially since the enactment of the Omnibus Crime Control and Safe Streets Act. That act and the U.S. Supreme Court case of *Warden v. Hayden* provide the basis for a court to issue a search warrant to search for and seize evidence of a criminal offense (e.g., a taxpayer's records).

Failure to correctly report income or any other information required by the tax code is a violation of federal criminal law. Tax fraud and tax evasion are likewise crimes. The Internal Revenue Code, Section 7201, provides that:

> Any person who willfully attempts in any manner to evade or defeat any tax imposed by this title or the payment thereof shall, in addition to other penalties provided by law, be guilty of a felony and, upon conviction thereof, shall be fined not more than $100,000 ($500,000 in the case of a corporation) or imprisoned not more than five years, or both, together with the costs of prosecution.

In addition to the use of a search warrant, the government may compel the production of documents through the use of an administrative summons or through a grand jury summons. The advantage of a search warrant over a summons is that the search warrant takes the taxpayer by surprise and may prevent destruction of the documents. Unlike summonses, warrants require no advance warning.

To obtain a search warrant, the IRS agent must first establish probable cause that a crime has been committed and that the place requested to be searched will contain items that may be seized pursuant to a search warrant. A judge must determine that the agent has sufficient probable cause to support the request for a warrant and that it is reasonable to issue a warrant in this case. Legal search warrants may be issued only by neutral and impartial magistrates (judges). The warrant must specify the place to be searched and the items to be searched for. A general search warrant violates the Fourth Amendment of the U.S. Constitution, which prohibits unreasonable searches and seizures.

After the judge issues the warrant, the agents are then required to search within a reasonable period of time and return the warrant and any items seized to the court that issued the search warrant.

Normally, before a special agent's oath of knowledge that certain incriminatory evidence is located at a certain place, will be accepted by a judge as sufficient cause to support the issuance of a warrant, the agent must show how this knowledge was obtained. The four most common situations are as follows:

1. The agent has observed the documents and has good reason to believe that they contain evidence of tax evasion or fraud. For IRS investigations, this possibility is unlikely.

2. The agent has obtained from a third person information that indicates the presence of the records and that the records contain evidence of tax crimes. In addition, the agent normally must demonstrate why the information of this third person (an informant) is probably correct. (This latter requirement may be accomplished by showing that the third person either has observed the documents or has heard the taxpayer talk about them.) This situation is common with IRS search warrants. The IRS has in the past used angry spouses and girlfriends or boyfriends, paid informants, and other persons who for one reason or another are upset at the taxpayer and want to "get even."

3. The agent has observed or perceived facts from which the presence of records and their contents may be inferred. This possibility is also very likely. For example, a taxpayer may file a tax return indicating low income, but the taxpayer lives in an expensive home and drives an expensive car. In this case, seizure of bank records may be sup-

ported by the facts because it appears that the taxpayer is receiving money from unexplained sources.

4. In many cases, the agent uses a combination of the above three situations to establish probable cause. For example, in one court case, the IRS received an anonymous tip that a couple were cheating on their income taxes. A check of the neighborhood revealed that the couple probably had an unexplained source of income (from sale of drugs). This information was considered sufficient to establish probable cause to issue a search warrant.

A second requirement for obtaining a search warrant is a description of the items to be seized. In this area, the IRS has an easier time than other criminal justice agencies since what the IRS is attempting to obtain—taxpayer records, bank records—are fairly uniform nationwide.

Another requirement is that the agent must demonstrate that the information which establishes probable cause is not stale. For example, evidence that the suspect possessed drugs 6 months ago cannot be used alone to justify an inference that the taxpayer possesses drugs now. This requirement is also not a big problem for IRS agents since, unlike much evidence of criminal conduct, a taxpayer's records are usually retained for long periods of time. On this point, one court stated that "Since taxpayer documents and records, unlike fruits of a bank robbery, are normally innocuous in themselves and are not evanescent in nature, a longer time would presumably be required before information as to their existence and whereabouts would be considered stale." In this case, the court held that a 3-month delay in the execution of the search was harmless.

After a search warrant is issued, the scope of the search must not exceed the limitations set forth in the warrant. For example, a warrant to search a taxpayer's business office does not justify the search of the taxpayer's home since this exceeds the scope of the search. A similar limitation involves the type of items seized. For example, authority to search for a taxpayer's bank records does not justify the seizure of telephone records of the taxpayer discovered during the search.

Many taxpayers are under the assumption that the Fifth Amendment to the U.S. Constitution protects them from being required to produce documents that would incriminate them, i.e., their tax records. This is in error for two reasons: First, the tax code requires the taxpayer to establish (i.e., prove) the amount of income that the taxpayer makes and the deductions and exclusions that the taxpayer is claiming. Second and more important, the courts have traditionally held that the Fifth Amendment protects a person from being required to make or from originating incriminating evidence, but it does not prevent a person from being required to produce presently existing evidence (like tax records).

Steps to Take If Faced with a Search Warrant

1. Do not consent to the search. Consent removes the need for a search warrant and waives legal recourse to any defects in the search warrant. A taxpayer may show where the records are, but should make it clear that he or she is doing so only because of the warrant.

2. Make no statements to the agent. It's too late to talk the agent out of anything. Allow your attorney to do all the talking. Contrary to popular belief, the special agent has no duty to warn you that anything you say may be used against you, unless you are under arrest.

3. Make a detailed record of all documents and materials that the IRS agent obtained and of any statements made by the agent. This will assist your attorney in preparing your case.

4. Consult with an attorney who is knowledgeable in this area as soon as practical.

Leading Court Cases

There are two leading U.S. Supreme Court cases dealing with IRS criminal investigations that are set forth below to provide taxpayers some general guidance in this area.

Beckwith v. United States. Chief Justice Warren Burger delivered the opinion in this case.

The issue in this case is whether a special agent of the Internal Revenue Service, investigating potential criminal income tax violations, must, in an interview with a taxpayer not in custody, give warnings called for by this Court's decision in *Miranda v. Arizona.* (The Miranda case was the case in which the Court established the requirement for the police to advise suspects in custody of their rights against self-incrimination.)

The testimony in this case indicates that after considerable amount of investigation, two special agents of the Intelligence Division of the Internal Revenue Service met the taxpayer at the taxpayer's residence. The special agents knocked on the taxpayer's door at 8 a.m. The taxpayer opened the door and invited the agents in. He then excused himself and went into his bedroom to finish dressing. Then the taxpayer and the agents sat down in the dining room. The special agents informed the taxpayer of their investigation and of his right not to answer questions that might incriminate him. The agents improperly advised him as to his rights to counsel.

The taxpayer then got into a discussion with the agents. During the discussion, the taxpayer made several incriminating statements that the government used against him in a trial for criminal tax evasion. The taxpayer's counsel objected to the admission into evidence of the statements made by the taxpayer to the special agents on the grounds that the agents improperly advised the accused of his rights under the Fifth Amendment.

The Court first determined that the mistaken advice on right to counsel was not intentional and didn't mislead the accused. The Court next looked at the question of whether or not the agents had a duty to advise the accused of his rights. In holding that the agents had no duty to warn the accused of his rights under the Fifth Amendment, the Court opined that unlike police interrogation in a police-dominated atmosphere, here the accused was not in custody and the questioning took place in his dining room. Therefore, the custodial nature of the interrogation was lacking, and there appeared to be no inherently coercive conditions.

Andresen v. Maryland. Justice Blackmun delivered the opinion in this case. The issue in this case is whether the introduction into evidence of a person's business records, seized during a search of his offices, violates the Fifth Amendment's restriction on requiring a person to be compelled in a criminal case to be a witness against himself.

In this case, the State Attorney's office began an investigation of real estate settlement activities in the Washington, D.C., area. During the investigation, Andresen's activities came under scrutiny. The investigators, concluding that there was probable cause to believe that the accused had committed the state crime of false pretense, applied for and got a search warrant to search Andresen's offices. The petitioner's office was searched and about 2 percent of his files were seized by the police.

He was then convicted. Three documents from the petitioner's office were used in evidence against him. His counsel objected on the grounds that the use of the documents was equivalent to self-incrimination in violation of the Fifth Amendment. The Court noted that the constitution provides that "no person shall be compelled in any criminal case to be a witness against himself." The "historic function" of the privilege against self-incrimination has been to protect a "natural individual from compulsory incrimination through his own testimony." There was no question that the records seized from the petitioner's office and introduced against him were incriminating. More-over, it was undisputed that some of these business records contained statements made by the petitioner. The question, therefore, was whether the seizure of these business records, and their admission into evidence at the petitioner's trial, compelled testimony in violation of the Fifth Amendment. The Court held that there was no violation of the Fifth Amendment because the accused was not asked to say or to do anything.

The records seized contained statements that the petitioner had vol-untarily committed to writing. The search for and seizure of these records were conducted by law enforcement personnel. When the records were admitted into evidence, they were authenticated by a handwriting expert, not by the petitioner. Any compulsion by the pe-titioner to speak, other than inherent psychological pressure to respond at trial to unfavorable evidence, was not present.

A contrary determination that the seizure of a person's business records and their introduction into evidence at a criminal trial violates the Fifth Amendment would undermine the general rule that there is no sanctity in papers as distinguished from other forms of property. In addition, permitting the introduction into evidence of a person's busi-ness records seized during an otherwise lawful search does not offend or undermine any of the policies underlying the privilege against self-incrimination.

13
Tax Audits

In this chapter, IRS audit policies and tactics to reduce the chances of a tax audit, audit procedures including preparing for a tax audit, and appeals from adverse rulings of a tax auditor are discussed. A brief introduction to the rules and procedures of the U.S. Tax Court is included.

Audit Policies and Reducing Tax Liability

Each of us has the feeling that our return will be selected and scrutinized individually by the IRS. What we fail to realize, however, is that there are approximately 100 million individual income tax returns of the Form 1040 "family" processed by the IRS each year. Using past history as a guide, it is noted that only about 1 percent of individual tax returns are, in fact, selected for audit. There are roughly 100 million tax returns filed each year, and rarely does the IRS audit more than 1 million returns. For the past decade, the percentage of income tax returns audited has never exceeded 3 percent. Accordingly, most tax returns are not selected for audit by the IRS. If your adjusted gross income is less than $15,000, you have about 1 chance in 248 of being audited. If, however, your adjusted gross income is over $100,000, you have 1 chance in 24 of being audited. The IRS estimates that it has enough staff support to audit only 11 of every 1000 returns (an all-time low). The IRS also indicates that it is trying to collect over $50 billion in back taxes owed. This amount is up 50 percent from 1987.

IRS Audit Policy

Traditionally, the United States has succeeded in an income tax collection system based primarily on the concept of voluntary compliance— that taxpayers, in the majority, will promptly report income, deductions, and credits and pay taxes legally due. To encourage voluntary participation, the IRS has established an audit selection policy designed to increase the individual taxpayer's subjective belief that their returns will be targeted for examination. In addition, the IRS has lobbied Congress to reduce the dependence upon voluntary tax collection by instituting a series of tax reporting and collection mechanisms such as reporting of required information, involuntary withholding of a certain portion of wages, and the use of computerized analysis.

In order to increase the subjective belief that individual tax returns will be audited, the best strategy would appear to be to maximize audit coverage without regard to the amount of taxes owed. However, a second factor involved is the IRS's desire to establish their cost-effectiveness to the members of Congress and to the public in general. To establish cost-effectiveness, the IRS needs to select those returns where the possibility of the largest additional tax liability and collection of tax is possible. Accordingly, the current IRS tax audit policy is a codification of the two competing strategies, one for broad coverage as possible and one for cost efficiency.

Approximately 75 percent of all income tax returns filed each year are from the Form 1040 family. The other 25 percent consists of S corporation, gift tax, estate, and regular corporation returns.

The General Accounting Office (GAO) of the U.S. government has concluded that the level of voluntary compliance of non-Form 1040 returns is lower than that of returns in the Form 1040 family. As a result of recommendations of the GAO, the IRS now allocates over half its available auditing resources to an examination of non-Form 1040 family forms, which result in higher yields per audited return than in the Form 1040 family. This also means that audit percentages for non-Form 1040 returns are higher.

The IRS has devised a complicated, multitiered audit selection system for Form 1040 returns in order both to maintain adequate emphasis on overall coverage and to maximize the audit yield. The procedures used are as follows:

1. All returns in the Form 1040 family are preliminarily screened by computers to select returns that have a potential for significant changes following an audit.

2. The returns are then screened by a computer to detect special compliance problems that the IRS has considered to be worthy of special scrutiny.

3. Next, the computer-selected returns to be audited are made available for manual review by IRS personnel at various office levels.

4. From the computer-selected returns that are manually reviewed by IRS personnel, certain returns are then selected for distribution to IRS agents for actual audits.

In selecting returns to be audited, the IRS uses national standards. Thus, individual taxpayers are measured against nationwide standards during the computer selection process. The IRS has attempted, but as of this date, has been unable, to develop a successful system that would permit a localized audit selection system whereby taxpayers are measured against local rather than nationwide standards.

IRS Processing

When the return filed by the taxpayer is received at one of the IRS service centers, it is opened and stamped with the date of receipt. It is then routinely prescreened. The prescreening includes a mathematical check, a comparison of the amount of tax enclosed, if any, with the tax indicated as due on Form 1040, and a check to make sure that the forms are signed and contain identification numbers and sufficient information to determine tax liability. Next, the information from the forms is encoded into computer data by data processors. During this process, the mathematics are corrected, if necessary. Next, the data is entered into the national computer bank.

The following information is normally transferred to the computer bank: the taxpayer's identifying number as well as any professional tax preparer's number, line items on the forms, the type of return, and any other information on the schedules. Information not encoded does not affect the computer audit screening process. The information may, however, be used during the manual selection after a return has been preliminarily selected by the computer. Included in this category are the name and occupation of the taxpayer, and information submitted by the taxpayer to justify certain deductions or credits that are not normally contained on the form.

The computer screening divides the returns into two groups: one with a large number of returns that have a low potential for significant tax changes on audit and one with a smaller number of returns with a high potential for significant tax changes on audit. In order to do grouping by computer, the IRS uses a mathematical statistics package called DIF, which originally stood for discriminate function and was developed in the early nineteenth century by a botanist to classify plants.

The purpose of the DIF is to discriminate against those returns that are likely to have a high potential for significant tax change on an audit. The DIF statistical package assigns a numerical score to each return. The higher the DIF score, the more likely that the return will be selected for audit since it indicates the higher potential for significant change on tax audit.

To establish standards for numerical values, the IRS conducts a statistical survey of taxpayer compliance known as the taxpayer's compliance measurement program (TCMP). Its purpose is to determine the percentage of voluntary compliance with tax requirements. Under TCMP, the IRS randomly selects a sample of taxpayers and audits every line item on these returns. While the chances of random selection by a taxpayer are very minimal, less than 1 out of 2000, each taxpayer has equal opportunity to be selected.

By use of the random selection program, the IRS arrives at DIF formulas by assigning weights to line items which correlate to their relative ability to indicate audit potential. If, under the TCMP, it is determined that taxpayers are more likely to understate their tax liability on certain items than others, different weights will be assigned to the individual line items which correspond with the relative history of voluntary taxpayer compliance.

The IRS selects a certain number of returns—approximately 250,000— for reasons other than DIF scores. These are considered special targeted groups and include returns indicating illegal activity, tax protesters, illegal refund schemes, excessive number of dependents claimed, missing schedules, and tax preparer if that person or agency is considered a problem.

At certain periods of time, the IRS determines that particular types of programs should be targeted. For example, one year the IRS targeted for audit those returns claiming a one-time exclusion of a $25,000 gain on the sale of personal residential property with previous tax returns under the taxpayer's identifying number to determine if other subsequent exclusions had been indicated.

Other items that the IRS has used to select returns for audit include the document matching program, i.e., returns that do not match with information documents filed by other institutions such as banks or other businesses and the delinquency control programs. This latter program is aimed at that group of taxpayers that the IRS has identified as problem taxpayers. In addition, a limited number of tax returns are selected for audit because of information reports received by the IRS. Included in this group are the audits triggered by informants and "angry" ex-spouse returns whereby a separated or divorced spouse provides convincing details of a taxpayer's failure to comply with the voluntary tax program.

Taxpayer's Compliance Measurement Program

As noted earlier, there are certain randomly selected tax returns audited to determine the level of voluntary compliance with the tax program. Approximately 50,000 taxpayers are involved in the Form 1040 compliance program survey. Once selected for audit by the National Computer Center, these returns may not be rejected by a district office without special permission. This restriction is based on the concept that for a survey to be valid and reliable it must utilize a certain sample size that has been randomly selected.

During a compliance program audit, the auditor is required to verify every single item on the form. For example, taxpayers must prove the ages and identity of their dependents and must substantiate all deductions with adequate records; in some cases, they have been required to prove marital status. Any adjustments on the return are noted and reported to the National Computer Center.

After completion of the compliance measurement program results, the IRS then, using statistics, provides an estimate of the frequency and amount of deviation from verified values of every line item reported by taxpayers. For example, the IRS may conclude that there is a 15 percent chance that a casualty loss deduction is overstated by $100 or a 30 percent chance that a $100 deduction for charitable contributions is overstated by at least 10 percent. Using this information and other indicators of audit potential, the IRS then develops the DIF scoring package. If the compliance measurement program indicates that charitable contributions is a problem area, then it will assign a higher DIF score to that line item than nonproblematic line items. Accordingly, taxpayers with large deductions on a problem line will receive a higher DIF score than a taxpayer with a similar deduction for a nonproblematic line item.

There is indication that future directions of the IRS regarding problem areas may shift the audit selection system toward detecting unreported income rather than overstatement of deductions.

Nonaudit Triggers

According to information published by the IRS, poor mathematics on a return is not an audit trigger. This is based on the concept that of the 9 percent of returns that are annually corrected for math, the correction takes place before the audit screening and before the information is entered into the computer banks.

The IRS also states that, contrary to the popular belief, use of the preprinted labels contained on the blank returns mailed each year to taxpayers does not increase your chances of being selected for audit. The rumor has persisted that the labels contain coded information that will be compared with the present return and thus may trigger an audit. The IRS contends that the information on the labels is used only to process the return and is not considered in the audit selection process.

Withholding Noncompliance Study

The IRS is conducting a study to determine the level of withholding noncompliance by employers. The data obtained from the study will be examined for possible modifications in the withholding system to ensure greater compliance with regulations.

Plans are to examine and audit tax returns of 3500 employers to determine if questionable Forms W-4 ("Employee Withholding Allowance Certificate") are being reported to the IRS. In addition, selected employees will be examined regarding the correctness of the W-4s filed by them. Also, a study will be made of persons incorrectly classified as independent contractors. A search will also be made to determine the degree of misclassified workers and nonfilers.

Elements of a Tax Audit

The Internal Revenue Service defines an *audit* as "an impartial review of the taxpayer's return to determine its completeness and accuracy." Most of us, however, when we receive notice that our return has been selected for audit, immediately feel a sense of panic. We recall such IRS horror stories as the one where the IRS agent threatened to seize the iron lung of a taxpayer stricken with polio unless taxes claimed to be due were immediately forthcoming. The attitude is often "Why me?"

A common complaint by taxpayers is, Why did the IRS wait so long to question my return? Part of the delay is caused by the procedures discussed earlier in this chapter regarding computer screening. The audit groups usually receive the returns selected for audit approximately 6 months after their due date. For example, returns due to be filed in

April will normally go to the audit group the following October or No-vember. By law, any additional tax assessed may be assessed only within 3 years after the date the return was filed or was required to be filed, whichever is later. The 3-year statute of limitation, however, can be waived by a taxpayer. For practical purposes, if you are not notified that your return has been selected for an audit within 18 months after it is filed, the chances are good that it has not been selected for audit.

Audit Letter.   Taxpayers whose returns are selected for audit will re-ceive an audit letter. Typically, the audit letter will ask you to do one of three things: (1) mail in your receipts for verification of certain items; (2) set up an appointment with the local IRS examination office; or (3) re-quest that you appear at an examination audit at the time indicated on the notice. The type of letter received by the taxpayer depends upon the type of audit and the needs or the preferences of the audit group.

The notification letter should also inform you which items on your return have been selected for audit. This may consist of a separate page which lists the most common deductions with checkmarks made in those boxes next to the issues selected on your return. If your return is a nonbusiness return (does not contain a Schedule C), often you will receive attached to the letter blue information notices.

The notices tell you what records are needed to verify the deductions or line items being audited. However, you should bear in mind that they represent the ideal types of records. Other items of evidence or other types of record keeping may be sufficient depending upon the facts and your situation. If the audit is questioning the claimed exemp-tions, normally a questionnaire about your dependents or exemptions will be included in the letter. You will be requested to complete the questionnaire and return it or bring it at the time of your appointment.

If you have filed a business return, you may receive an appointment letter that lists the records you need to produce. It is not uncommon for business owners to be required to bring in all journals and ledgers for the business. In addition, often owners are required to bring in bank statements for all savings and checking accounts to verify the business income.

If you have any questions about what records to bring, if the appoint-ment time is not convenient, or if you need additional time to gather your records, you should call the telephone number listed and request either assistance or rescheduling of your appointment. Bear in mind that the clerk who answers the phone and provides any assistance probably will not be an auditor assigned to your case. Normally, audi-tors are not assigned to a case until you appear for your appointment;

therefore, the clerk can answer only simple questions regarding record-keeping requirements. The taxpayer, also, should not rely upon the clerk for tax law advice.

Normally, a taxpayer has a right to change the appointment one time. However, don't expect to receive an appointment time other than during normal business hours. When requesting a rescheduling of your appointment, if possible, provide the IRS with as much notice as possible. Some offices will consider appointments confirmed if they do not hear from you at least 7 days before the appointment.

In some cases, audits are conducted by mail. If this is appropriate in your case, then you should include in any correspondence with the IRS examination office a copy of the appointment letter. If you are mailing your records to the IRS examination office, they should be arranged in a logical sequence so that the auditor may be able to examine them quickly and ascertain the validity of your deduction. Simply mailing the IRS a shoebox full of receipts not arranged in any logical order is an open invitation for a more in-depth audit. Normally, time taken to arrange your receipts and records in a logical order will be cost-effective for you in the long run.

If the time selected for your audit is inconvenient or if it is at an inappropriate time of the year, you may request an extension of time. The IRS in the past has been reasonable on those matters, providing you can establish a logical reason for the delay. Substantial delays, however, will come under closer scrutiny.

Repetitive Audits.   If taxpayers have been audited for the same classified issues in either of the 2 preceding tax years, and the audits assessed no change in tax liability, then those taxpayers are exempt from being audited on those issues. If this occurs in your case, notify the examination office as soon as possible; present any proof that you may have which establishes the fact of the previous audit and that there has been no change in tax liability. If, however, during the previous audit year, either your tax liability was changed or you received a letter stating that your return was accepted as filed, then you may be subject to reaudit. In fact, the odds are fairly high that if you are audited 1 year and there is some significant change in tax liability, you will be placed on the problem taxpayer list and be subject to more frequent future audits. The "accepted as filed" letter for a previous tax year indicates that your file was previously screened for audit but the audit for some reason was not completed. For repetitive audit purposes, you will need to establish that a "no-change" letter was issued. The no-change letter means that your return was audited and no significant change in tax liability resulted.

Nonreceipt of Notification Letters.   A taxpayer cannot be assessed additional taxes without prior notice. Therefore, an appointment letter that is returned is not considered sufficient notification for audit purposes. In most cases, when the letter is returned with no forwarding address, a postal tracer and a check with last known employer is made for a more current address. In some cases, the IRS checks for a more current address on newly filed tax returns. Undelivered mail that was merely refused or unwanted by the taxpayer is considered notice to the taxpayer. If an audit notice is forwarded and not returned, then the IRS may assume that you have received notification.

Transfer to a Different Examination Office.   If you have moved since the return was filed, or if another IRS agent would be more appropriate for you, then you may request that your file be transferred to the other IRS examination office. Normally, the IRS has been cooperative in transferring for valid reasons. Their policy, however, is that the convenience of the government is the principal consideration in the decision as to where the examination will be conducted. If your file is transferred to a new examination office, the IRS will either send you a new appointment letter or notify you that no further action will be taken on your return.

Power of Attorney.   If you wish to have someone represent you at the IRS examination procedures, then you must give that individual a written authorization to represent you and to receive private confidential information regarding you from the IRS. This is accomplished by use of a power of attorney.

The IRS has special forms for this purpose. Use of a power of attorney bought through a commercial bookstore normally will not be adequate unless it is specifically tailored to meet the requirements under the IRS regulations and statutes regarding the necessity to keep taxpayer personal and financial data confidential.

Any person who represents you must have a valid power of attorney. This rule applies even to attorneys and members of your own family. While there are no reported test cases on what constitutes a valid power of attorney, the standard IRS practice is to rely only on those that contain all the criteria set forth in IRS Forms 2848 and 2848D. In addition, it is usually much easier to complete the prescribed forms than to attempt to draft your own.

Significant Potential Change in Tax Liability

In determining whether a return has a high potential for significant tax change on audit, there are several factors that the IRS considers. The factors are:

1. Comparative size of the item with regard to other items on the return. For example, a questionable expense item of $5000 would be significant in a tax return where total expenses are under $50,000, but probably insignificant if total expenses were in excess of $500,000.

2. The absolute size of the item even though it may represent only a small percentage of the taxable income.

3. The type of item. For example, a large deduction for professional books claimed on a Schedule C of a truckdriver may be questionable.

4. The manner in which the item is reported. For example, itemized deductions claimed as business expenses may cause a return to be selected for audit.

5. Evidence of fraudulent intent or intent to mislead. Included in this category would be missing and/or incomplete schedules.

6. The relationship of one item to other items on the returns. For example, deductions for real estate taxes claimed with no deduction for mortgage interest expense, or failure to report dividends when a Schedule D indicates significant sales of stock.

Reducing Tax Audit Liability

The information in this chapter is intended not as a method or blueprint for avoiding tax audits. Each of us is subject to tax audits. It is presented in order that an individual may to some degree assess potential for a tax audit. A word of caution is that the IRS has in the past, without notice, changed their procedures for selecting returns to be audited.

Some steps that will reduce your chances of an audit include the following:

1. Report all income. Any unexplained income noted in a match of withholding and information returns from employers, banks, saving and loans institutions, etc., with information contained on your return can trigger an audit.

2. Examine copies of any information returns filed with the IRS by your bank or savings and loan institution to verify their accuracy.

3. Explain unusual items in your return. This action may not prevent your return from being selected by the DIF process since the explanation will not be coded. After the DIF selects potential returns to audit, however, the selected returns are then manually examined for final audit selection and your explanations will be considered at this time.

4. Double-check the return and all the schedules to ensure that they are properly completed. Missing schedules or incomplete schedules are considered as audit triggers during the manual selection process.

Audit Procedures

Preparation for Audit

After receiving notification of an audit, the taxpayer should prepare for the audit by assembling all records and working papers that in any way relate to the items being examined. If some records are not available or cannot be located, attempt to obtain backup records from other places. For example, if interest paid is being challenged, ask for backup records from the businesses to which you paid the interest in question.

The records should be indexed in a manner that will permit instant referral to the correct one. This is not the time to appear with a shoebox full of receipts. If you are asked to submit receipts by mail, make copies and submit the copies. Do not mail your original receipts. As noted earlier, any time you mail anything to the IRS, include a copy of the letter requesting the items to enable the IRS to identify the incoming material.

One decision that you, as taxpayer, must make is whether or not to be represented by a professional, i.e., an attorney, CPA, or enrollee. An enrollee is a person who is not an attorney or a CPA but has passed the required examination to represent taxpayers before the IRS.

If your audit is in person, at either your home or place of business, ask for the auditor's identification before talking to him or her. There are two classes of the IRS field auditors—special agents and revenue agents. Normal audits are conducted by revenue agents. Special agents normally audit those returns involving tax fraud. Ascertain which type of agent you are confronting by an examination of their identification. Agents have an obligation to identify themselves and normally will do so even without being asked. If they flash their badges, ask for a closer examination of it.

If the agent is a special agent and you are not represented by an attorney, it is highly recommended that you request a halt in the proceedings until you have time to obtain legal representation.

Field Audit

In any discussions with an examiner, be polite and act in a professional manner. Answer the questions directly, but do not volunteer any additional information. Additional information could open the examination to additional items. In most cases, full cooperation will produce the best results.

After the audit is complete, the examiner will present the taxpayer with a proposal. If there is no doubt that the tax is due, it may be best to agree to it to quickly end the audit. If there is reasonable doubt, consider the proposal by the agent as one that is probably most favorable to the IRS.

When confronted with an unfavorable proposal, first, attempt by persuasion to change the agent's opinion. This may be an appropriate place to bargain with the agent by compromising on disputed items. Settling with the agent avoids the time and energy of further proceedings and may avoid raising other issues on the return. In addition, settlement at this stage usually permits a claim to be established with less evidence than at other stages of the examination.

At the end of the examination, the agent prepares a report of examination. The report contains proposed adjustments, reasons for the adjustments, and additional assessments, if any. The taxpayer will then be asked to sign the waiver agreeing to the report. Next, the report with taxpayer's waiver (if the taxpayer signs one) is forwarded to an IRS approving officer. If the taxpayer signs the waiver, then normally approval of the report is routine.

Generally, the taxpayer should sign the waiver if the tax is clearly owed or an agreeable compromise is reached with the agent. Otherwise, the taxpayer should follow the appellate procedures.

IRS Appeals Office

When there is a disagreement between the agent and the taxpayer, the next step is an administrative appeal with the IRS appeals office. The appeals office is not a part of the district office. The district directors have no authority over the appeals office. The office is directly responsible to the regional commissioners.

The appeals office has broad authority to settle cases. The office can also increase the extent of the audit and raise new issues if requested by the district office. If a settlement is reached, it is considered a final settlement.

In some cases, it is to a taxpayer's advantage to waive the administrative appeal, pay the amount requested, and then submit a request for refund. If the request for refund is denied, then the taxpayer can sue in Federal District Court or the U.S. Court of Claims. Under this method, it is not possible for the IRS to assert new claims or to increase the deficiency.

If settlement is reached with the appeals office, that settlement is final and the taxpayer is precluded from suing in court for a refund or reassessment of the deficiency. If, however, no settlement is reached with the Appeals Office, then the taxpayer can pay the amount claimed and sue in either Federal District Court or the U.S. Court of Claims for a refund. An alternative procedure is to file a timely petition with the U.S. tax court.

Res Judicata

A taxpayer will not be allowed to present a cause of action against the IRS if the same question or issue has been previously decided adversely to the same taxpayer under the doctrine of *res judicata* (stands decided). For this doctrine to apply, it must be for the same issues, i.e., the same tax return and the same taxpayer.

In cases involving the same issues over different tax years, a taxpayer would be precluded from relitigating the issues previously litigated on the basis of a somewhat similar doctrine called *collateral estoppel*. The collateral estoppel doctrine applies only if the taxpayers are the same. For example, it would not apply where separate returns are filed one year by a married couple and the next year joint returns are filed. However, a decision which binds a taxpayer would also bind his or her estate or the beneficiary of that estate.

IRS determinations are not *res judicata* nor are they subject to the collateral estoppel limitation since IRS determinations are not court decisions. Accordingly, if the IRS makes a determination one year that a certain tax deduction is not permissible, a taxpayer would not be estopped from presenting the same issue the next year. The taxpayer may, however, be inviting a subsequent audit. In addition, state court decisions on federal tax matters are also not normally binding on either the taxpayer or the federal government in tax court or other federal courts.

When to Go to Court

In considering whether or not to go to court, the following factors should be considered:

1. Time, effort, and expense involved.

2. Chances of a favorable decision, including the fact that the IRS has a history of appealing adverse decisions.

3. Consequences of a favorable decision; a favorable decision this year may save a taxpayer taxes not only in the year in question but for future years for which the same issue will arise.

The Courts

U.S. Tax Courts

The tax court is a court of record established by the legislative powers granted by Congress pursuant to Article I of the Constitution. It has nationwide jurisdiction and is available to all taxpayers. The jurisdiction of the tax court extends to controversies over income, gift, and state taxes only. It is the only court available to a taxpayer without the taxpayer first paying the assessment.

About 90 percent of cases filed in tax court are settled out of court. As of 1986, there were 70,000 cases pending. During fiscal year 1986, out of approximately 1400 cases, only 54 taxpayers won outright victories in the tax court trials compared with 813 victories for the IRS. In the remaining cases, the taxpayers got partial relief.

It appears that taxpayers come out best when arguing over facts rather than challenging a disputed law. The tax court has shown a history of being more lenient involving factual situations than when the legality of a tax regulation is being questioned.

Approximately 55 percent of all taxpayers who sue in tax court are not represented by an attorney. As one noted New York lawyer stated, "If you can fight your own ticket in traffic court, there's no need to hire an attorney to fight a factual situation in tax court." The one thing that taxpayers should be aware of is that cases taken to tax court drag on for years and may be very exhausting for the taxpayer.

The tax court does have the authority to slap penalties on taxpayers who are involved in frivolous law suits. For example, in fiscal year 1986, the tax court fined 543 claimants with penalties averaging $3600. The maximum penalty in those cases was $5000.

Presently, there are 19 judges on the tax court, appointed by the President, by and with the advice and consent of the Senate. The terms of appointment for each judge is 15 years. A judge must retire at the age of 70. Most hearings before the tax court are held before a single regular tax court judge. Sometimes tax commissioners' cases are delegated to a tax commissioner. While the principal office of the tax court is in the

District of Columbia, the tax court regularly sits in some 50-odd cities scattered throughout the United States. Proceedings, pleadings, and other papers normally must be filed with the tax court in Washington, D.C. However, a judge at a hearing sometimes will permit papers to be filed at the location of the hearing.

As noted, the tax court is a court of limited jurisdiction. It has no jurisdiction to determine the propriety of any IRS motives or the constitutionality of an IRS statute. Its basic function is to serve as a court to litigate an assessment of deficiency claimed by the IRS.

To bring a case before the tax court, a taxpayer needs to file a petition within 90 days after receiving a deficiency notification from the IRS.

The tax court case will be limited only to the tax years covered by the IRS deficiency notice or reasonably included in the notice. Normally the tax court will not consider issues raised for the first time at trial by either the IRS or the taxpayer.

The tax court has a small claims division that handles tax deficiency case notices that do not exceed $10,000. In the small claims procedure, the decisions of the tax court are based on a brief summary opinion instead of formal findings of fact. Taxpayers who elect the small claims procedure have no right of appeal. Taxpayers electing the normal tax court procedures may appeal to the federal Circuit Court of Appeals.

Litigation in Federal District Court

To litigate the issue in federal District Court, the taxpayer must pay the assessment of taxes claimed by the IRS, then submit a request for refund. When the refund claim is denied, the denial may be litigated in the federal District Court. One of the advances of litigating an issue in federal District Court is that for questions involving facts, the taxpayer has a right to a jury trial. One of the disadvantages of litigating in federal District Court is the fact that the taxpayer must establish not only that the IRS erroneously denied the request for refund but also the amount of refund due. In this regard, the IRS may open records for other tax years to offset any claim for refund.

U.S. Court of Claims

As with the U.S. District Court, a taxpayer may litigate a case in the U.S. Court of Claims only on the basis that he or she has overpaid taxes, i.e., a refund suit. The U.S. Court of Claims sits in Washington, D.C. It consists of a chief judge and 15 associate judges appointed by the President by and with the advice and consent of the Senate. The tenure of office for a U.S. Court of Claims judge is 15 years. As with the tax court, a jury trial is not available in the U.S. Court of Claims. A taxpayer may appeal the decision of the U.S. Court of Claims to the federal Circuit Court of Appeals.

In determining which court to file your case in, the following factors should be considered:

1. The ability of the taxpayer to pay the tax assessment. The only way a taxpayer may bring a suit in federal District Court or U.S. Court of Claims is via the refund route.

2. Interest expense. By immediately paying the tax and filing for a refund, the taxpayer stops the interest expense on the deficiency.

3. The right to a jury trial. The right to a jury trial is available only in District Court, and only on disputed facts.

4. The allocation of the burden of proof. In general, this is less in tax court than in federal District Court or the U.S. Court of Appeals. In tax court, the taxpayer must establish only that the IRS's deficiency is erroneous, whereas in U.S. District Court, the taxpayer must establish first that the taxes were overpaid and second the amount of overpayment.

5. Speed of trial. The taxpayer will get the quickest trial in the U.S. Court of Claims and the next fastest in the tax court; whereas, in U.S. District Court, it may take the taxpayer 3 years before the case is eventually heard.

Attorney's Fees

Pursuant to federal taxation statutes, attorney's fees and court costs may be recovered by a successful taxpayer if the government's actions were not reasonably justified. In some cases where the court finds that the taxpayer's litigation was not in good faith, the court may award attorney's fees and court costs to the government. Under the Tax Reform Act, the maximum attorney's fees payable are $25,000. (See the discussion in Chapter 12 regarding the Equal Access to Justice Act.)

Appeals

For cases tried in the federal District Court or the U.S. Court of Claims, as noted, the taxpayer has a right to appeal to the Circuit Court of Appeals, and theoretically from the Circuit Court of Appeals to the U.S.

Supreme Court. However, the chances of a case being appealed to the U.S. Supreme Court are very slim.

Court Settlement

In all three courts discussed, the parties may settle during the court proceedings and, upon settlement, have the case decided pursuant to either a stipulation of the parties or an agreed-to judgment. In the case of these decisions, all parties will normally be bound by the stipulations since they were voluntarily entered into.

14
Significant
Court Decisions

In this chapter, court decisions and IRS rulings of interest to the business community are discussed. These cases should provide the reader with not only an insight into the philosophy of tax law, but also guidance regarding matters contained in the cases.

Evaluation of Charitable Gifts

In the tax court case, *Commissioner v. Sammons,* the taxpayer had purchased a sacred Native American pipe. In the 1930s, the pipe has been transferred without the traditional pipe-passing ceremony. The person who received the pipe shortly thereafter broke his leg and died from blood poisoning. His widow sold the pipe without the traditional ceremony to an individual who died less than 1 month later.

The Museum of Native American Cultures heard about the pipe in 1977 and attempted to obtain it for their collection. Mr. Sammons had agents buy it for $140,000. Prior to donating the pipe to the museum, he had it appraised at a value of $548,380. When the pipe was donated in 1979, Mr. Sammons deducted its appraised value for the years 1977 through 1979. The IRS that year questioned about 70 of the donations to that museum. His donation was one of those questioned.

The tax court held that the appraisal was inflated and that reliance on an inflated appraisal is negligence. Accordingly, the deduction in excess of $140,000 was disallowed and he was assessed a negligence penalty plus interest.

Casualty Deduction

Mr. and Mrs. Crowell purchased stock in the Equity Funding Corporation. When the stock went bad, they deducted the $55,942 paid for the stock as a casualty loss due to a theft. There were substantial questions regarding criminal activity on the part of the officers of the company during the period of time when the stock was sold to the Crowells. The Crowells, however, had purchased the stock on the "open" market, not from the company.

The tax court denied the deduction on the theory that the taxpayers could not prove that the crooks meant to defraud them specifically.

Tax-Free Award

Mr. Bent, a schoolteacher, lost his job because of his critical statements in public about the school board and certain key administrators in the school system. He sued the school system. A judge denied his claims for job reinstatement but awarded him damages for violation of his constitutional rights. The case was then settled for $24,000.

The taxpayer then deducted about $8000 for legal fees on his tax return, but did not report the $24,000 as income. The IRS denied the deduction and alleged a tax deficiency for the tax due on the $24,000. The IRS contended that the settlement was for lost wages and therefore was taxable. The taxpayer contended that the settlement was for personal injury, a violation of his constitutional right to freedom of speech, and thus was not taxable.

The tax court agreed with the taxpayer that the award was for personal injury and was therefore not taxable. The court also stated, however, that he could not deduct the legal fees since they were incurred to gain exempt income.

State Intercept Program

In one U.S. Supreme Court decision, *Sorenson v. Secretary of the Treasury* (54 U.S.L.W. 4391), the court held that a state could "intercept" money owed to the taxpayer by the IRS from a refundable earned income credit for past due child support. Mr. Sorenson fell behind in child support payments after becoming disabled. He and his second wife had a joint income of less than $10,000 for the tax year. Thus, they were eligible for earned income credit. The court held that the state could intercept the money and apply it to back due child support.

Unrelated Income Problem

In *United States v. American Bar Association,* the U.S. Supreme Court held that dividends earned by the bar's endowment group insurance program was taxable as unrelated income by a tax-exempt organization. In this case, the bar association used its insurance plan as a method to raise funds for the association, a tax-exempt organization. Members covered by the insurance allowed the "policy dividends" to be paid to the association.

The association claimed that the policy dividends were in fact charitable gifts from members and not taxable income. The high court disagreed and held that it was taxable income to the bar.

Magazine Advertising

A nonprofit organization, the American College of Physicians, may not avoid paying taxes on income from advertising in its journal by claiming that the purpose of the advertisements is education. The U.S. Supreme Court, in noting that 45 of the largest magazines in the United States are published by nonprofit, tax-exempt organizations, held that any income from advertising in a journal or magazine is taxable income.

Sufficiency of Proof

In a recent tax court decision, the taxpayer contended that the fair market value of the checks that he had received in payment for the sales of some gold coins were less than their face value. The taxpayer introduced no evidence of their face value or evidence that the checks had returned unpaid. The court held that the taxpayer had the burden to establish that the checks had a fair market value of less than their face value, and since he had not met that burden, the deficiency assessed by the IRS was sustained.

Reconstruction of Income

In a question regarding the taxpayer's gross income (a business), the tax court upheld the IRS's determination of the taxpayer's gross income based on total bank deposits made during the tax year. The court stated that the taxpayer, not the IRS, is required to establish that bank deposits are from other than taxable income.

Entertainment Expenses

Recently, in denying the deduction for entertainment expenses, the tax court held that the burden of proof was on the taxpayer to establish that the expenses qualified for the deduction and also to substantiate the amount, time, place, and business purpose of each expenditure. The taxpayer's generalized and uncorroborated testimony was insufficient to satisfy strict substantiation requirements.

Hobby Losses

One taxpayer was denied deduction expenses incurred through horse breeding and showing activities when the tax court held that he was not engaged in the business for profit. Factors that the court considered were as follows:

1. The activity was not conducted in a businesslike manner.
2. The taxpayer did not consult with experts regarding the business but relied instead on his limited knowledge and background.
3. The activity had lost money for the past 6 years.
4. The profit potential of the activity was never investigated.

Tax Protester

The Ninth U.S. Court of Appeals recently ruled that a California man could not use the federal Privacy Act to remove the designation of tax protester from his IRS records. The IRS had labeled him as a tax protester. The IRS defines a *protester* as one who refuses to pay taxes on constitutional grounds that the courts have held to be without merit, as well as schemes involving family trusts, alleged churches, and sham transactions designed to illegally reduce an individual's tax liability.

The IRS audit manual provides that once a person is labeled as a tax protester, his or her returns are automatically screened to determine if he or she is continuing to rely on illegal schemes to avoid taxes.

In denying the request to remove the protester tag, the court stated that the records in question related only to the determination of tax liability, not to how the taxpayer had exercised his First Amendment rights. The records, according to the court, are internally generated reports relating to the filing of facially illegal returns.

Failure to Report Cash

The Second Circuit Court of Appeals upheld the conviction of an employee for conspiracy and for causing his employer to fail to file required currency transaction reports. The court found that, although the employee had no duty to report the currency transactions, by structuring the customer's deposits so that no single deposit involved more than the required reporting amount of $10,000, the employee willfully caused his employer to fail to report in violation of the law. Accordingly, the finding of guilty with respect to the employee was upheld on appeal.

Casualty Loss

The Eleventh Circuit Court of Appeals ruled that a taxpayer may take a casualty loss deduction for the decline in fair market value of their property as the result of a flood that changed the character of the neighborhood. In this case, the taxpayers owned a home on a cul de sac in Mobile, Alabama. Although floodwaters damaged the home, they claimed additional damages for the decline in value since the city decided to eliminate, for safety reasons, seven of the homes on the street and required that the vacant lots be maintained as permanent open spaces. The taxpayers introduced evidence that the action diminished the attractiveness of their home and that the city has reduced the tax basis of the home after the flood. The court noted that loss in fair market value due to a flood was a casualty loss deductible under the tax regulations.

Failure of Employer to File Return
on Pension Plan

The Seventh Circuit Court of Appeals upheld the penalty assessment of an employer for failure to file the required Form 5500-C, "Annual Return Report of Employee Benefit Plan." The employer paid a penalty and appealed the assessment. The employer had employed an attorney to file the necessary form. The court held that that fact did not constitute a reasonable cause for failure to file the return.

De Facto Tax Preparer

The tax court held that a person does not have to be in the business of preparing tax returns to be liable for penalties. In one case, a used car dealer offered to fill out and review income tax returns for car buyers with any refund going to pay the down payment on the car. The dealer placed his address on the return so that the refund check would be mailed to his address. Then acting on a power of attorney, the dealer would endorse and cash the checks.

IRS regulations define a *preparer* as a person who prepares or employs others to prepare any return or refund claim for compensation. The court held that the dealer, in promoting the sale of cars, was in fact being paid for his preparation and thus was liable for incorrect returns. In addition, the court noted that the assignment by customers of their refund checks before the returns are processed by the IRS is invalid and that the IRS is not required to mail the checks to the preparer.

15
What the IRS Knows about You

Introduction

In this chapter, we will examine how the IRS obtains information from you and about you regarding your tax situation. In addition to the matching program discussed in Chapter 12, the most common methods by which the IRS obtains information about you include use of an administrative summons, informants, and statements obtained directly from you, the taxpayer. Also included in this chapter is a discussion of your legal rights, how to obtain information from the IRS, and IRS guidelines for gathering information.

Through the use of computers, the IRS can develop a complete profile of a taxpayer. If the IRS desires additional information, they may request it. Under the provisions of the Privacy Act of 1974 and the Paperwork Reduction Act of 1980, the IRS must tell you what major purposes they have in asking for information from you.

Your bank records and safe-deposit boxes may be open to IRS scrutiny without informing you. In addition, the IRS may gather information by using paid informers.

Administrative Summons

The IRS has considerable authority to issue administrative summonses. The scope of such a summons is limited only by the requirement that the IRS establish a legitimate purpose for the investigation. A summons is a judicial order.

For a summons to be effective, it must be valid and must be served on the taxpayer. For a summons to be valid, it must be issued for a proper purpose. In cases of doubt regarding the validity of the summons or its manner of service, consult an attorney.

In the context of IRS litigation, normally the summons is an order to produce accounting books, records, or other information regarding a taxpayer's business, income, or expenses. The IRS code provides that the summons issued by the IRS can require the taxpayer to produce for examination "books, papers, records, or other data." The statute also requires the taxpayer to appear for "testimony."

The IRS can issue a summons to examine records and books pertaining to the taxpayer that are in possession of a third person. For example, the IRS can summons the bank records from your bank that your bank retains on your account. *Note:* Any time the IRS summons records in possession of a third party, the IRS must notify the taxpayer of the summons.

Purpose of Summons

The Internal Revenue Code lists five purposes for which the IRS can issue an administrative summons:

1. To determine the correctness of any tax return

2. To prepare a constructive return for a taxpayer

3. To determine the tax liability of a taxpayer

4. To assist in the collection of any federal tax

5. To determine any transferee liability

What the IRS Cannot Do with a Summons

The purposes for which the IRS may issue a summons, listed above, are very broad. There are, however, limits to the summons power of the IRS. Those limitations include the inability to require taxpayers to prepare their own returns or to force taxpayers to give information that is protected by constitutional rights. Such rights include prohibition against self-incrimination and protection against unreasonable search and seizure. (See the section on legal rights later in this chapter.)

Who May Be Summoned

The tax law allows the IRS to summons any person liable for a tax, any person who has information regarding the tax liability of a taxpayer, any employee, officer, or tax entity whose tax liability is under investigation, or anyone who has information that will assist in the collection of taxes due. The reason for the summons must be to promote the assessment and collection of federal taxes. It cannot be a "fishing expedition."

Subject of a Summons

The summons must specify which records are being requested. In one case, a court held that an IRS summons that directed the taxpayer to produce all records, memos, and work papers pertaining to the taxpayer's tax returns for the past 3 years was too broad. One court, however, upheld an IRS summons that requested all the names of clients of a certain tax preparer.

There are several court rulings which found that business records that were not used in tax return preparation or to substantiate business income or expenses could not be the subject of a summons. In one case, the IRS attempted to obtain the proposed budget from a business. The court held that the proposed budget was a planning tool only and therefore could not be subject to the summons. A similar ruling was made when the IRS requested a copy of a business' memo which listed the possible liabilities of the company.

The IRS can examine property on which the taxpayer has claimed depreciation. One court limited this authority in a case where the property in question was needed to conduct the business. In this case, the taxpayer was in the business of renting videotapes. The IRS requested possession of the tapes for examination. The court concluded that turning over the tapes would destroy the taxpayer's business.

A summons by the IRS for a taxpayer to provide examples of his handwriting was upheld by the courts. In that case, there were some questions regarding the validity of certain records used by the taxpayer to substantiate business deductions. The court opined that the statutory duty to appear and give testimony included the duty to provide nontestimonial evidence.

In a case involving corporate books, the court allowed the IRS to examine all corporate stockholder meeting minutes for the year being audited. The taxpayer had contended that the IRS should be allowed to examine only those minutes that were the subject of a tax issue.

Enforcement of a Summons

The Internal Revenue Code provides that "If any person is summoned under the internal revenue laws to appear, to testify, or to produce books, papers, or other data, the district court of the United States in which such person resides or may be found shall have jurisdiction by appropriate process to compel such attendance, testimony, or production of books, papers or other data." Accordingly, when a taxpayer fails to produce books or records when ordered to do so by an IRS summons, the agent can then apply to the local district court for an order requiring the taxpayer to comply with the summons.

Failure to comply with the court order to produce such records may be punishable by contempt of court, either civil or criminal. If the taxpayer is charged with criminal contempt, he or she can be ordered to jail prior to trial. In civil contempt cases, normally the remedy ordered by the court is the attachment of property or the assessment of a tax liability against the taxpayer. Before a taxpayer can be punished for criminal contempt, the IRS must establish that the records are in existence and that the taxpayer has the ability to produce them.

In one case, the taxpayer was held in criminal contempt for failing to obey a court order to produce his tax records, despite the fact that he relied on the advice of his attorney not to produce the records. In some cases, self-incrimination is a justification for not producing records or books. (See the section on legal rights.)

In any proceeding before a district court where the IRS is seeking court enforcement of a summons, the taxpayer has an opportunity to present evidence as to why the summons should not be issued and to depose (ask questions of) the agent.

In most cases, before the taxpayer can be ordered to comply with a summons, the taxpayer must have been served with the summons. Service is normally accomplished by having a process server or other person handing the taxpayer a copy of the summons. In some cases, the service may be by posting the summons at the taxpayer's residence or place of business. If the taxpayer appears in court regarding the summons, this court appearance will normally constitute a waiver of the service requirement.

One of the leading U.S. Supreme Court decisions on the enforcement of a summons is *United States v. Rylander*, decided in 1983. In January 1979, the IRS issued a summons to Rylander ordering him to appear before an agent of the IRS in Sacramento, California, and to produce for examination, and testify with respect to, books and records of two corporations. Rylander was president of both corporations. When he failed to appear, the district court issued an order to show cause why the summons should not be enforced.

He was able to evade the service of the summons for several months. He finally appeared before the district court in January 1980, but failed to produce the records as ordered. At the contempt hearing, he stated that he did not possess the records and had not disposed of them to other persons. He refused to answer other questions regarding the records. He was held in contempt and appealed the decision.

The Supreme Court held that a proceeding to enforce an IRS summons is an adversary proceeding in which the defendant may contest the summons on any appropriate grounds, and that in a civil proceeding for contempt, a defendant may assert the defense of present inability to comply with the order.

The Court also held that the shield against self-incrimination could not be used by a defendant to shift the burden of proof to the government. Since the burden of proof was on the defendant to establish that he did not have the records in question and since the defendant refused to answer questions as to the location of the books, the conviction for contempt was upheld.

Third-Party Summons

As noted, the IRS may issue a summons to a third party to produce records, books, etc., pertaining to an individual taxpayer. There are special procedures that the IRS must use to enforce a third-party summons. For the most part, the special procedures are designed to allow the taxpayer to contest the production of third-party books, records, etc. *Note:* The special rules do not apply to testimony of a third-party or to collection action after a valid assessment.

The IRS is required to provide sufficient information in the summons to the third-party that will allow the third person to identify and locate the records in question. If the third person is a record-keeper, the taxpayer may bring court proceedings to cancel the summons.

In any third-party summons that identifies the taxpayer by name, the taxpayer is required to be notified within 3 days after the summons is served and at least 23 days before the date set for the production of the documents.

The taxpayer may within 20 days of receiving notice bring an action in court to cancel the summons. The taxpayer, if contesting the summons, must within the 20 days notify the third-party in writing not to comply with the summons. A certified copy of the notice not to comply must be mailed to the IRS agent who issued the summons. The IRS cannot examine the records within the 20-day period in order to give the taxpayer an opportunity to object to the summons.

The IRS can issue a "John Doe" summons if the IRS has knowledge that a particular transaction with tax consequences has been made and that the records are in possession of a third-party but does not know the name of the taxpayer. A John Doe summons, however, may not be issued without court approval in order to prevent IRS fishing expeditions.

Contesting the Summons

In the court proceedings to enforce the summons, the taxpayer will be provided an opportunity to establish why the summons should not be enforced. In one case, for example, the court refused to order the taxpayer to comply with the summons where there was evidence that the agent issuing the summons was being arbitrary. In several cases, the courts have refused to enforce summonses where IRS agents had refused to answer valid questions of the taxpayer.

Often when the taxpayer refuses to produce records, books, etc., as demanded by IRS, the IRS, rather than use court proceedings, merely assesses a tax liability against the taxpayer. This is based on the theory that the taxpayer is required to substantiate any information included on the taxpayer's tax return.

Grounds that taxpayers have used in the past to prevent the enforcement of a summons include the following:

1. The taxpayer established that the summons was issued merely to harass the taxpayer.
2. The IRS failed to establish a legitimate purpose for issuing the summons.
3. The information in question was already available to the IRS.
4. The IRS failed to follow required procedural steps in issuing the summons.
5. The records subject to the summons were privileged (see the discussion under legal rights of self-incrimination).
6. The agent refused to answer the taxpayer's relevant questions.
7. The IRS failed to produce records demanded by the taxpayer.
8. Production of documents is requested for unnecessary reexamination purposes.

Information from State Agencies

In most cases, the rules involving a third-party summons do not apply to state agencies. State agencies apparently can turn over information to the IRS without the necessity of a formal summons or notification of the taxpayer.

The leading case involving this issue was decided by the U.S. Court of Appeals for the Ninth Circuit in 1987. In that case, *United States v. Joseph,* the taxpayer was investigated by the Clark County, Nevada, district attorney's office for practicing dentistry in Las Vegas without a license. Joseph's case was concluded with a plea of guilty by Joseph. During the investigation, the assistant district attorney obtained possession of Joseph's records. It appeared that Joseph may have also failed to comply with the federal income tax requirements.

At the conclusion of the case, Joseph's records were turned over to the attorney for the Board of Dental Examiners. Next, the records were given to a special agent of the IRS. The taxpayer filed a notice to suppress the records and to prevent the IRS from using them. He claimed that his rights were violated and that the IRS had failed to comply with the notice requirements prior to obtaining the records.

The court stated that evidence obtained by one police agency may be made available to other agencies without a warrant, even for a use different from that for which it was originally taken, and that federal examination of evidence in the state's possession does not constitute an independent search requiring the execution of a search warrant.

The court next discussed the requirement that the IRS provide notice to the taxpayer of a request for records from a third-party. The court stated that for this requirement to be applicable, the third person must be a record-keeper for the taxpayer. Since the dental board and the district attorney's office were not third-party record-keepers according to this definition, the IRS was under no duty to issue a summons or to notify Joseph that it was seeking the records. (*Notes:* As discussed later in this chapter and in Chapter 10, there are additional restrictions on the IRS providing information to other agencies. The restrictions, however, do not apply to other agencies providing information to the IRS.)

Legal Rights

Self-Incrimination

Violations of the Internal Revenue Code can be criminal acts. Accordingly, in certain situations the taxpayer can claim the privilege against self-incrimination when ordered to produce certain records. For the taxpayer to assert the privilege against self-incrimination the following conditions must exist: (1) there must be a real risk of self-incrimination; (2) the privilege cannot be invoked for vague reasons; it must refer to specific books, records, questions, etc.; and (3) the books, records, etc., must be in the hands of the taxpayer at the time the summons is issued.

The records, books, etc., in most cases must be items prepared by the taxpayer. If the items are prepared by someone other than the taxpayer, then they can be the subject of a summons even if they are in possession of the taxpayer.

Records in possession of a third party normally are not protected by the self-incrimination privilege. In one case, records in possession of a corporation were required to be produced and were used against the only stockholder of the corporation. The court stated that the corporation and the stockholder are two separate parties, even though the stockholder owned all the shares of the corporation.

The IRS is restricted from using an administrative summons if the case has been referred to the Justice Department for prosecution. For purposes of this restriction, each tax year is considered as separate. Accordingly, if the case on one tax year has been referred for criminal prosecution, the IRS can still use the administrative summons for other tax years.

The Supreme Court requires that the taxpayer raise the defense of self-incrimination at or prior to the court proceedings to enforce an IRS summons. The taxpayer cannot wait until contempt proceedings to raise this issue for the first time.

One of the leading cases on requiring the taxpayer to produce records is the case of *United States v. Bellis*. This case, decided by the U.S. Supreme Court in 1974, involved a partner in a small law firm who was held in contempt for failure to comply with a subpoena requiring production of the partnership's financial records. Justice Thurgood Marshall held that Fifth Amendment privilege against compulsory self-incrimination is limited to its historic function of protecting only individuals from compulsory incrimination through his or her own testimony or personal records.

The Court held that a person could not rely on the privilege against self-incrimination to avoid producing records of a collective activity, even if the records might incriminate him personally. One of the key factors discussed in the case was the fact that the defendant (taxpayer) held the records in his representative capacity as a partner in the partnership. The Court stated that the rights against self-incrimination were personal rights, and that individuals, when acting as representatives of a collective group, cannot be said to be exercising their personal rights and duties.

Attorney-Client Privilege

Any communications between taxpayers and their attorneys are normally privileged and the government cannot force attorneys to testify regarding the communications. While attorneys cannot refuse to testify, they can refuse to answer specific questions because of this privilege. The attorney-client privilege is separate from the privilege against self-incrimination discussed previously.

Exceptions to this attorney-client privilege include situations where the attorney was retained in furtherance of continuing criminal activity or where the communication in question was overheard or disclosed to persons not included within the privilege. Secretaries or other individuals employed by an attorney are included under this privilege.

The privilege applies to both oral and written communications between the attorney and the taxpayer. It does not apply to taxpayer records being retained by the attorney. In most cases, the attorney can be required to turn over the taxpayer records.

The "work product" of an attorney made during a tax examination or litigation cannot be summoned by the IRS. Work products include memos, notes, conclusions, etc., regarding a taxpayer's case. The working papers of the person who prepared the taxpayer's taxes can, however, be summoned by the IRS.

In many situations, the attorney can be required to testify regarding the date and general nature of services performed for a taxpayer and as to fee received from a client.

Accountant-Taxpayer Privilege

The IRS does not recognize any privileges between an accountant and the taxpayer. Even those privileges available to accountants under state law are not available in IRS proceedings. If the accountant is an employee of the taxpayer, any records in possession of the accountant are considered as in possession of the taxpayer. Accordingly, the privilege against self-incrimination may be available.

Withdrawal of Consent

If the IRS' possession of records is the result of a voluntary turnover by a taxpayer and if the taxpayer subsequently withdraws consent, the IRS must promptly return the records. In many cases, the IRS may then issue a summons for the records.

Informants

In criminal cases, the U.S. Supreme Court has stated that the IRS is not required to provide the taxpayer with the name or names of any informants who have provided information to the IRS regarding a taxpayer's tax situation. There is one U.S. Court of Appeals case which held that in civil proceedings, like criminal proceedings, the IRS is not required to reveal the source of its information. Accordingly, in many cases, the taxpayer has no indication of the extent of knowledge in possession of the IRS auditors who are acting on tips from informants.

Tips from informants account for about 15 percent of all government fraud investigations. Many times the informants are ex-spouses, former lovers, or former employees. The problem in many cases, is that the informants provide information that the government would otherwise not have available. Accordingly, conducting an audit defense can be difficult in these cases.

Obtaining Tax Information

Records from the IRS

In some situations, the taxpayer may need to obtain records from the IRS or other governmental offices. The Internal Revenue Code provides that a taxpayer has the right to inspect his or her tax returns, including any amendments, attachments, etc. In addition, under the Freedom of Information Act, taxpayers may obtain many documents from the IRS, such as IRS policy manuals, audit manuals, etc. Much of the information used in research for this book was obtained from the IRS under this act.

Courts have required the IRS to provide the taxpayer with documents that indicate how the IRS arrived at certain positions with regard to the taxpayer's tax liability. In some cases, however, discovery has been refused as an exception to the Freedom of Information Act. An example of the latter involved an auditor's report. The court stated that it was prepared for litigation purposes and therefore not subject to discovery.

Nontax Situations

This section explains how others can get information from the IRS on individual taxpayers. Discussed are some of the situations in which others can obtain information on taxpayers from IRS files.

Criminal Investigations. A federal judge or magistrate may order that any tax return or return information in possession of the IRS be turned over to officers or employees of any federal agency that is conducting an investigation pursuant to nontax criminal proceedings. The Secretary of the Treasury may also release information within the possession of the IRS that indicates that persons are involved in nontax criminal activity. In addition, the secretary can release information where it appears that there is imminent danger of an individual's death, physical injury, or flight from prosecution.

The IRS will release information to the Social Security Administration to prevent the payment of social security benefits to illegal aliens. The IRS can, also, release information in order to assist in the locating of fugitives from justice. The IRS will not, as a matter of policy, release any information that will hamper or impair a criminal or civil fraud tax investigation. Nor will the IRS release information that will identify an informant.

Any federal or state agency that administers certain social security and food stamp programs may obtain information regarding unearned income of individual taxpayers.

Deceased Taxpayers. The IRS often relaxes the rules on the disclosure of information in the cases of deceased taxpayers. In one recent case, the IRS was forced to release information regarding the tax return of a deceased taxpayer. In this case, the requester of the information was the mother of an illegitimate child. She was trying to locate assets of the deceased taxpayer, who was the father of the child.

Unauthorized Disclosure. If a taxpayer's returns or any information from his or her return is disclosed either knowingly or negligently except as permitted by law, the taxpayer may sue both the IRS and the individual who released the information. Court actions brought regarding unauthorized disclosure must be commenced within 2 years of the taxpayer's discovering the disclosure.

Taxpayers may receive compensation for their damages for the unauthorized disclosure in the amount of their actual damages or $1000 for each disclosure, whichever is greater. If the disclosure was willful or the result of gross negligence, then actual damages plus an additional sum (punitive damages) may be awarded to punish the person disclosing the information.

In one case, a chief criminal investigator was held liable for the unauthorized disclosure of tax information when he indicated that the taxpayer was subject to a criminal tax investigation regarding "oil thefts." The indication that the taxpayer was involved was based on information from the taxpayer's Form 1040. In another case, the IRS mailed out information that the taxpayer was a promoter in an abusive tax shelter. In this case, the court held that the information on which the conclusion was based was taken from tax records of the taxpayer. Since the release was not made pursuant to a court order or other exception, the release by the IRS was held to be wrong.

IRS Information-Gathering Guidelines

The IRS has issued guidelines for the gathering of information regarding taxpayers by IRS personnel. The guidelines are set forth in the IRS Manual 4100-217, "Classification, Screening and Identification for Examination of Tax Returns, Claims and Information Items." The guidelines are set forth below:

1. All examination employees will be alert for indications of noncompliance with the tax laws. They will continue to seek facts and evidence necessary to resolve issues in assigned cases and projects; however, care must be taken to ensure that only directly tax related information is sought. Employees will not maintain any individual files or background information on taxpayers other than project files which they have been specifically authorized to maintain by the district director.

2. Tax-related information, other than potential fraud and informants' communications, received by examination employees will be forwarded with a Form 5346 to the chief, (code: PSP) for processing.

3. Information received indicating noncompliance by a large number of taxpayers should be forwarded through channels to the chief of the examination division, and as appropriate, to the district director, the assistant regional commissioner (ARC) (examination) or assistant commissioner (examination), for consideration and appropriate action.

Under the provisions of the Privacy Act of 1974 and the Paperwork Reduction Act of 1980, when the IRS requests information from a taxpayer, they must advise the taxpayer of these items:

1. The legal right to ask for the information.
2. The major purposes in asking for the information and how the information will be used.

3. What the penalties or results are if the information is not provided.

4. Whether a response is required to obtain a benefit, is voluntary, or is required by statutes.

In most cases, the IRS's legal authority to ask for information is contained in the Internal Revenue Code, Sections 6001 and 6011.

16

International
Tax Issues

This chapter covers key concepts in international tax issues. U.S. citizens are generally subject to tax on their income from foreign countries. Resident aliens are generally taxed on their worldwide income, and nonresident aliens are generally taxed on income from U.S. sources.

If you paid foreign or U.S. possession income taxes, you may be eligible to claim a tax credit against your U.S. income tax. Instead of taking a tax credit for foreign tax, you may elect to take a regular deduction for the tax.

Tax Liability of U.S. Citizens

Every person born or naturalized in the United States and subject to U.S. jurisdiction is a U.S. citizen. A person who has filed for citizenship but has not received the final order of a naturalization court is considered an alien.

As a general rule, all U.S. citizens and resident aliens are liable for U.S. income tax on their income even if the income is from non-U.S. sources. This rule applies to U.S. citizens even if they reside abroad.

There are certain additional deductions and tax credits available for individuals with income from non-U.S. sources to offset possible double taxation problems. Income tax treaties between the United States and other countries are designed to limit double taxation (U.S. and foreign) for certain types of income.

Resident Aliens

Aliens who are U.S. residents generally must compute their income taxes just like citizens. There are special rules that apply to "dual status" aliens who change their status during the calendar year. Certain aliens may elect to be taxed as U.S. residents. To qualify for the election to be taxed as a resident, the individual must meet the "substantial presence" test in the following calendar year. To qualify for the election, the taxpayer must (1) not be a U.S. resident on the year preceding the election year; (2) have been in the United States for at least 31 consecutive days in the election year; and (3) have been in the United States for at least 75 percent of the days during the period beginning with the first day of the U.S. presence and ending with the last day of the election year.

The election is made by attaching a statement to the taxpayer's income tax return for the tax year for which the election is to be in effect, the election year. If the individual has not satisfied the substantial presence test for the year following the election year as of the due date for the election year return, an extension of time to file may be requested. With the request for extension, the taxpayer must pay the amount of tax that he or she expects to owe for the election year computed as if the taxpayer were a nonresident alien for the year.

A resident alien is treated as a U.S. resident with respect to any calendar year if the individual meets one of three requirements: (1) the individual meets the "green card" test; (2) the individual meets the substantial presence test; or (3) the individual elects to be taxed as a U.S. resident.

The green card test requires that the individual have the status of having been lawfully accorded the privilege of residing permanently in the United States as an immigrant under the U.S. immigration law and that status has not been revoked or abandoned. These stipulations apply only to tax-related questions and cannot override provisions of U.S. treaties.

The substantial presence test requires that an individual maintain presence in the United States on at least 31 days during the calendar year, and that the number of days on which the individual was present during the current calendar year, when multiplied by an applicable multiplier, equals or exceeds 183 days.

First Year of Residency

There are special rules covering the first year of residency. For example, if an individual is a U.S. resident in any calendar year but was not a resident at any time during the preceding calendar year, the individual is treated as a resident for only the actual portion of the year he or she was a resident.

Last Year of Residency

An alien is not considered a resident for any part of the tax year if he or she had closer connections to a country other than the United States; he or she is not a resident at any time during the next calendar year; and he or she was not a resident during the last part of the tax year.

Foreign-Earned Income

There are foreign-earned income exclusions available for qualified U.S. citizens and resident aliens. If qualified, the individual may elect to exclude from gross income up to $70,000 of foreign-earned income; and if employee housing is not furnished by his or her employer, may exclude a portion of gross income based on foreign housing expenses. *Note:* These exclusions must be claimed separately.

To qualify for the exclusions, the taxpayer must have his or her "tax home" in a foreign country and must have been a bona fide resident of one or more foreign countries for an uninterrupted period that includes an entire tax year; or during any 12-month consecutive period was present in a foreign country at least 330 full days.

A *tax home* has the same meaning as an individual's home for travel expense deductions. *Foreign-earned income* is defined as earned income from foreign sources attributable to services performed by the individual during a "qualified" period. Foreign-earned income does not include salaries paid to an employee by the United States or a U.S. agency, amounts received as pensions or annuities, or amounts received from a nonexempt trust. *Note:* Amounts paid by the United States or U.S. agencies to nonemployees may be excludable.

To meet the bona fide resident test, the individual must establish that he or she has been a bona fide resident of one or more foreign countries for at least 1 entire tax year. Residence should indicate an intent to live in that place for a period of time. Under certain circumstances, the foreign presence requirement may be waived. In most cases, a waiver is granted only when the individual is required to leave the foreign country because of war or other hostile conditions.

Nonresident Aliens

Nonresident aliens must pay a 30 percent tax (unless a lower rate is established by a treaty) on investment income from U.S sources. There is also a 4 percent tax imposed on transportation income from U.S. sources. Former U.S. citizens who gave up their citizenship to avoid taxation are subject to special alternative graduated taxes on income from a U.S. source or income that is "effectively connected" to the United States.

A nonresident is considered engaged in a U.S. business if the individual is a member of a partnership that is engaged in U.S. business. In addition, a nonresident who is the beneficiary of a trust or estate that is engaged in U.S. business is also considered as engaged in U.S. business.

A nonresident who must file is required to file Form 1040NR. A joint return is not permitted where one spouse is a resident and the other a nonresident unless the nonresident elects to be treated as a resident. Nonresidents who are engaged in a business in the United States need a tax identifying number. If the nonresident is a limited partner in a partnership engaged in U.S. business, the nonresident may use the IRS tax number provided to the partnership. Nonresident aliens who are required to file must file by the fifteenth day of the sixth month after the close of the tax year (in most cases, June 15).

U.S. Government Employees Abroad

Government employees stationed in foreign countries are subject to U.S. income taxes if they are U.S. citizens or U.S. residents. Often, however, they receive tax-free allowances. For example, cost-of-living allowances received by civilian employees stationed outside the continental United States are generally tax free.

Residents of Puerto Rico, the Virgin Islands, Guam, American Samoa, and the Northern Mariana Islands are normally not required to pay U.S. income taxes on income from those locations. Individuals residing in those locations are normally subject to local taxes on their worldwide income.

International Trade

Domestic U.S. corporations who derive income from Puerto Rico or other U.S. possessions may qualify for a special tax credit. To qualify, the corporation for the 3-year period immediately preceding the close of the tax year must receive 80 percent or more of its gross income from sources within a U.S. possession, and must receive 75 percent or more of its gross income from the active conduct of a trade or business within the possession.

Foreign Sales Corporations

U.S. exporters can obtain tax advantages for exports by the use of a foreign sales corporation (FSC). FSCs have no corporate-level tax on their export income and are eligible for a 100 percent dividends-received deduction. To qualify for these tax advantages, the FSC must satisfy foreign presence and economic activity tests. To qualify as an FSC, the corporation must meet the six requirements listed below:

1. The FSC must be created under the laws of a jurisdiction outside U.S. customs territory.

2. The FSC must have no more than 25 shareholders at any one time.

3. The FSC must not have any preferred stock outstanding.

4. The FSC must have an office located in a foreign country that is certified for FSC purposes.

5. The board of directors must have at least one board member who is not a U.S. resident.

6. During the tax year, the FSC may not be a member of any group having a domestic international sales corporation (DISC).

An FSC may elect to be treated as a "small FSC." To be a small FSC, the FSC must not be a member at any time during the tax year of a controlled group which includes an FSC that has not made an election to be treated as a small FSC. Small FSCs are not required to meet the foreign management and foreign economic requirements.

Domestic International Sales Corporations

Domestic international sales corporations (DISCs) are tax-exempt domestic corporations a portion of whose profits are sheltered against U.S. income tax until the profits are withdrawn from it. A DISC is a "paper" corporation with its major expense being the keeping of detailed records of its profits, distributions, etc. The DISCs, except for the "interest charge" ones, have largely been replaced by FSCs. An interest charge DISC can defer interest on $10 million of qualified export receipts. A DISC is exempt form U.S. income taxes but is subject to the excise tax on tax-motivated foreign transfers.

Taxation of Foreign Corporations

Foreign corporations are subject to regular U.S. corporate tax rates on income received through the conduct of business in the United States. In addition, they are subject to a tax of 30 percent on their investment income from U.S. sources. Treaty obligations, however, may require a tax rate of lower than 30 percent. The foreign corporation may also be subject to a "branch profit" tax (defined below). For IRS purposes, a foreign corporation is one that is organized outside the United States or under the laws of a jurisdiction other than that of the United States, a state, or the District of Columbia.

A foreign corporation engaged in a U.S. trade or business through a branch office is liable for a branch profit tax in addition to other taxes. The tax is roughly 30 percent of the profits associated with the branch operations and income. Branch profit taxes do not apply to international organizations. In addition, corporations formed under the laws of U.S. territories are also not subject to branch profit taxes.

A foreign corporation may in some cases elect to be treated as a domestic corporation and pay the same taxes as a domestic corporation. To qualify for the election, the corporation must use a calendar year for U.S. tax purposes unless it merges its return with a parent corporation or files a consolidated return with another tax entity.

Corporations formed in American possessions will not be treated as foreign corporations if less than 25 percent of the stock is owned by foreign persons (directly or indirectly), and at least 65 percent of the gross income is U.S. income or income directly connected to the United States.

17

Taxpayer's Bill of Rights

This chapter contains a discussion of the Taxpayer's Bill of Rights, the legislation that provided certain rights to taxpayers and established a problems resolution office within the IRS. The chapter will also discuss how legislation can be used to assist taxpayers who are having problems with the IRS. Most of the information for this chapter is taken from IRS Publication 1 (revised in October 1990).

As a taxpayer, you have the right to be treated fairly, professionally, promptly, and courteously by IRS employees. One of the stated goals of the IRS is to protect your rights so that you will have the highest confidence in the integrity, efficiency, and fairness of our tax system. To ensure that you always receive such treatment, you should know about the many rights you have at each step of the tax process.

Information and Help in Preparing Returns

You have the right to information and help in complying with the tax laws. In addition to the basic instructions the IRS provides with the tax forms, the IRS must make available a great deal of other information.

Taxpayer Publications

The IRS publishes over 100 free taxpayer information publications on various subjects. One of these, Publication 910, "Guide to Free Tax Services," is a catalog of the free services and publications offered by the IRS. You can order all publications and any tax forms or instructions you need by calling the IRS toll-free at 1-800-TAX-FORM (829-3676).

Other Assistance

The IRS provides walk-in tax help at many IRS offices and recorded telephone information on many topics through their Tele-Tax system. The telephone numbers for Tele-Tax and the topics covered are listed in certain publications and tax form instructions. Many of their materials are available in braille (at regional libraries for the handicapped) and in Spanish. The IRS also provides help for the hearing-impaired via special telephone equipment.

The IRS has informational videotapes that you can borrow. In addition, you may want to attend their educational programs for specific groups of taxpayers, such as farmers and those with small businesses.

In cooperation with local volunteers, the IRS offers free help in preparing tax returns for low-income and elderly taxpayers through the volunteer income tax assistance (VITA) and tax counseling for the elderly (TCE) programs. You can get information on these programs by calling the toll-free telephone number for your area.

Copies of Tax Returns

If you need a copy of your tax return for an earlier year, you can get one by filling out Form 4506, "Request for Copy of Tax Form," and paying a small fee. However, you often only need certain information, such as the amount of your reported income, the number of your exemptions, and the tax shown on the return. You should be able to get this information free if you write or visit an IRS office or call the toll-free number for your area.

General Rights of Taxpayers

Privacy and Confidentiality

You have the right to have your personal and financial information kept confidential. People who prepare your return or represent you must keep your information confidential.

You also have the right to know why the IRS is asking you for information, exactly how they will use any information you give, and what might happen if you do not give the information.

Information Sharing.   Under the law, the IRS can share your tax information with state tax agencies and, under strict legal guidelines, with the Department of Justice and other federal agencies. The IRS can also share tax information with certain foreign governments under tax treaty provisions.

Courtesy and Consideration.   You are always entitled to courteous and considerate treatment from IRS employees. If you ever feel that you are not being treated with fairness, courtesy, and consideration by an IRS employee, you should tell the employee's supervisor.

Protection of Your Rights

IRS employees should explain and protect your rights as a taxpayer at all times. If you feel that this is not the case, you should discuss the problem with the employee's supervisor.

Complaints.   If for any reason you have a complaint about the IRS, you may write to the district director or service center director for your area. The IRS should give you the name and address if you call their toll-free phone number.

Representation and Recordings.   Throughout your dealings with IRS, you can represent yourself or, generally with proper written authorization, have someone represent you in your absence. During an interview, you can have someone accompany you.

If you want to consult an attorney, a certified public account, an enrolled agent, or any other person permitted to represent a taxpayer during an interview for examining a tax return or collecting tax, the IRS should stop and reschedule the interview. The IRS will not suspend the interview, however, if you are there because of an administrative summons.

You can generally make an audio recording of an interview with an IRS collection or examination officer. Your request to record the interview should be made in writing and should be received 10 days before the interview. You must bring your own recording equipment. The IRS also can record an interview. If they do so, they should notify you of their intent 10 days before the meeting and you can get a copy of the recording at your expense.

Payment of Only the Required Tax.   You have the right to plan your business and personal finances so that you will pay the least tax that is due under the law. You are liable only for the correct amount of tax.

The IRS's stated purpose is to apply the law consistently and fairly to all taxpayers.

If Your Return Is Questioned.   The IRS accepts most taxpayers' returns as filed. If the IRS inquires about your return or selects it for examination, this does not suggest that you are dishonest, according to IRS claims. Despite such claims, you should consider the inquiry as an investigation of your tax compliance status. The inquiry or examination may or may not result in your being required to pay more taxes. The IRS may close your case without change, or you may receive a refund (this is rare).

Examination and Inquiries by Mail.   The IRS handles many examinations and inquiries entirely by mail. They should send you a letter with either a request for more information or a reason why the IRS believes a change needs to be made to your return. If you give the IRS the requested information or provide an explanation, the IRS may or may not agree with you and should explain the reasons for any changes. You should not hesitate to write to them about anything you do not understand.

If you cannot resolve any questions through the mail, you can request a personal interview. You can appeal through the IRS and the courts. You will find instructions with each inquiry or in Publication 1383, "Correspondence Process."

Examination by Interview.   If IRS notifies you that they will conduct your examination through a personal interview or if you request such an interview, you have the right to ask that the examination take place at a reasonable time and place that is convenient for both you and the IRS. If the time or place the IRS suggests is not convenient, the examiner should try to work out something more suitable. However, the IRS will make the final determination of how, when, and where the examination will take place. You should receive an explanation of your rights and of the examination process either before or at the interview.

If you do not agree with the examiner's report, you may meet with the examiner's supervisor to discuss your case further.

Repeat Examinations.   The IRS should try to avoid repeat examinations of the same items, but this sometimes happens. If the IRS examines your tax return for the same items in either of the 2 previous years and proposes no change to your tax liability, contact the IRS as soon as possible to request that it discontinue the repeat examination.

Explanation of Changes.   If the IRS proposes any changes to your return, it should explain the reasons for the changes. It is important that you understand these reasons. You should not hesitate to ask about anything that is unclear to you.

Interest

You must pay interest on additional tax that you owe. The interest is generally figured from the due date of the return. But if an IRS error caused a delay in your case, and this was grossly unfair, the IRS should reduce the interest. Only delays caused by procedural or mechanical acts not involving the exercise of judgment or discretion qualify. If you think the IRS caused such a delay, discuss it with the examiner and file a claim for refund.

Business Taxpayers

If you are in an individual business, the rights covered in this chapter generally apply to you. If you are a member of a partnership or a shareholder in a small business corporation, special rules may apply to the examination of your partnership or corporation items. The examination of partnership items is discussed in Publication 556, "Examination of Returns, Appeal Rights, and Claims for Refund." The rights covered in this publication generally apply to exempt organizations and sponsors of employee plans.

Appeals

If you don't agree with the examiner's findings, you have the right to appeal them. During the examination process, you should be given information about your appeal rights. Publication 5, "Appeal Rights and Preparation of Protests for Unagreed Cases," explains your appeal rights in detail and tells you exactly what to do if you want to appeal.

Appeals Office

You can appeal the findings of an examination within the IRS through the appeals office. Most differences are normally settled through this appeals system without expensive and time-consuming court trials. If the matter cannot be settled to your satisfaction in the appeals office, you can take your case to court.

Appeals to the Courts

Depending on whether you first pay the disputed tax, you can take your case to the U.S. Tax Court, the U.S. Claims Court, or U.S. District Court. These courts are entirely independent of the IRS. As always, you can represent yourself or have someone admitted to practice before the court represent you.

If you disagree about whether you owe additional tax, you generally have the right to take your case to the U.S. Tax Court if you have not yet paid the tax. Ordinarily, you have 90 days from the time the IRS mails you a formal notice telling you that you owe additional tax (called a *notice of deficiency*) to file a petition with the U.S. Tax Court. You can request simplified small tax case procedures if your case is $10,000 or less for any period or year. A case settled under these procedures cannot be appealed.

If you have already paid the disputed tax in full, you may file a claim for refund. If the IRS disallows the claim, you can appeal the findings through the appeals office. If you do not accept their decision or they have not acted on your claim within 6 months, then you may take your case to the U.S. Claims Court or U.S. District Court.

Recovering Litigation Expenses

If the court agrees with you on most issues in your case and finds that the IRS's position was largely unjustified, you may be able to recover some of your administrative litigation costs. To do this, you must have used all the administrative remedies available to you within the IRS. This includes going through their appeals system and giving them all the information necessary to resolve the case.

Publication 556, "Examination of Returns, Appeal Rights, and Claims for Refund," will help you more fully understand your appeal rights. Figure 17-1 charts the income tax appeal procedure.

Collection of Taxes

Whenever you owe tax, the IRS should send you a bill describing the tax and stating the amounts you owe in tax, interest, and penalties. Be sure to check any bill you receive to make sure it is correct. You have

Income Tax Appeal Procedure

At any stage
- [ ] You can agree and arrange to pay.
- [ ] You can ask for a notice of deficiency so you can file a petition with the Tax Court.
- [ ] You can pay the tax and file a claim for refund.

*Further appeals to the courts may be possible, except there is no appeal under the Tax Court's small tax case procedure.

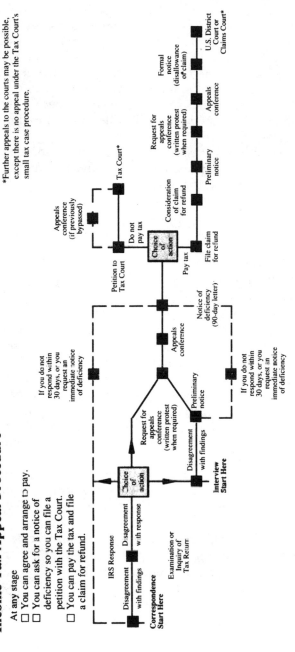

Figure 17-1. Income tax appeal procedure.

the right to have your bill adjusted if it is incorrect, so you should let the IRS know about an incorrect bill right away.

If the IRS informs you that you owe tax because of a mathematical or clerical error on your return, you have the right to ask them to send you a formal notice (a notice of deficiency) so that you can dispute the tax, as discussed earlier. You do not have to pay the additional tax at the same time that you ask the IRS for the formal notice, if you ask for it within 60 days of the time the IRS tells you of the error.

If the tax is correct, the IRS should give you a specific period of time to pay the bill in full. If you pay the bill within the time allowed, the IRS should not have to take any further action.

The IRS may request that you attend an interview for the collection of tax. You will receive an explanation of your rights and of the collection process either before or at the interview.

Payment Arrangements

You should make every effort to pay your bill in full. If you cannot do so, you should pay as much as you can and contact the IRS right away. They may ask you for a complete financial statement to determine how you can pay the amount due. On the basis of your financial condition, you may qualify for an installment agreement. The IRS can arrange for the payments to be made through payroll deduction. The IRS should give you copies of all agreements you make with them.

If the IRS approves a payment agreement, the agreement will stay in effect only if you give correct and complete financial information, you pay each installment on time, you satisfy other tax liabilities on time, you provide current financial information when asked, and the IRS determines that collecting the tax is not at risk.

Following a review of your current finances, the IRS may change your payment agreement. They should notify you 30 days before any change to your payment agreement and tell you why they are making the change.

The IRS should not take any enforcement action (such as recording a tax lien or levying on or seizing property) until after they have tried to contact you and given you the chance to voluntarily pay any tax due. Therefore, it is very important for you to respond right away to their attempts to contact you (by mail, telephone, or personal visit). If you do not respond, the IRS may feel that they have no choice but to begin enforcement action.

Liens

If the IRS places a lien on your property (to secure the amount of tax due), they must release the lien no later than 30 days after finding that you have paid the entire tax and certain charges, the assessment has become legally unenforceable, or they have accepted a bond to cover the tax and certain charges.

Recovery of Damages.   If the IRS knowingly or negligently fails to release a lien under the circumstances described above and you suffer economic damages because of their failure, you can recover your actual economic damages and certain costs.

If the IRS recklessly or intentionally fails to follow the laws and regulations for the collection of tax, you can recover actual economic damages and certain costs.

In each of these two situations, damages and costs should be allowed within the following limits. You must exhaust all administrative remedies available to you, the damages will be reduced by the amount which you could have reasonably prevented, and you must bring suit within 2 years of the action.

Incorrect Lien.   You have the right to appeal the IRS's filing of a Notice of Federal Tax Lien if you believe they filed the lien in error. If the IRS agrees, they should issue a certificate of release, including a statement that they filed the lien in error.

A lien is incorrect if (1) you paid the entire amount due before the IRS filed the lien, (2) the time to collect the tax expired before the IRS filed the lien, (3) the IRS made a procedural error in a deficiency assessment, or (4) the IRS assessed a tax in violation of the automatic stay provisions in a bankruptcy case.

Levy

The IRS will generally give you 30 days' notice before they levy on any property. The notice may be given to you in person, mailed to you, or left at your home or workplace. On the day you attend a collection interview because of a summons, the IRS cannot levy your property unless the collection of tax is in jeopardy.

If your bank account is levied, the bank will hold your account up to the amount of the levy for 21 days. This gives you time to settle any disputes concerning ownership of the funds in the account.

Property That Is Exempt from Levy.   If the IRS must seize your property, you have the legal right to keep the following items:

- Necessary clothing and schoolbooks
- A limited amount of personal belongings, furniture, and business or professional books and tools
- Unemployment and job training benefits, workers' compensation, welfare, certain disability payments, and certain pension benefits
- The income you need to pay court-ordered child support
- Mail
- An amount of weekly income equal to your standard deduction and allowable personal exemptions, divided by 52
- Your main home, unless collection of tax is in jeopardy or the district director (or assistant) approves the levy in writing

Release of Levy.   The IRS generally must release a levy if you pay the tax, penalty, and interest for which the levy was made; the IRS determines the release will help collect the tax; you have an approved installment agreement for the tax on the levy; the IRS determines the levy is creating an economic hardship; or the fair market value of the property exceeds the amount of the levy and release would not hinder the collection of tax.

Taxpayer Rights during the Levy Process.   If at any time during the collection process you do not agree with the collection officer, you can discuss your case with his or her supervisor.

If the IRS seizes your property, you have the right to request that it be sold within 60 days after your request. You can request a time period greater than 60 days. The IRS should comply with your request unless it is not in the best interest of the government.

Access to Your Private Premises.   A court order is not generally needed for a collection officer to seize your property. However, you don't have to allow the employee access to your private premises, such as your home or the nonpublic areas of your business, if the employee does not have court authorization to be there.

Withheld Taxes

If the IRS believes that you were responsible for seeing that a corporation paid income to and withheld social security taxes from its employees, and the taxes were not paid, the IRS may look to you to pay an amount based on the unpaid taxes. If you feel that you do not owe this amount, you have the right to discuss the case with the collection officer's supervisor. You may also request an appeals hearing within 30 days of any proposed assessment of employment taxes. You generally have the same IRS appeal rights as other taxpayers. Because the U.S. Tax Court has no jurisdiction in this situation, you must pay at least part of the withheld taxes and file a claim for refund in order to take the matter to the U.S. District Court or U.S. Claims Court.

The amount of tax withheld from your wages is determined by Form W-4, "Employees Withholding Allowance Certificate," you give your employer. If your certificate is incorrect, the IRS may instruct your employer to increase the amount. The IRS may also assess a penalty. You have the right to appeal the decision. Or you can file a claim for refund and go to the U.S. Claims Court or U.S. District Court.

The Collection Process

Publications 586A, "The Collection Process (Income Tax Accounts)," and 594, "The Collection Process (Employment Tax Accounts)," will help you understand your rights during the collection process.

To stop the collection process at any stage, you may pay the tax in full. If you cannot pay the tax in full, contact the IRS right away to discuss possible ways to pay the tax. Figure 17-2 lists the steps in the collection process.

First notice and demand for unpaid tax

  10 days later

    Enforcement authority arises (a notice of a lien may be filed)

    Up to 3 more notices sent over a period of time asking for payment

    Notice of intent to levy is sent by certified mail (final notice)

  30 days later

    Enforcement action to collect the tax begins (levy, seizure, etc.)

Figure 17-2. The collection process.

Refund of Overpaid Tax

Once you have paid all your tax, you have the right to file a claim for a refund if you think the tax is incorrect. Generally, you have 3 years from the date you filed the return or 2 years from the date you paid the tax (whichever is later) to file a claim. If the IRS examines your claim for any reason, you have the same rights that you would have during an examination of your return.

Interest on Refunds.   You will receive interest on any income tax refund delayed more than 454 days, after the later of either the date you filed your return or the date your return was due.

Checking on Your Refund.   Normally, your will receive your refund about 6 weeks after you file your return. If you have not received your refund within 8 weeks after mailing your return, you may check on it by calling the toll-free Tele-Tax number on the tax form's instructions.

If the IRS reduces your refund because you owe a debt to another federal agency or because you owe child support, it must notify you of this action. However, if you have a question about the debt that caused the reduction, you should contact the other agency.

Cancellation of Penalties

You have the right to ask that certain penalties (but not interest) be canceled (abated) if you can show reasonable cause for the failure that led to the penalty or can show that you exercised due diligence, if that is the applicable standard for that penalty.

If you relied on wrong advice you received from the IRS employees on the toll-free telephone system, the IRS should cancel certain penalties that may result. But you have to show that your reliance on the advice was reasonable.

If you relied on incorrect written advice from the IRS in response to a written request you made after January 1, 1989, the IRS should cancel any penalties that may result. You must show that you gave sufficient and correct information and filed your return after you received the advice.

Special Help to Resolve Your Problems

The IRS has a problem resolution program for taxpayers who have been unable to resolve their problems with the IRS. If you have a tax problem that you cannot clear up through normal channels, write to the problem resolution office in the district or the service center with which you have the problem. You may also reach the problem resolution office by calling the IRS taxpayer assistance number for your area. If you are hearing-impaired with TV and Telephone (TTY) access, you may call 1-800-829-4059.

If your tax problem causes (or will cause) you to suffer a significant hardship, additional assistance is available. A significant hardship may occur if you cannot maintain necessities such as food, clothing, shelter, transportation, and medical treatment.

There are two ways you can apply for relief. You can submit Form 911, "Application for Taxpayer Assistance Order to Relieve Hardship," which you can order by calling 1-800-TAX-FORM (829-3676). You can choose instead to call 1-800-829-1040, to request relief from your hardship. The taxpayer ombudsman, problem resolution officer, or other official will then review your case and may issue a taxpayer assistance order (TAO) to suspend IRS action.

Taxpayer Assistance Numbers

You can use the telephone number shown in the white pages of your local telephone directory under U.S. government, Internal Revenue Service, federal tax assistance. If no number is listed, call toll-free 1-800-829-1040.

You can also find these phone numbers in the instructions for Form 1040. You may also use these numbers to reach the problem resolution office. Ask for the problem resolution office when you call.

Assistance Abroad

U.S. taxpayers abroad may write for information to:

Internal Revenue Service
Attn: IN:C:TPS
950 L'Enfant Plaza South, S.W.
Washington, D.C. 20024

You can also contact your nearest U.S. embassy for information about what services and forms are available in your location.

Glossary

Accelerated Cost Recovery System (ACRS): A schedule of allowable depreciation that enables a taxpayer to deduct the cost of a capital investment at an accelerated rate. The ACRS was first used for assets placed in use after 1980.

Accountable Reimbursement Plan: An arrangement whereby the employer requires you to adequately substantiate business expenses and return any excess reimbursement to the employer.

Accelerated Depreciation: A method whereby an asset may be depreciated more quickly than permitted under the straight-line method.

Accrual Method of Accounting: Accounting method different from cash accounting in that income is report in the year earned rather than when paid and expenses are reported in the year incurred rather than when paid.

Acquisition Debt: A debt used to buy, build, or construct a principal residence which generally qualifies for a full interest expense deduction.

Active Participation: A test used by the IRS for determining the deductibility of certain items.

Adjusted Basis: The book value of property used in determining the gain or loss in the sale or exchange of property, usually the cost of the property adjusted to account for increases such as capital improvements and decreases such as depreciation.

Amended Return: A return filed on a Form 1040-X within a 3-year period to correct a mistake on the original return.

Adjusted Gross Income: Net gross income after adjustments to income have been figured.

Alimony: Payments made to a separated or divorced spouse as required by a decree or an agreement. Qualified alimony payments are deductible from taxable income by the payor and taxable to the payee.

Alternative Minimum Tax: A tax which is applied to a taxpayer who uses tax preference items which reduces the taxpayer's taxes below a certain amount.

Amortization: The writing off of an investment's intangible assets over the project life of the asset.

Amount Realized: The fair market value of property or money received in the sale or exchange of property.

Annuity: An annual payment of money to a person. The payment is for the fixed period or for the life of the person.

At-Risk Rules: Rules describing the loss deduction to cash investments and personal liability notes in real estate transactions.

Away from Home: In reference to business travel, that during which the taxpayer is required to spend at least one night before returning home.

Asset: Property that has some monetary value.

Basis: In most cases, the cost of an asset adjusted for depreciation or other deductions.

Boot: Generally cash or an exchange of property that is given in addition to the principal exchange of property.

Calendar Year: A tax year that ends on December 31.

Capital Asset: Generally property held for personal use or investment.

Capital Expenditures: The expenses incurred for permanent improvements or betterment of property.

Capitalize: To treat expenditure as the cost or additional cost of a property in order to increase the property's basis.

Capital Gain or Loss: The difference between the amount gained and the adjusted basis of the amount realized and the adjusted basis of the sale or exchange of capital assets. Long-term capital gain is gain on property held in excess of 6 months.

Capital Gain Dividend: A mutual fund dividend allocated to gains realized on a sale of capital assets.

Cash Method of Accounting: Accounting method in which income is reported when received and expenses when paid.

Casualty Loss: Loss from an unforeseen and sudden event, deductible subject to a 10 percent floor for personal losses.

Charitable Contribution: An itemized deduction that is allowed for qualifying charities.

Clifford Trust: A short-time trust in which the principal is reserved by the grantor and current income is paid to a beneficiary.

Community Property: Property acquired during a marriage that belongs equally to both spouses; used only in the community property states, which are Arizona, California, Idaho, Louisiana, Nevada, New Mexico, Texas, and Washington.

Condemnation: The taking of an individual's property for a fair price by a governmental unit for a public purpose.

Consumer Interest: Interest incurred on personal debts and consumer credit; in most cases, it is not deductible.

Declining Balance Method: One method of accelerated depreciation in which the yearly deduction for depreciation is a percentage of the basis of the asset.

Deductions: Items that directly reduce income. Personal deductions include mortgage interest, state and local taxes, and charitable contributions. In most cases, deductions are authorized or allowed only if itemized on Schedule A. Certain deductions, however, such as alimony and business losses, may be deducted from gross income even if itemized deductions are not claimed.

Deferred Income or Gain: Income or gain that is not recognized as taxable income or gain until a later time.

Defined Benefit Plan: A retirement plan that pays fixed benefits based on actuarial projections.

Defined Contribution Plan: A retirement plan that pays benefits based on contributions to individual accounts plus accumulated earnings.

Depreciable Asset: Property used in trade or business which has a useful life of more than 1 year.

Earned Income: Compensation that is received for services rendered. Earned income includes salaries, wages, professional fees, and other amounts received as pay for work actually performed; it does not include income received from annuities, pensions, and investments.

Earned Income Credit: A refundable credit based on earned income available to certain taxpayers whose income is below a certain level.

Fair Market Value: What a willing buyer would be willing to pay when there is no compulsion to sell or buy the article in question.

General Partner: A member of a partnership organization who is personally liable for the obligations of the partnership.

Gift Tax: A tax on gifts in excess of $10,000 per donee per year.

Green Mail Payments: Funds paid in excess of stock values in connection with the redemption of stock.

Head of Household: Unmarried taxpayer who pays more than 50 percent of the cost of maintaining a residence for the entire tax year for a qualifying individual.

Hobby Losses: Expenses associated with the pursuit of a hobby, deductible only up to the amount of income received from the activity.

Home Equity Debt: A debt secured by the principal residence or second home to the extent of the excess market value over the acquisition debt.

Imputed Interest: Interest that is imputed where the seller financed at a low interest rate and the parties' stated interest rate is below the IRS federal rate.

Indexing: A provision in the tax code that automatically adjusts deductions, benefits, or liabilities to account for either inflation or deflation of the economy in general.

Individual Retirement Arrangement (IRA): An account that permits a taxpayer to establish a retirement plan, subject to certain requirements.

Installment Sale: Sale of property that allows for tax deferment if at least one payment is received after the tax year in which the sale occurs.

Intangible Personal Property: Property such as bonds, stocks, notes, and accounts receivable whose value is in the rights conveyed.

Involuntary Conversion: Property lost as a result of fire, theft, flood, or condemnation.

Keogh Plan: A retirement plan set up by self-employed persons providing tax-deductible contributions to it.

Limited Partner: A partner whose potential personal liability for partnership debts is limited to the amount of money or other property that the partner contributed or is required to contribute to the partnership.

Limited Partnership: A partnership composed of at least one general partner and one or more limited partners.

Material Participation Test: Test for determining whether a person is actively or inactively involved in a business activity to determine whether a loss is a passive activity or is subject to the passive activity rule.

Modified ACRS (MACRS): Depreciation method applied to assets placed in service after 1986.

Nonrecourse Loans: Liabilities of a partnership for which none of the partners has any personal liability.

Partnership: An unincorporated business or income-producing entity organized by two or more persons. A partnership is not subject to tax but passes to the partners all incomes, deductions, losses, etc., according to the terms of the partnership agreement.

Pension: Regular payments made from an employer-funded retirement plan for past services rendered.

Personal Property: All property that is not considered real property.

Points: Charges made to a homeowner at the time of a loan; a point is equal to 1 percent.

Profit-Sharing Plans: A defined contribution plan under which the amount contributed to the employee's account is based upon a percentage of the employer's profit.

Qualified Charitable Organization: An organization that is approved by the U.S. Treasury to receive charitable contribution deductions.

Qualified Plan: An employee benefit plan that has been approved by the IRS, such as pension arrangements.

Real Estate: Land and fixtures permanently attached to the land.

Real Estate Investment Trust (REIT): An entity that invests primarily in real estate and mortgages and passes income and losses through to the taxpayers.

Recognized Gain or Loss: The amount of gain or loss realized and included in the individual's taxable income for that year.

Residential Rental Property: Rental property in which 80 percent or more of the gross income is obtained from dwelling units.

Rollover: Distributions received from a retirement plan that are reinvested in another retirement plan within 60 days.

Royalty Income: Amounts received from property such as books, movies, and mineral rights.

S corporation: A small corporation that meets the IRS requirements for S corporation treatment and is therefore taxed through its shareholders; a small corporation that elects the S status in order to receive tax treatments similar to a partnership.

Section 179 Deduction: First-year expensing of an asset.

Section 1231 Property: Depreciable property used in trade or business and held long term.

Short-Term Capital Gain or Loss: Gain or loss on the sale and exchange of assets for 6 months or less.

Simplified Employee Pension Plan (SEP): : An IRA type of plan set up by an employer rather than an employee.

Sole Proprietorship: The simplest form of business organization, it has no existence apart from the owner.

Straddle Provisions: Rules regarding the tax treatment of offsetting investment positions used by taxpayers to reduce the individual's risk of loss.

Sum-of-the-Year's-Digits Depreciation: A method of depreciation which is based on a formula developed from the anticipated useful life of the property.

Tangible Personal Property: Personal property that has a value because of its character and not the rights associated with the property, e.g., books, cars, etc., but not stocks, bonds or accounts receivable. Tangible personal property is also defined as personal property that can be moved.

Tax Credit: A credit that is applied directly to tax liability.

Tax Home: A taxpayer's principal place of business or employment.

Taxable Income: Net income after claiming all deductions from gross income and adjusted gross income; adjusted gross income less personal exemptions and less standard or itemized deductions.

Tax Straddle Rules: Rules intended to prevent the manipulation of offsetting positions in actively traded personal property such as stocks, securities, commodities, and foreign currency.

Useful Life: The estimated time in which a depreciable asset will be used, pertaining to property not depreciable under ACRS or MACRS.

Wash Sales: Sales on which the loss is disallowed because market position was recovered within a 61-day period.

Appendix
Business Tax Calendar

January 15. Final payment of estimated taxes for the prior year is due. Payment is made using Form 1040-ES.

January 31. W-2 forms sent by employers and copies of any information returns, 1099s, should have been received by this date from all institutions, and so forth which paid you money during the prior year.

February 28. Employers should file copies of information returns, W-2 and 1099s, with IRS by this date. Other forms required to be filed by employer with IRS include the W-2P Form, Statement for Recipients of Annuities, Pension Retired Pay, or IRA Payments, and Form 1099R, Statement of Distributions from Profit-sharing and Retirement Plans and IRAs.

March 15. Tax returns, Form 1120 or Form 1120S for S corporations, for corporations using the calendar tax year should be filed with IRS by this date.

April 15. Personal income tax returns, Form 1040s; requests for extensions, Form 4868; gift tax returns, Form 709 and 709A; and the declaration of estimated tax for first quarter, Form 1040-ES should be filed by this date. Information income tax information returns of partnerships, Form 1065, for those partnerships using a calendar year are also due at this time.

June 15. Second quarterly payment of estimated tax, Form 1040-ES, is due.

August 15.   This is the due date for filing of those taxpayers receiving a filing extension for prior tax year. For those taxpayers needing additional time, a further extension may be obtained by filing Form 4868 by this date.

September 15.   The third quarterly estimated tax payment is due. Corporate tax returns, Form 1120 or Form 1120S, are also due for those corporations who previously submitted a request for an automatic six-month extension. Corporations needing more time should file for an additional extension, Form 7004, by this date.

December 15.   This is when new W-4 Forms should be filed with the employer to adjust withholding payments for next year.

Note: If any of the above dates is a holiday or other nonbusiness day, Saturday or Sunday, then the due date is the next business day.

Index

About the Author

Cliff Roberson is a practicing attorney in California and Texas, tax expert, and Professor at the University of Houston-Victoria. His previous books include *Fight the IRS and Win: A Self-Defense Guide for Taxpayers; Avoiding Probate: Tamper-Proof Estate Planning; The Business Person's Legal Advisor*, Second Edition; *Staying Out of Court: Manager's Guide to Labor Law*; and *The McGraw-Hill Personal Tax Advisor*, Second Edition.